Twayne's United States Authors Series

EDITOR OF THIS VOLUME

Lewis Leary
University of North Carolina

Lydia Maria Child

TUSAS 380

Lydia Maria Child

LYDIA MARIA CHILD

By WILLIAM S. OSBORNE

TWAYNE PUBLISHERS
A DIVISION OF G. K. HALL & CO., BOSTON

Published in 1980 by Twayne Publishers,
A Division of G. K. Hall & Co.
All Rights Reserved

Printed on permanent/durable acid-free paper and bound
in the United States of America

First Printing

Frontispiece of Lydia Maria Child from *Letters of Lydia Maria Child*, ed. John Greenleaf Whittier. (Boston: Houghton Mifflin and Company, 1882.)

Library of Congress Cataloging in Publication Data

Osborne, William S.
Lydia Maria Child.

(Twayne's United States authors series; TUSAS 380)
Bibliography: p. 191–93
Includes index.
1. Child, Lydia Maria Francis, 1802–1880
Criticism and interpretation.
PS1293.Z508   818'.209   80–432
ISBN 0-8057-7315-0

Once again, for Ruth

Contents

About the Author

William S[tewart] Osborne is a professor in the Department of English at Southern Connecticut State College, New Haven, Connecticut. He graduated from the University of North Carolina (Chapel Hill) and earned his advanced degrees at Columbia University. Formerly chairman of the Department of English at Southern Connecticut State College, he now devotes himself to full-time teaching and writing. His particular areas of interest are nineteenth-century American literature and Southern literature.

He has written the TUSAS study on *Caroline M. Kirkland*; has written articles on American literature which have appeared in *American Literature*, *Maryland Historical Magazine*, *West Virginia History*, *American Notes and Queries*; has supplied introductions and notes for recent editions of John Pendleton Kennedy's *Swallow Barn* (Hafner Publishing Company) and *Rob of the Bowl*, Caroline M. Kirkland's *A New Home—Who'll Follow?*, and William Hill Brown's *The Power of Sympathy* and Hannah Foster's *The Coquette* (all College and University Press). He is also General Editor of the Masterworks of Literature Series, published by the College and University Press, New Haven, Connecticut—a series which concentrates primarily on reprints of works of less well-known writers in nineteenth-century American literature.

Preface

When Lydia Maria Child died in 1880, she was eulogized as one of the most capable women of her generation: humanitarian, social critic, editor, fiction writer, and occasional poet. A person who spoke frankly her thoughts, frequently championing controversial causes, she roused in people either great admiration or violent, even abusive, ridicule. James Russell Lowell in a soberer moment in "A Fable for Critics" remembered:

> Yes, a great heart is hers, one that dares to go in
> To the prison, the slave-hut, the alleys of sin,
> And to bring into each, or to find there, some line
> Of the never completely out-trampled divine. . . .
> What a wealth would it bring to the narrow and sour
> Could they be as a Child but for one little hour!

On the other hand, Henry James in *The Bostonians* may have had Mrs. Child in mind as he drew the portrait of Miss Birdseye—a "poor little humanity hack" who "belonged to any and every league that had been founded for almost any purpose whatever. This did not prevent her being a confused, entangled, inconsequent, discursive old woman, whose charity began at home and ended nowhere, whose credulity kept pace with it, and who knew less about her fellow-creatures, if possible, after fifty years of humanity zeal, than on the day she had gone into the field to testify against the iniquity of most arrangements."[1] With such a dour portrait James obviously argued his own ignorance of American society—like Winterbourne, "he had lived [in Europe] so long as to have got morally muddled" about his native land—and scoffed at the contribution impassioned women of the age like Mrs. Child provided their country.

Mrs. Child's humanitarianism—her crusade for reform and brotherhood—cannot be challenged and is carefully documented in her biographers' works, most notably in Helene G. Baer's *The Heart Is Like Heaven: The Life of Lydia Maria Child* (1964), and also in Milton Meltzer's *Tongue of Flame: The Life of Lydia Maria Child*

(1965).[2] A recent study that discusses Mrs. Child as a woman activist is Susan P. Conrad's *Perish the Thought: Intellectual Women in Romantic America, 1830–1860* (1976). To date, however, no biographer has concentrated on Mrs. Child's contribution to our literature. Such an emphasis is the province of this study.

During that portion of her life given over to the purely literary, she wrote four novels as well as shorter tales and relatively undistinguished verse, published in the magazines of the day. More often she used her pen—to her way of thinking, more purposefully—in writing two volumes of "letters" containing social and literary commentary and a number of domestic manuals, as well as other pieces of nonfiction also published in the magazines. Explicit in all this writing were a personal creed, early formulated—service to others—and an urgent desire to make her countrymen and countrywomen more responsive to the social needs of those among them less fortunate: the poor, the oppressed, the underprivileged.

The first novel was *Hobomok, A Tale of the Times* (1824), an account of the Puritans and the Indians in the Massachusetts Bay Colony. The second novel also dealt with colonial life, a romance of the Revolutionary period—*The Rebels, or Boston before the Revolution* (1825)—relating some of the events leading to the Stamp Tax crisis and the Boston Tea Party. Although the style of these novels, which reflects the author's youthful exuberance, is overwrought and turgid, there are clearly novelistic successes: the minor characters are effectively drawn; their conversation is sprightly, colloquial, often appropriate; the domestic life of seventeenth-century Salem in *Hobomok* is imaginatively suggested.

The third novel, *Philothea, a Romance* (1836), showed greater ability in novel construction; style and character, setting and action blend harmoniously. By today's standards, it is probably her best piece of fiction. The romance, set in the Age of Pericles, was an enchanting evocation of "the glory that was Greece"; and the heroine, the other-worldly Philothea, was a lovely dream of Mrs. Child's rich imagination. The fourth novel, *A Romance of the Republic* (1867), was based on incidents "which [grew] out of slavery"—the horrible blight of nineteenth-century American society. This novel should have been her best effort, for she was writing about her own times. However, devoted as she was to political and civil freedom for all men and women, she was unable to subordinate propaganda to the subtler demands of fiction. Worse, she employed an outdated novel tradition—the domestic romance so popular in America in the 1850s.

In this study I have devoted a chapter to each of these novels—

evaluating strengths and weaknesses, commenting on themes and ideas, suggesting a reader's perspective both in Mrs. Child's day and ours. *Hobomok* has been reprinted (Garrett Press, Inc., 1970); *The Rebels* and *A Romance of the Republic* have long been out of print; *Philothea* is available through private subscription, in an edition prepared by Kenneth W. Cameron (Transcendental Books, 1975). Nevertheless, since the books are not easily obtainable, I have summarized the stories and on occasion excerpted passages for discussion.

It was ultimately her practical interests in society which led Mrs. Child away from novel-writing and into books and essays on social problems. Her commitment to society was much stronger than it was to literature. Service to others. Among these ephemeral pieces are significant works which may command the modern reader's attention. *The Frugal Housewife* (1830) and *The Mother's Book* (1831) were household manuals devoted to domestic concerns. *The History of the Condition of Women in Various Ages and Nations* (1835) was a report of women's contributions to society, with a tacit statement that women worked equally with men in the mainstream of life. *The Progress of Religious Ideas through Successive Ages* (1855) was a two-volume handbook to the world's religions written for the popular market. In a style often forceful, utterly unpretentious, and astonishingly uncluttered—when compared with that of some of her contemporaries, Margaret Fuller and Elizabeth Peabody among them—she established her particular thesis, announcing her liberal views and obliquely her humanitarian sentiments. The style in these nonfiction pieces was remarkable in another sense, in that it was plainer, homelier, than that which she customarily wrote in her fiction. In these works she was very much the practical writer who like Franklin chose a simple style to convey "instruction among the common people."

Soon she became far more deeply involved in social reform. *An Appeal in Favor of That Class of Americans Called Africans* (1833) brought her widespread notice, even national reputation. The book won considerable support for the abolitionist movement and angered a number of her contemporaries, who quarreled if not with her partisan sympathies at least with her aggressive tone and sharp language, her emotional fervor and common sense.

These nonfiction pieces as well as gift books and annuals of shorter prose and verse, compiled for the seasonal trade, are discussed in another chapter of this study. I have been deliberately selective in presenting Mrs. Child's ephemeral works and have quoted liberally from certain materials since they are not readily accessible. A selective bibliography of the more important ephemera appears at the end of this study; a more extensive bibliography of this kind of work is given in Mrs. Baer's biography.

She published two volumes of *Letters from New York* (1843, 1845), among the best-selling books of the 1840s, where in precise style she directed her readers' attention to serious social issues: women's position in society, education for women, economic status for women, capital punishment, poverty, the plight of the under-privileged. In addition, there were essays, often rhapsodic, on the delights of nature, her deep appreciation for music, and personal responses to transcendentalism and Swedenborgianism. An analogy can be drawn between Mrs. Child's observations and Cooper's in *The American Democrat* because both writers decry the American tendency to ape the manners of Europe and to establish a caste consciousness based on material wealth. Although she noted many of the same symptoms of an ailing society Cooper described, her diagnosis was sharply different. She saw evils in American society not from the provincial view of men of property but from the clear-sighted view of the social worker. Poverty was the greatest menace to American society. "If we can abolish *poverty*," she firmly believed, "we shall have taken the greatest step toward the abolition of crime." She was, as George F. Whicher remarked, "a dangerous woman" for her conservative times.[3]

The discursive essays in *Letters from New York* provide material for another chapter in thus study. Finally, an introductory chapter establishes, by means of a biographical sketch, Mrs. Child in the larger social context of her times and prepares the way for a chronological discussion of the major work in subsequent chapters. A summary chapter suggests her contribution to American literature and estimates her importance to the modern reader.

As informative as her fiction may be in the perspective of America's developing literary consciousness, Mrs. Child undoubtedly appeals most strongly to the modern reader as a dedicated humanitarian—a person whose concern for the status of women in American society, for the poor and the oppressed and the underprivileged in America, and for the human dignity of minorities marks her as a woman well in advance of her own day. As a fiction writer, she is rarely an innovator; as a social critic, she anticipates in her range of subject matter and in her work for various reforms the themes of later writers in America—the muckrackers, Henry George, and Edward Bellamy, among others.

Mrs. Child is confessedly a minor writer in American literature. But, as Tremaine McDowell put it in the *Literary History of the United States*, referring to Mrs. Child and several of her New England contemporaries, reformers all, "their lives speak more loudly than their books. And their books, lacking in literary distinction as they are, speak more loudly of America than do the more polished writings of their bookish contemporaries."4 Mrs. Child, who had "great heart," is hardly the "humanitary hack" James may have caricatured. It is this life as reflected in her writing that this study hopes to convey to the modern reader.

On more than one occasion during her writing career, Mrs. Child referred to "walk[ing] out in stormy weather without a cloak"— having published an appeal or written an essay that provoked indignant protest among her contemporaries because she had not forewarned them of her intention. To forestall "stormy weather," at least in respect to the limits and the scope of this study, I will define my method. As I have said, this is a study of Mrs. Child's principal work with emphasis on her fiction and on her social commentary. Although she wrote a great deal of verse, it is not good verse— sentimental "household" poetry which does not approach even the feebler efforts of Bryant, Longfellow, and Whittier. Therefore, I have to a large extent omitted it, citing only those poems which illustrate a particular idea or satisfy a particular end.

Primary source material other than the works themselves is correspondence. The bulk of this correspondence is found in various collections in the Northeast: Boston Public Library, Cornell University Library, Harvard University Library, Library of Congress, Massachusetts Historical Society Library, New York Historical Society Library, New York Public Library. Additionally, there are fugitive letters in Henry E. Huntington Library and Syracuse University Library, among others. Whittier published a selection of the correspondence: *Letters of Lydia Maria Child* (1882). All this correspondence is concerned principally with Mrs. Child's public life; it is relatively poor in details of her literary life. What has been relevant in my opinion I have referred to throughout this study and have further identified in the Appendix. Frequently I have quoted from these letters liberally because they help to characterize a woman positive in conviction.

I wish to thank Sylvia E. Bowman, who first encouraged me in this study, Lewis Leary and Alice D. Phalen of Twayne Publishers, who provided incentive and understood missed deadlines. I am indeed grateful for permission to quote from the letters of Mrs. Child, letters in collections found in Boston Public Library, Cornell University Library, Library of Congress, and New York Public Library; I appreciate as well permission from Gail C. Levin, Assistant to the Director of the University of Pennsylvania Press, to quote excerpts of Mrs. Child's letters appearing in Mrs. Baer's biography. And most especial thanks are due the reference librarians of Hilton C. Buley Library, Southern Connecticut State College; Professor Kenneth Florey, Chairman of the Department of English; and Professor Ira M. Leonard and members of the Sabbatical Leave Committee, whose recommendation for a sabbatical leave made easier the completion of this study.

WILLIAM S. OSBORNE

Chronology

1802   Lydia Maria Francis born on February 11 in Medford, Massachusetts; youngest of six children born to David Convers Francis and Susannah Rand Francis.

1806–   Acquires rudiments of education in a dame's school and in
1814   a local seminary; her intellectual growth is monitored by an older brother, Convers Francis, who shapes her opinion of literature.

1814–   Makes her home with sister, Mary Preston, and her husband
1820   in Norridgewock, Maine Territory; attends local academy staffed by student-teachers from Bowdoin College, preparing herself to be a teacher.

1820–   Teaches school in Gardiner, Maine; in her reading in
1823   eighteenth-century philosophers becomes acquainted with the work of Swedenborg.

1824–   Makes her home with Convers and his wife in Watertown,
1825   Massachusetts; opens a girls' school; *Hobomok* and *The Rebels*.

1826   Begins editing *The Juvenile Miscellany*, a bimonthly magazine for children; meets David Lee Child, sometime lawyer and journalist.

1828   Marries Child on October 18; supplements his meager income with teaching and with articles for magazines; continues editing the *Miscellany*.

1829   *The First Settlers of New England.*

1830   *The Frugal Housewife.*

1831   *The Mother's Book* and *The Girl's Own Book.*

1832   *The Coronal* (an anthology of her prose and verse).

1833   *An Appeal in Favor of That Class of Americans Called Africans*, announcing her commitment to the abolition of slavery.

1834   The *Miscellany* ceases publication, one of the casualties of her commitment to abolitionism.

1835   *The History of the Condition of Women.*

1836 *Philothea*; husband in Europe for a year and a half, to observe process of turning beets into sugar.

1841– Editor of *National Anti-Slavery Standard*, New York organ
1843 of American Anti-Slavery Society; husband with help of her father buys farm in Northampton, Massachusetts, and commences growing sugar beets; *Letters from New York*.

1845 *Letters from New York*, Second Series.

1846– For remaining New York years earns livelihood through
1849 writing for magazines and newspapers; husband acknowledges failure with sugar beets project, loses farm, engages in a number of other shortlived projects.

1852 Establishes permanent residence with her husband again in Wayland, Massachusetts, in home she inherits from her father.

1855 *The Progress of Religious Ideas.*

1856 *Autumnal Leaves* (another anthology of her prose and verse).

1861 Supplies introduction for Harriet Brent Jacobs's *Incidents in the Life of a Slave Girl.*

1864 *Looking Toward Sunset* (an anthology of her and her friends' prose and verse).

1865 *The Freedmen's Book.*

1867 *The Romance of the Republic.*

1874 Husband dies on September 18.

1878 *Aspirations of the World: A Chain of Opals* (the last anthology of her work).

1880 Dies October 20.

CHAPTER 1

"I Never Work on the Winning Side . . ."

"I have been busily engaged in [re]reading 'Paradise Lost' . . . such astonishing grandeur of description, such heavenly sublimity of style," Maria Francis wrote her brother Convers. However, she added, "[D]on't you think that Milton asserts the superiority of his own sex in . . . too lordly a manner?"[1] Even though Convers might "smile at the freedom with which I express my opinion," Maria confessed that "when I write you, I feel perfectly unrestrained."[2] Convers might have smiled, but he was probably not surprised by his sister's frank opinion. Six years her senior, he had stimulated her fondness for books since they first shared readings in literature while superintending the ovens in their father's bakeshop. He had observed too her ideas about the status of women. Had he not encouraged in his tutoring such freedom of expression which could bring her to spurn Milton's patronizing manner. Liberality of opinion—even unorthodox opinion—and largeness of heart had been fostered in the Francis home.

I *". . . I Shall Be Independent"*

Born in Medford, Massachusetts, a prosperous village with thriving shipyards at the turn of the century, on February 11, 1802, Lydia Maria Francis was the youngest of six children. One of her earliest recollections was of her father, David Convers Francis, recounting the story of a fugitive slave who had been given sanctuary in the village. She remembered her father's anger against men who thought that they had the right to own other men, just because of the color of their skin.[3] Another early recollection was of her mother, Susannah Rand Francis, and her older sisters preparing the meal for Thanksgiving Eve, which they shared with less well-off neighbors—

sometimes as many as twenty or thirty. And after the dinner of chicken and pumpkin pie, the villagers returned to their homes with bread and crackers and doughnuts and turnovers for the children, made in the family bakeshop.[4] The Francis family lived simply, advocates of the doctrine that it was more blessed to give than to receive. Doubtless, Maria's antislavery convictions and her dedication to the needs of others less fortunate than herself were early lessons in life. "[A]ll true excellence and happiness consist in living for *others*, not for *yourselves*," she wrote some years later.[5]

The rudiments of learning Maria acquired in a dame's school in Medford, while her mother supervised the practical lessons in the home: how to be thrifty in managing a household, among others. But it was Convers who was the dominant teacher in these formative years. They read and talked together during leisure moments in the bakeshop and throughout evening study sessions. When he went off to Harvard to study for the ministry, she was left with the books they had read together—the classics and Shakespeare, English poetry and prose of the seventeenth and eighteenth centuries.

With Convers gone, she felt alone for the first time. Mary, the only older sister now living at home, did not share her brother and sister's love of literature; besides, she was preoccupied with her own plans for marriage to a young man living in the district of Maine. Before the marriage could take place, however, Mrs. Francis became ill; the illness, diagnosed as a form of tuberculosis, was terminal, and in a few months she was dead. A few months later Mary was off to Maine, the bride of Warren Preston, while Maria remained at home with her father, applying those lessons her mother had taught her and reading again the books she and Convers had shared. Mr. Francis, apparently a man of sober mien, was incapable of showing much affection to his twelve-year-old daughter; he spent his days in the bakeshop and his evenings dozing in front of the open fire. Although he enrolled Maria in the village's seminary, she found no friends to share her interest in literature, much less her startling ideas. She resented the instruction in the dull proprieties young ladies, she was told, practiced in society. She wanted a change.

Changes were occurring in Medford in 1814 as well. The war with Great Britain, now in its second year, had closed the shipyards; unemployment was high. Fearful that the economy was slipping, Mr. Francis determined to sell the bakery for an inflated price before the market fell. Concern for Maria may have prompted the decision, too, the father realizing that the young woman needed sympathy and guidance and schooling which he was unable to provide. Thus he wrote his daughter in Maine, asking her to open her home to the lonely child. Mary's response was immediate: she and her husband welcomed Maria.

Norridgewock, in the district of Maine, an inland village of several hundred people on the banks of the Kennebec River, was a prosperous village; unlike Medford, its economy was not suffering from the effects of the war. It was the mart for the local farmers and the shire town where the district's court convened three months out of the year. During court time judges and lawyers and their families provided business for merchants and innkeepers. Warren Preston was custodian of a rather well-stocked library which had been established primarily for the legal professionals; yet volumes of history and literature were on the shelves as well. Maria had access to the library and enrolled in the academy staffed by students on leave from nearby Bowdoin College. She was pleased that she could now study French and German, languages Convers was also studying at Harvard; the hope of reading Virgil "in his own tongue" eluded her, however. Surprisingly, none of the teachers who came to the academy knew the language, she wrote her brother; yet she was determined to learn Latin, "look[ing] forward to a certain time when I expect that hope with many others, will be realized."[6] She kept Convers informed of her reading and offered him her opinion of Scott's novels and Gibbon's history, the *Spectator* papers and *Rasselas, Prince of Abissinia*; and she turned to Convers when the student-teachers in Norridgewock could not satisfy her questions. "Do you know," she admonished, "you have a great many questions to answer me? Do not forget that I asked about the 'flaming cherubims,' the effects of distance, horizonal or perpendicular, 'Orlando Furioso,' and Lord Byron."[7]

She fretted that her reading was so haphazard, so undisciplined. She told Convers that she was "too indolent in examining the systems of great writers," that she had not "cultivated habits of thought and reflection upon any subject." The consequence, she felt, was that her imagination "[had] ripened before her judgment; I have quickness of perception, without profoundness of thought." And as proof of her lack of judgment, in one respect at least, she added: "[John] Neal must be condemned . . . without mercy, because his poem was one of genius' wildest, most erratic flights. Were every one as devout a worshipper at the shrine of genius as I am, they would admire him, even in his wanderings."[8]

In spite of what Maria regarded as her desultory studying, she believed herself well read enough in a few years' time to teach school.

She was anxious for new experiences, she had imposed on the Prestons long enough, she wanted her freedom. She informed Convers of her decision: ". . . I leave Norridgewock, and take a school in Gardiner. . . . All I expect is, that, if I am industrious and prudent[,] I shall be *independent*."⁹ Young perhaps to assert that independence, yet Maria was a determined young woman.

In Gardiner she boarded in the home of the schoolmaster. A lonely man with an invalid wife, he was infatuated with his youthful assistant—offering to teach her the guitar and to give her drawing lessons, which she refused. She preferred to spend her time away from the classroom in reading, so he supplied her with books of the eighteenth-century philosophers—Kant, Locke, Paley, and Swedenborg—assuming that she would turn to him with her questions. She did not; she turned to Convers, by now an ordained minister in a church in Watertown, Massachusetts, who grew somewhat alarmed over her philosophical speculations, warning her particularly against becoming a disciple of Swedenborg. "You need not fear my becoming a Swedenborgian," she promised him. "I am in more danger of wrecking on the rocks of skepticism than of stranding on the shoals of fanatacism." Although she was apt "to regard a system of religion as I do any other beautiful theory," she did believe that she had discovered a significant fact: "the spontaneous growth of goodness in the human heart." "If we oftentime commit good actions without time to reflect on their tendency," she queried Convers, "does it not argue a natural impulse to good which takes root in the heart before we have time to calculate its growth?"¹⁰ Although Maria's earnest belief in "a natural impulse to good" in the hearts of men would be severely shaken in the years ahead, her interest in the "fanaticism" of Swedenborg would remain with her throughout her life.

Convers was sufficiently concerned about his "undisciplined" sister's speculating over the theories of suspect philosophers that he invited her to make her home with him and his wife. Maria gladly accepted: to be in Convers's constant company, to be near Boston and Cambridge, to share in the intellectual stimulation he and his friends enjoyed. In her brother's home she met and argued with the bright young men who themselves sought out the popular and well-read minister: Theodore Parker, John Weiss, George Ripley, Whittier, and Emerson. Although Convers habitually saw all sides of an issue, Maria was consistently outspoken in her opinions, denouncing what she believed was wrong, defending what she believed was right. Parker reportedly said that he enjoyed her frankness and her "cheering words to a young fellow fighting his way to education."¹¹

To give herself an income, she opened a girls' school, where, in addition to teaching the conventional subjects, she provided lessons in home management and a vigorous program in physical education. Preparing lessons and written exercises for the girls was something Maria had enjoyed since she had written out her first assignments in Gardiner. She developed the habit of writing little stories to prove a point or to show a moral. It occurred to her that she might write a longer tale. Convers had been talking about a book he intended to write on the work of John Eliot, the seventeenth-century New England missionary among the Indian tribes. Although Maria knew relatively little about the Indians in New England, she believed that a romance could be fashioned which would have reader appeal. Then, too, she had read an article in the *North American Review* in which the author had suggested that the aspiring novelist in America might well find materials in the country's past. She wrote *Hobomok* (1824) in six weeks, a tale of the Puritans and of an Indian's love for a white woman—a love that was consummated by marriage and the birth of a child. The tale of miscegenation disturbed some of her contemporaries, even though the white woman eventually left Hobomok and returned to her former lover thought dead; yet Maria stressed the moral nature of man which rests in his conscience and not in the color of his skin or with the dictates of society. *Hobomok* proved, nevertheless, to be quite popular with Boston readers, and Maria was for the moment a literary ingenue.

Success prompted her to write another novel immediately: *The Rebels* (1825). Again setting her story in New England, recounting some of the events that preceded the Revolution, she probably owed something to *Lionel Lincoln,* Cooper's abortive romance of the Massachusetts agitations, although she gave greater attention than Cooper did to the local patriots. The story line of the novel did tax the readers' ability to keep the characters straight, but once again Maria showed how men of conscience differed from the British magistrates, even from their rebel colleagues, in an attempt to do what was right. Although it was popular with Boston readers, reviewers complained about its shoddy construction, one reviewer questioning her skill in "novel-making," and adding that if the author continued to write she would, "sooner or later, discover [her] proper employment, and produce valuable and honourable works."[12] Disappointed, even embarrassed, she turned again to writing children's stories, conceiving the idea of publishing them bimonthly in *The Juvenile Miscellany* (1826–1834)—the first periodical for children appearing in the United States. The magazine was as popular with young readers as her novels had been with their older sisters and mothers.

Teaching and writing and editing now occupied her waking hours.

She seemed content, writing an acquaintance in an animated tone:

What do you do with yourself in these days? Hold high converse with Plato, or feed your sheep with turnips? Snarl with Diogenes, or laugh at neighbor Paris and his Sampson's riddle? I wish I could pop down upon you, and enjoy one or two quiet days, but quiet does not seem to be in reserve for me. "How can you expect it," you will say, "when you are always engaged on some mad-cap enterprise or other? When Hobomoks, Rebels, Miscellanies, succeed each other, thick as hail?"[13]

II   ". . . *Living for Others, Not for Yourselves*"

Among Convers's circle of friends there now appeared a young man to whom Maria was particularly attracted—a serious young man, David Lee Child, who had given up his teaching in Boston Latin School to become secretary to the American consul in Lisbon and who had joined in the latter years of Napoleon's reign the Spanish revolutionaries "defending what he considered the cause of freedom against [the] French invaders."[14] When he had returned to the United States, he commenced the study of law in an uncle's office in Watertown and ultimately made his way to Convers's home. Maria was impressed with him because he shared her enthusiasm for reading and writing and endorsed her liberal ideas. When he told her that farmers in Spain and Italy still used the kind of plow described by Virgil, she confessed her hope of reading the poet in the original. He immediately offered to translate any passages for her and to teach her Latin and Greek.

In an autobiographical fragment Maria sets down her early impressions of Child, who "captivated my imagination, and soon interested my heart."

He is the most gallant man that has lived since the sixteenth century; and needs nothing but helmet, shield, and chain armour to make him a complete knight of chivalry.[15]

Child himself was "captivated" with Maria as well, as other excerpts in the autobiographical fragment reveal: ". . . the etherial [*sic*], high-souled, high-reaching Maria! the elegant, [wise], powerful-minded Maria! . . . I know of no mind with which [it] seems to me, my soul could hold such sweet converse as with the elegant, susceptible, correct, and brilliant spirit which animates the form of Maria. I could [love] her dearly if the fates were not adverse to it. She [is] the only lady in Watertown, who has made any [im]pression upon me of a serious and enduring kind[:] i.e., [nay?] of a tender kind."[16]

A heady idealism infected Child's estimate of the "high-souled" Maria, just as it did his attitude toward life. Family and friends frankly spoke their reservations about him to her, condemning him for being a visionary, a drifter, admonishing her to choose a man more settled, less quixotic. Child's practical sense, to these sober New Englanders, was about as effective as "cutting stones with a razor," she was told.[17] He had no regard for money, no commitment to the routine matters of life. Maria ignored the warnings; her saving ways, her practical sense, were enough for them both. Child's idealism was not a flaw but a sign of near perfection: "a complete knight." When she agreed to marry him, Child erupted in the pages of his journal:

Oct. 19, 1827. . . . Yesterday Eveg., after an ineffectual attempt to see Miss *L. M. Francis*, I sat down & indited a letter, in which I told her that I loved her, & was lying at her feet. Today I received an answer, which, much—as I loved & respected her, has raised still higher my opinion of her. It was favorable. I am ACCEPTED; I am too happy. The letter was (as might have been expected from her noble character), as far above the affectation & prudery & silliness of many women, (most I might say) as the Heavens are above the earth. I have at last found a treasure. . . . [18]

He did add a sobering reflection: "I have but one source of unhappiness, & that is a distrust of my power to make my Maria as happy as she deserves to be."[19]

The autobiographical fragment carries the brief statement: "David Lee Child and Lydia Maria Francis were united in matrimony Oct. 18, 1828."[20]

Child was, like Bronson Alcott, the stubborn idealist, whose appalling lack of common sense caused his wife as much anguish as Alcott caused his wife and daughters. But Maria, like Alcott's daughter Louisa May, at least, could on occasion command a ready wit to get her through the hard moments.

Child's distrust was well founded. From the beginning, he and his wife lived in a succession of tiny houses, apartments, and cottages. His income from lawyering was erratic at best, and what he earned he often lent to friends and acquaintances less well provided for or gave away to the destitute or contributed to causes he was espousing. Mrs. Child's income from teaching and writing—and her frugality—was at first sufficient for them both. They lived in genteel poverty.[21] But Child's philanthropy put them in debt in less than a year, and she had to borrow $500 from her father, humiliated to learn that the family's reservations about her husband were apparently all too true. But she refused to let the loan jeopardize their marriage: Child was still "a complete knight." Nevertheless, a friend wrote some years later that from "a worldly point of view, [she] ought to have had a different lot, but [she] never faltered or failed in her duty to her husband . . . and was, beyond all doubt, perfectly happy in her relations with him."[22]

It was during the first year of marriage that she wrote *The Frugal Housewife* (published the following year, 1830) for "those who are not ashamed of economy." Her own predicament undoubtedly gave the book its authenticity. She continued to teach and to edit *The Juvenile Miscellany*; wrote a "novel" in dialog, *The First Settlers of New England* (1829), in which a mother instructed her daughters about the mistreatment of the Indian tribes by seventeenth-century Puritans; compiled an anthology of her published verse and stories, *The Coronal* (1831); and served as literary editor of the *Boston Traveller*. The pressure for money to repay her father's loan took its toll, so much so that Child in some panic for her health insisted that she take a brief holiday.[23]

In spite of anxieties, frustrations, disappointments, and adversities, the marriage was in the early years at least as Child had envisioned. The autobiographical fragment records its progress. More books came from Mrs. Child's pen to shore up the income. Already ten editions of *The Frugal Housewife* had been sold in the United States, with editions printed in England and in France as well. Companion volumes—*The Mother's Book* (1831) and *The Girl's Own Book* (1831)—were selling nearly as well. Such books were apparently the "valuable and honourable works" she would supply her readers—not fiction contrived in plot and weak in execution as the reviewer in the *United States Literary Gazette* had somewhat reluctantly concluded, but nonfiction informative and instructive to the workaday world. Nonfiction seemed appropriate to Mrs. Child, too, as she expanded her spheres of concern. She began projects of more immediate interest—informal biographies of eminent women and good wives,[24] using as her library the Boston Athenaeum, where she held a complimentary card given her after the publication of *Hobomok*. The Athenaeum was a men's library. Only Hannah Adams, the eccentric Boston historian, recognized as the first professional woman author in America, and Mrs. Child were accorded card privileges by the members, who respected the "men's minds" of these two women.[25] Other people, too, respected the minds and the company of Mrs. Child and her knight errant. Visitors sought out the occupants of the little home in Cottage Place, as they had come to Convers's study some years earlier: Parker and Whittier and Emerson, the poets Frances Osgood and Celia Thaxter, Margaret Fuller and Elizabeth Peabody. The security the Childs felt during the three years spent in the little home in Cottage Place made for the happiest years of their marriage.

The appearance of William Lloyd Garrison's *The Liberator* in Boston in 1831 signaled the end of that security, although for the Childs a greater benefit accrued. Along with Garrison, Child had been a correspondent for the *Massachusetts Whig Journal*; along with Garrison, he had reflected on the evil of slavery and the threat it posed to the moral health of the nation. The evil of slavery was not new to Mrs. Child, having heard her father condemn "the peculiar institution" when she was a child. Now Whittier and William Henry Channing, among others, were actively discussing ways in which the issue could be resolved; and, as Whittier and Channing were discovering, to espouse a cause—as yet not a popular cause except in casual conversation or in an idealistic editorial—was sure to bring criticism. Regardless of almost certain disapproval, the Childs made their choice. Child was one of fifteen men, along with Garrison and Ellis Gray Loring, among others, who formed the American Anti-Slavery Society in Boston, in January 1832—dedicated to the immediate emancipation of the slaves. When Convers cautioned his sister about involvement in the cause, she replied with characteristic confidence: "Firmness is the virtue most needed in times of excitement. What consequence is it if a few individuals do sink to untimely and dishonored graves? . . . I have examined the history of the slave too thoroughly, and felt his wrongs too deeply, to be prudent in the worldly sense of the term."[26]

Mrs. Child now set herself a plan of study in the books and pamphlets available to her in the Athenaeum. When she concluded her investigations, she wrote *An Appeal in Favor of That Class of Americans Called Africans* (1833), "fully aware," she announced in the preface, "of the unpopularity of the task I have undertaken . . . expect[ing] ridicule and censure." She received both in fullest measure. Subscriptions to *The Juvenile Miscellany* ceased, sales of *The Frugal Housewife* and *The Mother's Book* dwindled; the Athenaeum trustees revoked her card privileges, making it patently clear that she was persona non grata.[27] Friends and acquaintances snubbed her; editors refused her articles; and angry Bostonians thought that a prominent young matron, whose work—"useful . . . [for] its good sense"—[28] was so much admired, deliberately antagonized them by declaring that black men and women were in fact Americans. Mrs. Child steeled herself for the abuse, accepted the censure, and announced without rancor to her young readers in the final issue of the *Miscellany*, now a casualty of the outspoken *Appeal*, that "all true excellence and happiness consist in living for *others*, not for *yourselves*." With these words Mrs. Child established her creed, a creed she rarely veered from for the rest of her long life; henceforth, hers was a life devoted to the service of others. She committed herself, joining what one Boston Brahmin called that "squad of blue-stockings and abolitionists, both of whom are my abhorrence."[29]

III   "... I Am Thankful That My Work Is for the Anti-Slavery Cause ..."

Child and Garrison, like some visionaries, were not men of business sense. Mrs. Child, like many reformers, was a woman of common sense—if on occasion misguided by earnestness of the current cause. More conservative New Englanders were alarmed by Garrison's aggressive—even abrasive—insistence that slavery be immediately abolished. He went so far as to advocate a boycott of all goods grown by slave labor—among them cotton, to the dismay of mill owners and bankers who saw that economic ruin for the region might result from his proposal. Child, too, surveyed the marketable goods produced by slave labor, wondering whether any might be grown satisfactorily in the North. One came to his mind: sugar. He had read articles on the success of Belgian manufacturers in extracting sugar from beets. Beets grew in New England. Perhaps beet sugar, produced by free labor, could become a substitute for cane sugar. With this idea in mind, he determined that he must go to Belgium and study the process of turning beets into sugar; but he needed money. Mrs. Child, still confident in her husband's schemes, took up her pen once again to earn the funds required for the venture. She had set aside a study on the status of women when the more urgent issue of slavery demanded her attention in the *Appeal*; now she returned to the earlier research and painstakingly amassed her evidence to prove that women from ancient times were indeed the equal of men. *The History of the Condition of Women in Various Ages and Nations* (1835) was published at an auspicious time, when women were voicing their protest against laws that prohibited them from administering property and entering the business world. Not so curiously, the call for the emancipation of slaves accompanied the agitation for the emancipation of women. Mrs. Child, a reluctant participant in causes,[30] but always a willing worker by means of her pen, analyzed—logically, if a bit heavy-handedly—the role of women through the ages. The book clarified women's position; letters came from appreciative readers, but sales were feeble.

However, the charge leveled against her by the *Literary Gazette* reviewer at the time *The Rebels* was published—that she had failed to achieve "eminent success as a novel-writer"[31]—still rankled; she turned again to fiction, finishing a romance, *Philothea* (1836), which she had been working on for some four or five years. It proved to be more popular with readers and reviewers than statistics about the condition of women. The romance was her tribute to the glory that was Greece, set in the age of Pericles and Aspasia, the wife of great beauty and political wisdom who had advocated new freedoms for women. And once again Mrs. Child depicted men of conscience victimized by the state for the fervor of their beliefs. It was obliquely a comment on the times in America as well. Although the publisher gave her an advance on the book, part of which would be used for Child's expenses in Belgium, she felt that in good conscience she must assign any royalties from the romance to her father, to discharge a portion of the debt still outstanding since the first year of the marriage. She had another conscious motive in mind, too, informing Convers: "I am glad if this work adds to my reputation, because it will help to increase my influence in the anti-slavery cause. It will be another mite added to the widow's fund for the treasury of the Lord. Every day that I live, I feel more and more thankful for my deep interest in a cause which carries me out of myself."[32]

Yet funds for the trip were still wanting. Mrs. Child asked friends and acquaintances in the growing abolitionist circle for money, the Society contributed to the small reserve, and ultimately the little home in Cottage Place was sacrificed. With barely sufficient money for one passage, Child set out in the fall of 1836 for New York and the ship to Europe, only to be delayed dockside with the threat of a lawsuit for nonpayment of bills. Friends paid the bills, and he was off to realize his dream.

In the year and a half Child was in Europe, Mrs. Child lived for a time with her mother-in-law and then with her elder brother James Francis, who, though unsympathetic to her husband's schemes, granted asylum to his sister. To pay her way she cared for his children, wrote stories for the few magazines that now accepted her material, and compiled another manual, *The Family Nurse* (1837), a mother's guide to home nursing, a glum book reflecting the despair of its editor.

Child returned in 1837, at the height of the panic which was hitting the country, his head full of theories and notions for converting beets into sugar. He thought that he had studied the process carefully. He even contracted for machinery to be sent to him, even though he had no money to pay for it. With Cottage Place sold, they were homeless. Ellis Gray Loring and his wife offered them a temporary home. It was humiliating for Mrs. Child to accept the charity, but she had no choice, vowing to pay Loring rent when she was able. "My strongest peculiarity," she told him, "is pride of personal independence."[33] Loring was an able friend, later acting as her business adviser.

The autobiographical fragment summarizes the years immediately ahead: "After my beloved husband returned from Europe, we met with many worldly disappointments and discouragements; and for several years pecuniary necessities compelled us to labor far apart from each other."[34]

The "disappointments and discouragements" were due to Child's stubborn commitment to sugar beets. Persuading Mr. Francis to lend him money, he bought a farm in Northampton, Massachusetts, 100 rocky acres with soil hardly conducive to growing any crop let alone sugar beets, which he had seen growing in rich sandy soil in Belgium. For several years he struggled to make the soil productive and the beet crop plentiful. "His soul has been almost worried out of him," his wife wrote a friend, "by want of funds and by delay after delay. . . ." Yet she was supportive, assuring her friend that "his skill [is] in no way deficient to the task he has undertaken."[35] The machinery he purchased rusted on the wharves in New York before he was able to secure enough money, once again through Mr. Francis, to pay for its release from the consignee. Although Child's pioneer work was recognized by a state agricultural society in 1839 with the award of a silver medal, it was a Pyrrhic victory. Farmers simply would not devote their rocky acres to growing sugar beets. Nevertheless, he persisted, even refusing the position of editor of the *National Anti-Slavery Standard*, the Society's New York-based newspaper, at a salary of $1,000 a year. Mrs. Child, more in touch with reality, saw the editorship as a means of discharging debts; and when he refused, she offered herself as editor and was accepted—though she had some reservations about curbing her "natural temperament."[36]

Mrs. Child went to New York in the spring of 1841, the Society having arranged lodging and board for her in the home of Isaac Hopper, the Quaker friend of the poor and the oppressed. Although she looked forward to the assignment, the task was in some respects "irksome," as she told a correspondent. ". . . It was not zeal for the cause, but love for my husband, which brought me hither. But since it was necessary for me to leave home to be earning somewhat, I am thankful that my work is for the anti-slavery cause. . . . I trust this weary separation from my husband is not to last more than a year."[37]

But to Loring she revealed her deeper anxiety: "Nothing *but* Mr. Child's pecuniary distress would keep me here another month. . . . Out of it, I *will* get, by hook or by crook. I question the morality of letting one's soul thus be ground up for a cursed reform!"[38]

She ran almost immediately into difficulty with the Society over its policy for the paper. Mrs. Child, although committed to the abolition of slavery, did not endorse the firebrand tactics now being encouraged by the more ardent Society members in Massachusetts. She did not condone violence[39] as a means of eradicating the evil of slavery. Her approach—as it had been in the *Appeal*—was to present facts honestly and objectively, appealing through the reasonableness of the argument to winning converts. She addressed her editorials in the paper to the perceptive reader—women, the Quakers, and "liberal sects"—since, she told Loring, "the orthodox will be shy of us, do what we may to please them."[40] As editor, she would be an independent agent, willing "to do *hard* work, but not *dirty* work for any cause."[41] She explained her position to Maria Chapman in Boston, one of the Society's members urging her to a more petulant editorial policy—in a letter severe, even sardonic, in tone:

> . . . I care not the turning of a copper, whether the Channingites and the Quakers approve of my course, or not; and I care *as* little whether the Chapmanites and the Garrisonites . . . give me a blowing-up; I am glad that they should do it, if it is any relief to their minds. . . . I am obliged to the Society for being willing to do my thinking for me, and graciously decide whether I shall live in N. York, Philadelphia or Boston. The *Standard* is theirs to move where they will. *I* am my own. . . . An agitator I am not, and never will be. . . . I feel at liberty to wash my hands of anybody, and anything, I please. . . . I hope you will not think this letter is in a threatening spirit, originating in an unique estimate of my own importance. No such thing. I merely wish it understood that I am emphatically an *individual*; and that you must choose your agent with reference to the work you want done.[42]

She wrote out her anger to Loring as well, to whom she was turning more often now than she was to her husband. She was indignant that, as a member of the Society, she was told to support this policy or to denounce that one. "I have no sectarian ties whatever," she fumed; "[and] I resist this innovation upon my freedom. If I see fit to contribute toward the hire of a Catholic Cathedral, or a Mahometan mosque, I have an undoubted right to do so. As if anti-slavery were the *only* idea in the universe!" Her experience convinced her that henceforth she would have "nothing to do with reforms . . . [as] organized machinery." Never again would she "join *any* association, for *any* purpose."[43] She kept her vow. Volunteer her services, endorse a particular reform, write in behalf of humanitarian endeavors, she did. But she would not subscribe to any association and work exclusively for its goals. She was hurt by the Society's intractableness, but she was not resentful. "You need not be afraid," she told Loring, "of my turning *against* the anti-slavery organizations. Those who leave old associates, from personal or selfish feelings, are prone to *attack* those they leave; not so with those who withdraw [because of] honest dictates of conscience or reason."[44]

In the end it was Mrs. Child's impatience[45] more than the hurt that prompted her resignation, that and her sincere reluctance to see the *Standard* become an organ of a faction of the Society. There was an irony in this devotion to antislavery and to the husband who tried futilely to make the rocky soil of New England produce sugar beets. Although she put in long hours as editor—"one demnition grind," she called it;[46] was separated "many a house-sick and husband-sick hour"[47] from what she held dear; had to live largely on the charity of her friends the Hoppers, whom she repaid as best she could by caring for the younger children and assisting the fugitive slaves who stopped at the Hopper way station on the Underground Railway, she was never paid the salary the Society promised her.[48] At one time she had only 37½ cents in her purse for three months; her winter coat was so shabby that she was fearful she would not be able to make her rounds newsgathering.[49] And when she did resign, the Society offered the editorship to her husband. At last recognizing the failure of his experiment, Child gladly turned to this venture: one that, at least, he was better suited to discharge. He also promised to admit "more controversial matter" into the paper.[50] Mrs. Child was provoked, pointing out to her husband that she could not see both of them "depending on the precarious support of *any* benevolent or reforming society."[51] He was adamant. She was right. He was never paid.

When Child gave up the farm, even more heavily in debt, he declared bankruptcy. The forced sale of what few possessions they had, the aggravation over his ineptness, the years of denial and poverty where they existed so often on the charity of friends—a fact which seemed not to bother Child but stripped her of pride and independence: all these considerations made her see one thing clearly. Although she loved her husband, he was a hopeless failure, an "incurable flaw."[52] Therefore, she asked Loring to separate her income from her husband's, a step "absolutely necessary in order to make my earnings of any use." Wherever the winds blew her husband, she was now determined to "make a nest in New York," to be close to editors and assignments. If Child wanted to make his home in New York as well, she would "find a warm corner . . . always . . . ready for him." For herself, she could no longer "float about" and "lose her capacity for business." She had to have a sense of security, and only she could build that security. She concluded, remorsefully or bitterly: "To pump water into a sieve for fourteen years is enough to break the most energetic spirit. I must put a stop to it, or die."[53]

IV "... A Feeling of Sadness . . ."

In keeping with her opinion that the *Standard* ought to be a "good family anti-slavery newspaper," Mrs. Child had written a number of familiar essays for the paper: impressions of New York and vicinity, her romantic delight in nature, vignettes of city life, her love of music and art, as well as articles on more vital subjects—women's rights, temperance, prison reform, hospital reform, capital punishment. These "letters" had been widely reprinted, in the *Boston Courier* by contract and in other papers in the East and in the South. Their popularity with readers encouraged her to publish them in book form, as *Letters from New York* (1843). The first collection was so well received that she garnered a second series from the articles, publishing them in 1845. Both collections went through a number of editions, and she was identified to an even larger reading public not only as a warm and sensitive woman but as a compassionate and eloquent champion of the poor and the oppressed. The volumes brought praise from friends[54] but, more importantly, provided a basis for that security which had eluded her since her marriage. She was, in fact, not even disturbed that pirated editions were being circulated nor that her "reform" essays had caused some editors not to invite her "to write for the popular periodicals of the day," as she told Rufus W. Griswold; ". . . *this* effect of unpopularity is no inconvenience . . . for I [w]ould not write for such publications if I were ever so much urged. Life is growing too earnest with me to admit of my writing 'pretty stories.'"[55] For the first time in her life she was truly independent.

Yet she did not give up "pretty stories" altogether because they brought in money: she edited *Flowers for Children* (1844, 1846), anthologies of her verse and stories for young readers; contributed other stories and essays to the antislavery organs, the *Liberty Bell* among others, and to the gift books and annuals.[56] The years she spent in New York—sometimes with her husband, more often alone—gave opportunity to indulge Lydia Maria Child. She renewed

her acquaintaince with Margaret Fuller, who had recently come to
the city as an editor for Horace Greeley's New York *Tribune*. They
still shared from their earlier association in Boston an interest in the
classics, literature, music and art, and reform, although Miss Fuller
was never the active abolitionist her friend was. Particularly on the
subject of women's rights were they of one mind; and they deeply
resented women's auxiliary position in society, more especially their
frequent inequity before the law. In fact, Miss Fuller had praised
Mrs. Child's work in just such an instance in *Woman in the
Nineteenth Century*—Mrs. Child's support of a young woman who
had stabbed her seducer.[57] However, Margaret Fuller largely in-
tellectualized women's rights while Mrs. Child sought to implement
practical changes. Although Mrs. Child sought equality, women—
like the Negroes—must be educated to the responsibility, and she
exhorted her women readers to prepare themselves for it. When she
was not otherwise occupied, she was spending time reading and
researching material for her most ambitious work to date, a history of
the world's religions.

Nevertheless, separation from one's husband in nineteenth-century
American society was not condoned. Friends were discreet, but
Convers, her father, and other members of the family strongly
questioned their living apart. She wavered, confessing to a friend
". . . a feeling of sadness . . . that I can not see my way clear for a
permanent home" with her husband.[58] Child's follies pretty well
corroded the tenderness she had felt for him. When he arrived in New
York in the spring of 1849 for a visit, the time for a final assessment
came; and when he returned to Northampton, it was agreed that she
would return, too, as soon as she could see her way clear of the New
York commitments. The "feeling of sadness" ultimately prevailed.
"Domestic love," she professed to her friend Marianne Silsbee, "is the
best of earth's blessings and worth having even at the price of many
drawbacks."[59] "At last," Mrs. Child writes in the autobiographical
fragment, "in 1852, we made a humble home in Wayland, Mass[ts],
where we spent twenty two cozy years, entirely alone, without any
domestic, mutually serving each other, and entirely dependent upon
each other for intellectual companionship. I always depended on his
richly-stored mind, which was always able and ready to furnish
needed information on any subject. He was my walking Dictionary of
many languages, my Universal Encyclopedia."[60] No doubt adjust-
ments were made, and compromises were worked out, by both of
them.

V   *". . . Pardon Me for Being So Ready to Rear
My 'Porcupine Quills'"*

The Wayland years were relatively quiet ones, in the beginning devoted to the needs of Mrs. Child's father, who now shared his home with them. Her reading in the history of the world's religions went on slowly, deliberately paced, unhurried. She needed time to sift fact from dogma, tenets of faith from fanaticism. Sectarianism, it seemed to her as she did her research, was not the answer to one's personal religion, but commitment instead to good works such as her friends the Hoppers espoused. As she worked her way through the books of the world's religions, often in foreign languages, analyzing, comparing, digesting, it was Child's command of languages that constantly amazed her—truly her "walking Dictionary . . . [her] Universal Encyclopedia." He translated passages so easily. After eight years, the book—*The Progress of Religious Ideas through Successive Ages* (1855)—was finished; the publisher accepted the manuscript without any change.

This is the second time [she wrote her friend Lucy Osgood] I have walked out in stormy weather without a cloak. My *Appeal*, in favor of anti-slavery and attacking colonization, marched into the enemy's camp alone. . . . Who can tell how many young minds may be so influenced by the *Progress of Religious Ideas* as to materially change their career?[61]

The book did not influence "many young minds," not even many mature minds, but it was for Mrs. Child at least "a real pilgrimage of penance" for her own defection from the Calvinist church of her forebearers and from Convers's Unitarianism.[62] Never one to accept cant and hypocrisy in the established sects, she had bemoaned to Lucy Osgood some years before the "spiritual isolation" she lived in, noting that so often she "wandered on most subjects, from the commonly-received opinions of mankind."[63] Her faith, she discovered, was a simple one: "Most devoutly do I believe in the pervasive and ever-guiding Spirit of God; but I do not believe it was ever shut up within the covers of any *book*, or that it ever *can* be. Portions of it, or rather breathings of it, are in *many* books. The words of Christ seem to me *full* of it, as no other words are. But if *we* want truth, we must listen to the voice of God in the silence of our *own* souls, as *he* did."[64] On another occasion she said: "I cannot say, as Lessing did, that if God offered him the truth with one hand, and the investigation [of truth] with the other, he would choose the latter.

I want to believe. . . . If I can only be sure that I do not accept delusion for truth. . . . Whether I shall ever get a sight of Canaan before I die, I know not."[65]

The "sight of Canaan," if it came to Mrs. Child, was her service to others—the lifetime commitment she made to good works. And now the abominable Fugitive Slave Law and the hateful Kansas-Nebraska Act gave her commitment incentive. "My own duty," she wrote Lucy Osgood, "I see very plainly. The voice of God in my soul says audibly, 'Stand by the slave, come what will!' That I *must* do. I cannot otherwise. . . ."[66] When Charles Sumner was caned unconscious on the floor of the Senate by an irate Prescott Brooks of South Carolina, her indignation spilled out in "The Kansas Emigrants," in *Autumnal Leaves* (1856), the anthology she had recently prepared. Then, too, she had long admired John Brown's efforts to prevent slavery in Kansas, even accepting the bloodshed he caused; in her eyes, and those of many New Englanders, he was a man with a mission, a self-appointed emissary of God. Although the raid on Harper's Ferry surprised her, she could only admire his bravery and courage, writing Garrison: "I think [that] this will prove [to be] that 'Concord Fight' of an impending revolution and that the 'Bunker Hill Battle' will surely follow. May God make us strong for freedom."[67] Like Melville, Mrs. Child saw in John Brown's action "the meteor of the war." Unlike Melville, she was not distressed: a holy war was better than an unholy Union. Heart full of compassion for the martyr, she wrote Governor Henry A. Wise of Virginia, offering to nurse the wounded hero if Brown wanted her. The governor answered that he would not prevent her coming to Virginia although certainly her reception would not be a friendly one, since in his opinion it was the prodding of abolitionists like her who had stimulated Brown's raid. Mrs. Child fired a rebuttal to the governor and awaited Brown's reply. She was disappointed when Brown refused her offer, on advice of counsel who apparently feared their client's case would be gravely jeopardized if a prominent abolitionist like Mrs. Child were too closely linked to the defense. The matter seemed to end, until Greeley printed the Child-Wise correspondence in the *Tribune*. Once again, Mrs. Child had gone out "in stormy weather without a cloak."

. . . You can hardly conceive of the violence and obscenity of those [letters] I receive from Virginia [she wrote a correspondent]. I did not suppose that even Slavery could produce anything so foul. . . . But *will* he be executed? Emerson writes me: "I have hopes for his brave life. He is one for whom miracles wait." And I confess I have a *little* of the same hope. . . . A little while ago, I thought I was growing drowsy and old; but these stirring times make me strong as an eagle.[68]

The "miracle" Emerson hoped for did not occur, and Brown was hanged. "[Whether] John Brown did wrong, or not; whether he was sane, or not," Mrs. Child declared, "all I know, or care to know, is that his example has stirred me up to consecrate myself with renewed earnestness to the righteous cause for which he died so bravely."[69]

Brown's martyrdom motivated her writing once again for "the righteous cause": the pamphlet *The Right Way, the Safe Way* (1860), in which she showed the Southern planter and the Northern businessman that slavery was not economical.[70] "You will perhaps wonder that I leave out the question of *justice* and *humanity*," she explained to a correspondent. "But you must remember that I wrote it especially for the *South*. It is strongly impressed upon my mnd that there are *reflecting* people at the South, who might be influenced by these statements, if we could only contrive to place them before them."[71]

VI   *"I Am Particularly Delighted with the Process of Saving with One Hand and Giving with the Other"*

The Childs rarely stirred from the home in Wayland during the war years. Child gave up the schemes which had kept them in debt so many years and concentrated on law practice and on writing. Mrs. Child remembers the "years of quiet companionship . . . far from the excitements and hurry of the World":

We had no leisure for ennui; being too constantly occupied with house-work, sewing, gardening, carpentering, and making various mechanical con-trivances, for which my dear husband had a wonderful degree of ingenuity and skill; from these employments we returned with never-failing zest to study, or to amuse ourselves with books.[72]

They now had a security which had eluded them in their younger years; with the death of Mr. Francis, Mrs. Child inherited the house and property.[73] She maintained an active correspondence, lengthy letters to friends and acquaintances on topics of the day—the conduct of the war, slavery, politics, her flowers, their domestic concerns and delights. She continued her writing, editing *Incidents in the Life of a Slave Girl* (1861), and submitted stories to the *Atlantic Monthly*, recalling incidents in her youth which served as a basis for the fictions. To a child who asked for an autograph, she wrote:

> To love one's family is good.
> To love one's country is better.
> To love one's fellowman is best.[74]

It was service to others that guided her pen and her sharing. The money coming into the house was rarely spent on themselves but given instead to friends and acquaintances, to people in need as they had once been, and to charities and relief societies and always associations which provided funds for fugitive slaves. The routine, she recounted to a friend:

... I work like a beaver the whole time. Just now I am making a hood for a poor neighbor; last week I was making flannels for the hospitals; odd minutes are filled up with ravelling lint; every string that I can get sight of, I pull for my poor oppressed brother Sambo. I write to the "Tribune" about him; I write to the "Transcript" about him; I write to private individuals about him; and I write to the President and Members of Congress about him; I write to Western Virginia and Missouri about him, and I get the articles published too.[75]

Although she expressed "calm confidence" that God, "ruling the whirlwind," would deliver the North through the crisis of war, she sometimes questioned the conduct motivating men—"merchants alarmed about depredations on commerce," citizens fearful of government's collapse into anarchy, even fellow abolitionists more interested in restoring the country's "national vanity . . . in the eyes of the world."[76] Who was concerned about the slave? She reported to her friend Lucy Osgood that when Child, "attend[ing] one of the fashionable meetings for furnishing aid" to the war effort, spoke of the responsibility of the government toward the slaves, he was "almost mobbed" and "was told the war had 'nothing to do with the damned niggers; the war was to preserve the *Union*, that's what they were fighting for, and they wouldn't hear a word about the niggers.'"[77]

For Mrs. Child, the real reason for the war, the abolition of slavery, was being lost sight of because men viewed the conflict from their own perspective. "God knows I *want* to love and honor the flag and my country," she wrote a correspondent, "but while *such* things are done under it, how can I love or honor it?" She despaired of men's aims: "Oh, blind, blind selfishness!" The only way to secure freedom, she concluded, "[was] to protect the freedom of *all*. It would be the most *humane* policy."[78] She met Emerson "in the cars" to Boston. "He asked me if I prayed six hours a day. [My belief is that I pray twenty four hours a day.] 'All we can do just now,' said he, 'is to look toward the East and pray.'"[79] Such an attitude, she felt, was spineless—as if one did not work to make sacrifices come out right. Still, she saw the "moral sense of [the] nation"—not only the South but the North as well—"fearfully diseased":

As the war is now carried on [she wrote Sarah Shaw], I see little of moral grandeur in it; almost nothing that will be of value as a[n] historical lesson to the human race. We give generously and we fight bravely; but on both sides we rush furiously to battle trampling on prostrate millions, who look up imploringly to us for help. I do not see how a just God *can* save a nation in such a moral condition as this is.[80]

She fretted that the President took so long to free the slaves; and, when emancipation was announced in January 1863, she wrote a friend: ". . . I shall [now] . . . take hold of something else that is unpopular. I never work on the winning side, because I know there will always be a plenty ready to do such work."[81]

"Something else" became concern for the education of the free blacks. Although she wanted "to go and labor among the Freedmen," to teach in their schools, she realized that "paramount duties"—Child's declining health—prevented her. So, she told a friend, "the Kind Father" put the notion in her head of writing for them a simple textbook. "It is not *much*," she said, "but it is *something. . . .* Perhaps the good Lord will put some other means of usefulness into my head."[82] *The Freedmen's Book* (1865) contained essays in conduct and poems, hymns, and stories extolling the accomplishments of the Negroes. "By hook and by crook," she set aside $600 to defray the cost of printing and persuaded Ticknor and Fields to pick up the rest of the tab, refusing royalties and giving them instead to the Freedmen's Association. She prided herself, she told a friend, that she and Child lived so "wonderfully cheap" because it enabled her "*to dash out*, when I have projects for Sambo in hand." And she concluded: "I am particularly delighted with the process of saving with one hand and giving with the other. I don't think the golden streets of the New Jerusalem would give me much satisfaction, unless I could help make them."[83]

She wrote one more novel, "giving with the other [hand]" the royalties to the Freedmen's Association. In all her fiction, from *Hobomok* on, she had made the appeal to conscience; now, in *A Romance of the Republic* (1867), a sentimental tale with a topical theme, she called for fair treatment of the blacks. The novel, she hoped, might satisfy the literary taste of the day; but its mawkish plot and persecuted heroines held little interest for readers who now preferred burlier realism. The tale of foundlings was dated.[84] She would not serialize the novel in the *Atlantic Monthly*, feeling confident that royalties from sales would far surpass the $1,000 she was offered. She was chagrined that money for the charity was so meager.

When Child's death occurred in 1874, she was devastated; although he had been in poor health for a number of years, the reality of the separation was almost more than she could bear. She spent some months with various friends but finally returned to Wayland and to the home which they had shared so contentedly after the dark New York years. A source of consolation was her friendship with Whittier, who assured her that she and Child would be reunited. And in the last years, too, it was Swedenborg's thought, which she had long before endorsed in *Letters from New York*, that gave her ease. She told Whittier: "I'm a little anxious to be gone[,] for I have so many things to tell David. I believe [heaven] would be of small value to me if I were not united with him."[85]

She boarded a young man to satisfy friends and family who were disturbed that she lived alone. Still her concern was for others. A month before she died, she wrote a correspondent: "The worthy young man who comes here to sleep needs some help about learning a trade, and I am going to give him a lift. Divers other projects I have in my mind, and I expect to accomplish them all by the help of Aladdin's lamp. Oh, it is such a luxury to be able to give without being afraid. I try not to be Quixotic, but I want to rain down blessings on all the world, in token of thankfulness for the blessings that have been rained down upon me."[86]

A final verse appears in the autobiographical fragment:

> Life! we have been long together,
> Through pleasant and through cloudy weather.
> 'Tis hard to part when friends are dear;
> Perhaps't will cost a sigh—a tear.
> Then steal away; give little warning;
>   Choose thine own time;
> Say not Good Night; but in some brighter clime
>   Bid me Good Morning.[87]

She died with little warning, as she bent over to pull on her slippers, on getting out of bed one morning, October 20, 1880.

At the funeral Wendell Phillips, whom she had won to the antislavery cause, said: "She was the kind of woman one would choose to represent woman's entrance into broader life."[88]

CHAPTER 2

Hobomok, A Tale of the Times

MRS. CHILD came to fiction in much the same way as Cooper, who had apparently responded to a challenge laid down by his wife. She wrote *Hobomok, A Tale of the Times* as a result of reading an article in the *North American Review*, in which the author remarked how appropriate for the purposes of fiction was New England's past, particularly if the writer set the story in the stirring times of the Puritans—those "character[s] of stern, romantic enthusiasm" who had wrested from a savage wilderness their new home where they might freely worship God. "Whoever in this country," predicted the reviewer, "first attains the rank of a first rate writer . . . will lay his scene here."[1] Mrs. Child wrote the first chapter of the novel "one summer Sunday noon . . . [b]efore attending the afternoon [church] service" and finished the novel in six weeks.[2]

Hobomok is not the first-rate fiction the reviewer called for: it was too hastily written, uneven in development, immature in style. Yet there is remarkable skill in creating characters and in depicting the times, and Mrs. Child's earnestness in telling the story carries the reader along. Higginson probably goes too far when he observes that the novel "must be read in very early youth to give it any . . . attraction,"[3] as is Griswold when he complains that the basic plot "is not very skillfully managed."[4] Both men are imposing a standard of literary taste that was defined for the novel several decades later. *Hobomok* is a relatively early novel in America: its flaws can perhaps be overlooked. A fairer estimate is provided by the reviewer in the *United States Literary Gazette*: ". . . Its merit is greater than its pretension . . . with many faults which due culture may remove, there is a kind of graceful wildness which almost redeems [it]."[5] Thus, if the modern reader looks at *Hobomok* through the eyes of Mrs. Child's contemporary, he may discover in large part a satisfactory novel.

I   *". . . Stern Piety . . . Lofty and Genuine, though
Deeply Colored with . . . Ignorance and Superstition . . ."*

To give the story the semblance of truth, Mrs. Child announces
that it is drawn from a manuscript "written by one of my ancestors
who fled with the persecuted nonconformists from the Isle of Wight,
and about the middle of June, 1629, arrived in Naumkeak [Salem] on
the eastern shore of Massachusetts." She plans certain liberties with
the text: she will omit what is "dreary" in the account, she will
sometimes speak herself to the reader, she will concentrate on the
more interesting vignettes in the manuscript—the social history of the
Puritans whose lives were so strongly marked by "the pure flame of
religion . . . burning deeply and fervently" within them. Perhaps, as
Mrs. Child admits, in nineteenth-century New England, it has been
"fashionable to look back upon those early sufferers in the cause of
the Reformation as a band of dark, discontented bigots."

Without doubt, there were many broad, deep shadows in their characters,
but there was likewise bold and powerful light. The peculiarities of their
situation occasioned most of their faults, and atoned for them. . . . But the
heart pays involuntary tribute to conscientious, persevering fortitude, in
what cause soever it may be displayed. . . . [W]hatever might have been their
defects, they certainly possessed excellencies, which peculiarly fitted them for
a van-guard in the proud and rapid march of freedom.

Thus, somewhat in the manner of Gibbon whose pageantry of history
she had so recently admired, she reconstructs in "bold outlines" the
character of the Puritan—sometimes intolerant and contentious,
often unyielding and proud. It is the "passion of their religion which
gave purpose to their lives," she concludes. And as she writes her
history lesson, she soon forgets the "ancestor's" narrative and tells her
own story.

The "ancestor's" special friend in the village is Roger Conant, a
"rigid Calvanist" [*sic*] as much by circumstances as by religious
persuasion, it seems. A lowly man in the eyes of Old World society, he
had married a gentlewoman whose father immediately disinherited
her and thereby curtailed any aspirations the young husband had for
a life among the gentry. "Frustrated in his plans, thwarted by his
rivals," he and his wife emigrate to the Massachusetts colony where
they cast their lot among the Puritans. Their sober view of life affects
Conant, "misanthropy and gloom [sinking] down into the soul of the
disappointed man." Their prejudice affects him as well; and he too
rails against the common enemy, the Church of Rome and the

Church of England—the "abomination" of kneeling and the "mummery of common prayer." When their daughter Mary, who at birth became the ward of her grandfather, comes to Salem to care for her mother, Conant criticizes her "vamp[ing] up [her] frail carcase in French frippery" and scorns her Anglicanism, reminding her that "the idle follower of Morton . . . was inwardly given to the vain forms of the church of England . . . [which] was the reason his God left him, and Satan became his convoy." Enraged by Mary's stubborn adherence to her faith, he throws her prayer book into the fire.

Conant is Mrs. Child's recollection of Nathaniel Ward's dyspeptic cobbler of Aggawam: "I tell you that whosoever is willing to tolerate any false religion, or discrepant way of religion, that his own may be tolerated, will for a need hang God's Bible on the devil's girdle." The matter of "God's glory" is the prerogative of the Calvinists alone, not to be entrusted to "the hands of the heathen or the popist." It is with certain finality that he intones, "[T]he Lord's will be done. He hath begun his work, and he will finish it." Conant's wrath is soon directed against a young Anglican recently arrived in the village, Charles Brown, an earnest suitor of his daughter. "Verily, in due time," Conant prophesies, "[the Lord] will send forth his fire and destroy [him] from the face of the earth." His brimstone religion and crude sentiments—notwithstanding his lack of formal education—have earned him the right of counsel in the village and the special sanction of the minister and the governor John Endicott.

Somewhat surprisingly, Conant's closest friend in Salem is one "neighbor Oldham," about whom there is some unexplained scandal; he speaks of "his own wanderings, mistakes, and sufferings . . . [and] his own disgraces with the most shameless effrontery" and "laugh[s] at them more loudly than any other man." Something of a maverick, even a charlatan, Oldham is a man whom the more pious villagers have wondered about: "they had doubted the vitality of his religion, and had felt themselves darkened by intercourse with him." Oldham is a born-again Calvinist—perhaps a reconstructed Morton reveler— who narrowly escaped banishment from Salem and only saw "the great light" after he was musket-whipped by the elders of the village. Profane humor lurks behind his accounting of the incident.

. . . It was a season of comfortable out-pouring. Two passages of Scripture came to my mind, and I was gifted with great light thereupon. David hath it, "By thee have I passed through a troop";—and Amos speaketh at a time when, "If a man fled from a lion, a bear met him; and if he laid his hand upon a wall, a serpent bit him." Well, it was much the same with me: but as I told you, it was a time of great light, though it was nothing like the first dawning.

I'll tell you how it was. I was sitting thus, with my mug of flip before me, and
one hand upon each knee, looking straight into the fire, when suddenly I
bethought that I was like that smoking brand, with none to pluck it from the
burning. So I took a draught of the good stuff, and all at once a light streamed
around me, ten times brighter than the [E]arl of Warwick's big lamp.

Although making light of the "mysteries of godliness" in a "spirit of
devilish mirth" is disturbing to the sterner Conant, Oldham seems
sincere in his "remarkable" piety—a piety he wears more easily than
does his friend. The "vitality of his religion" the villagers ought not to
wonder about, since his convictions are as deeply settled—and his
catechism as confidently proclaimed—as his neighbors'. "England is
no place now-a-days for christian folks to live within," he tells the
young man who comes to court his daughter Sally. "I tell you their
bishops, their deans, and their deacons, are all whelps from the
Roman litter. . . . It is a sad pity that king Charles (I mean no
disrespect to his majesty) should suffer those black coats from the
ninneversities to get upon his royal back. . . . England is full of
malignant enemies to the true faith; and . . . a body can [only] pithily
practise the great precepts of the gospel . . . which I take to be
mortification and sanctification." He fears the influence of the king's
"Romish" queen Henrietta Maria and her French ways: "God help
him, and Satan leave off helping the queen and his bishops." Like
Conant, he admonishes his daughter for "hankering after French gee-
gaws," which may turn her head from "sound sense and sober
godliness." Sally is, after all, a woman, one of the "weaker vessels"—
"the source of every evil that ever came into the world. I don't refer in
special manner to that great tree of sin planted by Eve; but I say they
are the individual cause of every branch and bud from that day
downwards."

Sally's suitor protests her father's views, but Oldham silences him.
Because of the waywardness of his daughter, Oldham is not at all sure
that she is included "in the covenant with her parents." "It is not every
child of a righteous man who is among the elect. . . . If there be a
good child in Jeroboam's family, he is specified; and if there be a
cursed Ham among the children of Noah, he hath his brand." He even
has doubts about the young man, "as I've been told you are falling
into some Antinomian notions." But he will not "stay and argue with"
the man because "I must go up to Governor Endicott's awhile, to see
how the cattle are to be divided atween us; and I must stop to see a few
of the poor sick souls about us."

Oldham is uneducated like his friend Conant, yet he too commands the special sanction of the minister and the governor: both men are good proselytes for the arduous work to be done in the new Canaan.

Of the two latter-day Puritans, certainly Oldham is the more likable. As severe in his opinion of women as the villagers of Hawthorne's Salem in their judgment of Hester Prynne, he nevertheless loves Sally—"as good as any of her kind, to be sure"—who reminds him of his own erring ways. He is a simple man with a simple philosophy: "God gave us laughter as well as reason," he remembers; "Solomon saith, 'There is a time for all things' . . . there is a time to smoke a pipe and crack a joke, as well as to pray and preach." Conant, on the other hand, is a misanthrope, proud without reason, bitter without real cause. Alienated from his wife and his daughter, he has reluctantly perhaps substituted the Calvinist faith for family ties. The conflict results in anguish as deep as Goodman Brown's. The droll Oldham and the stern Conant are well drawn, and Mrs. Child's insight into human nature—in these characters, at least—is sure.

As sure, too, is her use of pertinent detail for the story, the rivalry among men to establish their religious convictions. Although Thomas Morton's revelers have been a source of aggravation to the village elders, and the Indians are a threat to the slender security of the colony, particularly after Morton and his men have sold them guns and ammunition, the Salem elders are far more aggrieved with the presence of "false religion" in their midst. Rev. John Lyford has already been expelled from the neighboring Plymouth plantation for advocating nonconforming doctrines among the Pilgrims, and the recent arrival in Salem of Charles Brown and his brother with the expressed intention of establishing an Anglican community is greeted with contempt and fear. "To my mind," Conant observes "there is more danger of Satan's killing us with the rat's-bane of toleration, than the Lord's taking us off with the Indian arrows. It behoveth [sic] the watchmen of Israel to be on their guard, for false prophets and false Christs are abroad in the land." Critical of the "ruling elders there at Plymouth" who have countenanced Lyford's presence among them so long, even skeptical of the continuing compact between saints and strangers in the plantation, the Salem Puritans are determined that their village not become "a cage for every unclean bird[,] a free stable-room and litter for all kinds of consciences." And when the Brown brothers hold their service, they are summoned before the elders and tried in the meeting house in the presence of angry villagers.

. . . The Governor arose, as he said . . . "Have you, young man, upheld the ritual of the first-born daughter of the church of Rome, and maintained that the arm of royal authority ought to enforce obedience thereto?"

"I have said," replied Brown, "that 'Religio docenda est, non coercenda,' was a bad maxim of state policy; and that 'Haeresis dedocenda est, non permittenda' was a far better.[6] . . . I would rather," continued he, raising . . . [his] voice, "I would rather give my limbs to the wolves of your desert than see her sceptre broken by men like yourselves."

"Think you," said Governor Endicott, smiling, "that king James cared aught for the church, save that he considered it the basis of the throne? You forget his open declaration in the assembly at Edinburgh. 'The church of Geneva,' saith he, 'keepeth pasche and yule; what have they for them? They have no institution. As for our neighbour kirk of England, their service is an evil mass in English. They want none of the mass but the liftings.'"

"King James had not then come to the English throne," answered Brown. "He found cause to alter his opinion after he had felt the blessed influence of that church, and seen many of her corner stones, elect and precious."

"Nay, Mr. Brown," rejoined the Governor, "there is enow wherewithal to convince your reason, for you are not wanting in the light which leadeth astray, that it was 'king craft,' which made James turn his back upon a church whereunto he had given the name of the 'sincerest kirk in the whole world'; and, with all reverence to his royal memory, I cannot but think that his love of forms and ceremonies was but a taint of hereditary evil from his Moabitish mother. Forasmuch as I am a loyal subject of king Charles, it is neither wise nor safe for me to find specks and blemishes in his government; but to my thinking, there is but a fine-spun thread between the crosier and the liturgy, the embroidered mantle and the bishop's gown; and who does not know that the heart of the king is fastened to the rosary of Henrietta Maria? And that the mummeries of Rome are, at her instigation, within the palace of St. James? . . ."

"And I marvel that men of sense, like yourself, Governor Endicott, can expect the sword of the Lord to be quiet in its scabbard, when the robe of religion is torn, and her altars overturned," replied Brown; "and that too, by men unto whom you give your countenance—a parcel of separatists and anabaptists, covering their sins with the cloak of religion, and concealing their own factious and turbulent spirit therewith."

Upon this [Rev.] Higginson and [Elder] Skelton arose and made answer:

"Neither as factious men affecting a popular parity in the church, nor as schismatics aiming at the dissolution of the church ecclesiastical, but as faithful ministers of Christ, and liege subjects of king Charles, did we come hither, We have suffered much for nonconformity in our native land, and after much tribulation have we come to this place of liberty. Here the cap and the gown may not be urged upon us, for we consider these things as sinful abominations in the sight of God. So may the Almighty prosper us, as we have, in all humility, spoken the truth."

"'Credat Judaeus, non ego,'" replied Brown, scornfully.[7] "It is easy to talk about conscience and humility, but wherein have you shown it, in that you

judge the conscience of your brethren? . . . There are those who can tell of
your evil practices, and they shall be told in a voice of thunder."

Such incidents, fictionalized for the purposes of Mrs. Child's story,
were common enough in seventeenth-century New England, tactics
frequently employed to banish dissenters from the colony, as the
episodes of Anne Hutchinson and Roger Williams attest. The
"unclean" were not welcome.

Although the Salem Puritans are deliberately shown in a bad light,
Brown's light is hardly any brighter. The incident simply provides Mrs.
Child opportunity to underscore the hypocrisy she saw in organized
religion, no matter the persuasion. Conant, Oldham, and Elder
Skelton are ignorant men who without thinking spiel the litany of
Puritan intolerance, yet Endicott and Rev. Higginson and Brown are
ostensibly educated men who corrupt the conscience of men for
theological ends. The "cloak of religion" conceals the "sinful
abominations" of Puritan and Anglican alike. There is an implied
irony in Brown's comment: "It is easy to talk about conscience and
humility, but wherein have you shown it, in that you judge the
conscience of your brethren?" Sectarians are Christians in name
only when truth is proscribed.

"Conscience and humility," not one of the disputants in the village
can lay claim to. There is, however, one in Salem who can—Conant's
wife. Denied the comfort of the Anglican religion by the Puritan
elders, when she first came to the village with her husband, Mrs.
Conant comes to realize that reliance on "forms and ceremonies" is
an empty security at best. There is a touch of humor in the comment
she makes to her daughter Mary, but sober judgment as well: her
ailing health fortunately spares her the "exhilarating draught[s]" of
Rev. Higginson's Sunday services "with some dozens of *doctrines*,
and more *uses* than twenty sermons . . . and an *improvement* at the
close, and a *finally* at the end of that." Doctrines simply rationalize
religion but do not stimulate Christian precepts of conscience and
humility. Not "a strong mind" but "a simple heart" is Mrs. Conant's
way to get "right with God." Dogmatists mislead the pilgrim since
doctrines cannot satisfy spiritual needs. ". . . There is little good," she
tells Mary, "in being convinced, if we are not humbled; to know every
thing about religion, and yet to feel little of its power." Dogmatists
have even corrupted the Bible through their reading of it, so that God
can no longer speak to the heart: they "[guard] the tree of life from the
touch of man." Without religion, without the Bible, the pilgrim finds
God in the creation itself, where "one may read to their fill." "It is

God's library," Mrs. Conant concludes, "the first Bible he ever wrote." Here the heart responds to God, and conscience and humility inspire the heart with faith; unlike religion, which "appear[s] more and more like a vapor," such faith will not "[pass] away." Mrs. Conant's sentiment is hardly characteristic of the seventeenth century, but it was one Mrs. Child no doubt was hearing in Convers's study during her conversations with the young men from Harvard.[8]

However, Mrs. Child's intent in *Hobomok* is not to scorn the Puritans; she can understand that their "stern piety was lofty and genuine, though deeply colored with the ignorance and superstition of the times." In a more enlightened age, in nineteenth-century New England, the Puritans can be forgiven the conspiracy which assured them a practical basis for their New World theocracy. More important, in America's era of national consciousness, she apostrophizes their efforts to establish a way of life: "in two hundred years from that dismal period," a new nation, the rival of England, came "into life with all the impetuosity of youthful vigor." In a spurt of animated patriotism, Mrs. Child exonerates the Puritans for a greater good, since they "could not foresee the result of the first move which they were unconsciously making in the great game of nations— a game which has ever since kept kings in constant check."

II   ". . . A Tale of the Times"

New England's past provides the framework for Mrs. Child's story, but *Hobomok* is a romance. Undoubtedly, the novel is wrongly named, for it is more a tale of the Salem villagers than it is a story about the Indians. The activities of Mary Conant and Sally Oldham and their friends, not occasional scenes of Indian life, furnish Mrs. Child material for the domestic drama.

In Mrs. Child's mind, Mary Conant is the heroine of the romance. Reared in her grandfather's manor, accustomed to the genteel life of the gentry where she had been "the little idol of the brilliant circle" of friends, she is sent to Salem by her grandfather to care for her dying mother—a commitment she discharges only out of a sense of filial duty. In the Puritan wasteland she remembers the "fairy spot of her existence" and impatiently awaits the arrival of her fiancé Charles Brown, "who understood her feelings, and who loved, as she imagined love," to take her back to England. Meanwhile, she "endure[s] the mean and laborious offices which she [is] obliged to perform." Sally Oldham offers her companionship, but Mary demurs. A certain arrogance inbred by her former associates prevents her from responding to the social visits of "her untutored friend," who is "so vastly her inferior." In fact, there are no women in Salem whom she can comfortably socialize with. Mrs. Child urges the reader's concern for Mary's outcast state, but Mary does not encourage it.

When Brown arrives, he immediately antagonizes the elders by conducting Anglican services in the village, and he is banished. Mary remains. With Brown gone and "in the selfishness of . . . weighty sorrows," her "woman's heart" turns for "flattery and devoted attention" to the Indian Hobomok. Given her breeding, her insufferable snobbery, the reader finds Mary's interest in Hobomok unbelievable—and her subsequent marriage to him incredible. It is truly, in the words of the *North American* reviewer, "a catastrophe."[9]

Sally Oldham is the more likely heroine of the romance, far more appealing to the reader than Mary. Her father's estimate of her—"she is as good as any of her kind, to be sure"—is unjust. She is fun-loving, carefree, honest, outspoken, even loyal to her sometime friend Mary. Mrs. Child describes Sally as a "roguish damsel"; the "ancestor," whose manuscript Mrs. Child has ostensibly followed for her story, remembers Sally as "a promp [*sic*] and jolly damsell, much given to lightnesse of speeche, but withal virtuous." The few eligible men in the village and its environs all court her, and she shares confidences about them with Mary. "Did you ever see such a fellow?" she asks Mary, in reference to a newcomer to Salem.

Every day since [he] landed, he has been at my elbow, trying to make love by stammering and stuttering about the crackling thorns of worldly mirth; and I verily think he believes that I have been greatly delighted therewith. A plague on all such sanctified-looking folks. There was Mr. Lyford (I don't care if he was a minister)[,] he was always talking about faith and righteousness, and the falling-off of the Plymouth elders, and yet many a sly look and word he'd give me, when his good-woman was out of the way.

Another suitor she refers to as "that screech-owl . . . who . . . [is] forever bawling Old Hundred in my ears."

The courtship of Sally and John Collier is a reenactment of *another* Plymouth courtship, as Collier arrives at Sally's house with a proposal of marriage from the "screech-owl." Sally is in command of the situation.

"So you are really going to break poor James' heart?" inquired [John], after a moment's pause.

"If so be there is such a thing as a heart in his big carcase of clay," rejoined the maiden, "I'm willing it should be shattered a bit."

"Poor fellow, what will he think of all this?" inquired the young man, thoughtfully. . . .

"But,—hem—but what can I do?" said he.

"I know what you *can* do; but what you *will* do, is of your own choosing. I have heretofore told you what to say to Hopkins; and now I tell you, John Collier, if you had sent by him, instead of he by you, and my father had said to me, 'wilt thou go unto this man?' I should verily have said, 'I will go.'"

"And I," rejoined the Plymouth messenger, smiling as he rose and laid his hand upon her shoulder, "I would assuredly have come out to meet thee, and bring thee into my tent. But what perplexes me most is, how I am to account for this to my friend Hopkins and the church."

"You may tell James," replied she, "that you was blind, till I would put eyes into your head; and as for the church, it is enough for them to square and clip our consciences without putting a wedge atwixt folk's hearts."

"It is not well to give away to lightness of speech in speaking of the dignities of the church," observed her lover, "though I know well you mean no harm."

Sally's parents are well pleased with the match, although Hopkins accuses Collier of treachery and deceit in delivering his message and brings charges against him before the elders—the implication being that Collier has bewitched Sally for his own devilish ends. At the hearing he explains the predicament, interrupted by an angry, resentful Hopkins. The elders delay their decision until Sally has had opportunity to confirm her lover's explanation; then they render verdict.

Although we deem it unseemly for young women to pursue such like courses (indeed were she within our jurisdiction, we should give her public reproof therefor),[10] and though we do fear that the daughter hath much of the corrupt leaven of the father, yet we do not see that we have a right to constrain the consciences of men in these particulars, especially as the apostle saith "the believing husband may sanctify the unbelieving wife." Therefore, we do leave Mr. Collier to pursue whatsoever course he deemeth expedient, trusting that, whatever he doth, he will do it in the name of the Lord. Moreover, we do think it proper that Mr. Hopkins make an apology to him, inasmuch as he hath not been slow to anger, nor charitable concerning his brother in the church.

Here is a love affair, amusing yet believable. Sally and Collier are married—the ceremony and wedding festivities providing another vignette of village life.

III   "*. . . The Catastrophe of the Story*"

Sally is loyal to her friend Mary, even when the Salem villagers—and Mary herself—are shocked by her "error in judgment," her marriage to Hobomok. She tells Mary in all sincerity: "I always thought he was the best Indian I ever knew; and within these three years he has altered so much, that he seems almost like an Englishman. After all, I believe matches are foreordained." If there is a bit of bewilderment in Sally's remark, she is attempting to rationalize an incredible situation—the marriage of a white woman to the manor born to an Indian primitive. Although the unlikely union speaks well for Mrs. Child's liberal mind, her treatment of the circumstances leading to the marriage is the feeble effort of an inexperienced novelist working out the details of her plot. Nor does any trait in Mary's character suggest the possibility of such a marriage. In fact, at one point in the story, Sally, who is prattling about marriage and the scarcity of young men in the village, remarks that the only "chance a body has for a husband" is to "pick up some stray Narragansett." "'O, don't name such a thing,' said Mary shuddering." And in the ensuing conversation the young women even suggest that they, like their Salem neighbors, regard the Indians as agents of the devil. It was perhaps with these ideas in mind that led the *North American* reviewer to remark that "[the marriage] is in very bad taste . . . and leaves . . . a disagreeable impression."[11]

As a tale of New England, as social history of a seventeenth-century village—which matter constitutes two-thirds of the narrative, incidentally—*Hobomok* satisfies the reader. Mrs. Child justifies the tale with an intimate knowledge of the Puritans' conduct and thought; she comprehends their theological concerns, their fears and apprehensions; she captures through history and legend the spirit of the times. However, the marriage of Mary Conant and Hobomok, so crudely grafted onto the narrative, disturbs the reader.

Hobomok figures in the novel as a character of secondary importance; and as a character of secondary importance, the reader is duly informed about him. Conant and Oldham, Mary and Sally reveal themselves to the reader, through their conversations and through their actions. Mrs. Child speaks for Hobomok; she also reports his activities. There are conversations between Mary and her lover which the reader is privy to, reinforcing the romance that obviously exists. The reader is told that Hobomok has loved Mary from a distance, ever since that day when "Mary had administered cordials to his sick mother, which restored her to life after the most skilful [*sic*] of their priests had pronounced her hopeless; and ever since that time, he had looked upon her with reverence, which almost amounted to adoration." He watches over her in silence, shadow-like, as she makes her way through the woods for a secret meeting with her lover, or as she sits disconsolately beside her mother's grave. He observes her among the villagers or in her home where he has been summoned by the elders to report the latest movements of rebellious tribes. He proves his arrow marksmanship at a deer slaughter. And during the winter months—Mrs. Child again informs the reader—he frequently comes up from Plymouth to join the villagers in their hunts. "At such seasons, he was all vigor and elasticity; and none returned more heavily laden with furs and venisons, than the tawny chieftain. The best of these spoils were always presented to the 'child of the Good Spirit,' as he used to call Mary. . . ." He recites to her and her father stories of the Indian nations, "glowing as they were in the brief, figurative language of nature." Finally, Mrs. Child tells the reader, "love for Conant's daughter, love deep and intense, had sunk into the bosom of the savage."

Since love "deep and intense" for a white woman has struck the redman, Mrs. Child, to forestall her readers' protests over miscegenation, uncolors him. She makes him white. She apologizes for his Indianness. Here, for the modern reader, is "the very bad taste."

No longer a character in his own right, Hobomok becomes the novelist's pawn. Hobomok, "cast in nature's noblest mould . . . clever . . . and comely withal," is Indian in name only. To make him an acceptable suitor, she alienates him from his brothers. He has apparently spurned the daughter of Philip of Pokanocket: "he loathed the idea of marriage with her." He has earned thereby the enmity of the Narragansetts. As a staunch friend of the white men, he is berated by one of the Indian warriors: "Shame on you, Hobomok! The wolf devours not its own; but Hobomok wears the war-belt of Owanux [Englishmen], and counts his beaver for the white man's squaw." He makes his home in Salem among his white friends, only visiting in his own wigwam in Plymouth on occasion. He is privy to the white men's councils, advises them, joins them in their hunting parties, goes on forays with them against the hostile tribes. Conant expresses the community's esteem: ". . . I have sat by the hour . . . and gazed on his well fared [sic] face, till the tears have come into mine eyes, that the Lord should have raised us up so good a friend among the savages." And to make final the isolation from his brothers, she suggests that Hobomok in his heart is really a nascent Christian:

The star, which had arisen in Bethlehem, had never gleamed along his path; and the dark valley of the shadow of death had never been illuminated with the brightness of revealed truth. But though the intellect be darkened, there are rays from God's own throne, which enter into the peacefulness and purity

of the affections, shedding their mild lustre on the ignorance of man. . . .
[T]here was within him a voice loud and distinct, which spoke to him of
another world, where he should think, feel, love, even, as he did now. He had
never read of God, but he had heard his chariot wheels in the distant thunder,
and seen his drapery in the clouds. In moods like these, thoughts which he
could not grasp, would pass before him, and he would pause to wonder what
they were, and whence they came. It was with such feelings that he stopped,
and resting his head against a large hemlock, which lifted its proud branches
high above the neighboring pines, he gazed on the stars, just visible above the
horizon.

Hobomok is now a white man in thought and emotion, in deed and
association. The transformation is unforgivable. Ironically, Mrs.
Child has made him one of our literature's earliest alienated heroes.

With only thirty pages before the end of the novel, Mrs. Child
"arranges" her denouement: "the catastrophe" of the story, as the
North American reviewer termed. Mary's mother has died, and she
regards herself unwanted in her father's house. She lives for the return
of her lover, only to learn that he was apparently drowned at sea.
There comes "a partial derangement of [her] faculties. A bewilderment of despair that almost amounted to insanity." She visits her
mother's grave, under the watchful eye of Hobomok. With marvels
yet to relate, Mrs. Child explains to the reader:

There was a chaos in Mary's mind;—a dim twilight, which had at first made
all objects shadowy, and which was rapidly darkening into misery, almost
insensible of its source. The sudden stroke which had dashed from her lips the
long promised cup of joy, had almost hurled reason from his throne.
What now had life to offer? If she went to England, those for whom she most
wished to return, were dead. If she remained in America, what communion
could she have with those around her? Even Hobomok, whose language was
brief, figurative, and poetic, and whose nature was unwarped by the artifices
of civilized life, was far preferable to them. She remembered the idolatry he
had always paid her, and in the desolation of the moment, she felt as if he was
the only being in the wide world who was left to love her.

Thus, in her "insanity" she says to Hobomok, "I will be your wife,
Hobomok, if you love me." The marriage is performed according to
Indian custom, and "[n]ature too, was in her saddest robe; and the
breeze . . . sounded like the dismal roarings of the distant ocean.
Mary's meditations were more dull, and cold, and dreary still." For
the first time Mrs. Child echoes the reader's amazement when she
adds, "It is difficult to tell what the feelings could have been . . .
which led her to persevere in so strange a purpose."

In the months immediately following the wedding in Hobomok's
wigwam in Plymouth, "Mary remained in the same stupefied state in
which she had been at the time of her marriage . . . but there is a
happy propensity in the human mind to step as lightly as possible on
the thorns which infest a path we are compelled to tread." Hobomok
shows "the same tender reverence, he [has] always evinced," and
Mary "by degrees" learns "to [welcome] his return with something
like affection." She resists, however, becoming Indianized. The
villagers in Salem, recovering from the shock, attribute the marriage
to Mary's despair, Collier declaring that she is "bereaved of
reason." Only Oldham responds as the reader might expect a man
like him at least to respond: "A pretty piece of business . . . to have a
parcel of tawny grandchildren at your heels, squeaking *powaw*, and
sheshikwee, and the devil knoweth what all." His wife is apparently
more understanding: "I'm sure I never would have said a word, if
Sally had taken it into her head to marry a Pequod." Conant
despairs over his daughter's marriage—the stern Puritan "bowed
down" by his wife's death and his daughter's derangement: ". . . to
have her lie in the bosom of a savage, and mingle her prayers with a
heathen, who knoweth not God, is hard for a father's heart to
endure." Later, he "conjure[s] her not to consider a marriage law-
ful, which has been performed in a moment of derangement, and
invite[s] her to return to the arms of a parent who tenderly love[s]
her." Mary refuses her father's tardy offer of love, knowing that "she
should be considered an outcast among her brethren, and she
couldn't persuade herself that her marriage vow to an Indian was any
less sacred, than any other voluntary promise." In time a son is
born.

Brown returns to New England—he was not drowned at sea; when
he chances upon Hobomok in the woods, on his way to Salem, he is
informed of the marriage and responds nobly: "She is your wife. Keep
her, and cherish her with tenderness." But Hobomok demonstrates
an even nobler "cast": "The purpose of an Indian is seldom
changed. . . . My tracks will soon be seen far beyond the back-bone
of the Great Spirit. . . . Ask Mary to pray for me—that when I die, I
may go to the Englishman's God, where I may hunt beaver with little
Hobomok, and count my beavers for Mary."

The novel concludes hastily now. Mary is subdued when she learns
the news about her lover and her husband, appropriately remorseful,
perhaps contrite: ". . . to have Hobomok a wanderer, for my sake,
and to have him die among strangers, without one relation to speak
those words of comfort and kindness, which he has so often uttered to

me, I cannot—I cannot endure it. I only have sinned; and yet all the punishment has fallen upon his head. No; not quite all; for I know Brown must despise me." Yet she is quick to ask Brown's forgiveness—"lost and humbled as I have been"—when he comes to the wigwam. "My temptations were many," she hurries on. "I cannot tell you all now . . . when I heard you too were gone, my reason was obscured . . . but to this hour, my love [for you] has never abated." Of course, Mary is cautious in her confession: the question is not that Hobomok has renounced her but that Brown is willing to have a woman who has been married to an Indian. Brown wittingly perhaps supplies the answer. "Where is your boy?" he asks. When the lad is summoned, Mary says, "According to the Indian custom, he took the name of his mother. . . . I called him Charles Hobomok Conant." "He shall be my own boy," Brown replies.

When Brown proposes immediate marriage and a return to England, Mary protests vehemently: "My boy would disgrace me. . . ." However, marriage to Brown, even life once again in provincial Salem, are circumstances better than she had imagined. The return to the village and reunion with her father, Mrs. Child reports, is "one of mingled pain and pleasure." Conant holds her "in a long, affectionate embrace, and never to the day of his death, referred to a subject which was almost equally unpleasant to both." Not only is Conant transformed, but Brown is, too; "disputes" over religion "would sometimes arise," but "they were always brought to an amicable termination." Young Hobomok becomes in time "a distinguished graduate at [Harvard]; and when he left that infant university, he departed to finish his studies in England. His father was seldom spoken of; and by degrees his Indian appellation was silently omitted." His Indianness is obliterated, too, bereft of his birthright as his father had been denied his.

IV   *". . . Its Merit Is Greater Than Its Pretension . . ."*

The impression *Hobomok* makes on the modern reader is diminished by the love story grafted on this "tale of early times." The *North American* reviewer remarked that the novel "suffered much from the general prejudice against the catastrophe of the story."[12] In Mrs. Child's day it was no doubt the miscegenation which may have embarrassed her readers; today it is Mrs. Child's denial of Hobomok as an Indian—a denial Mrs. Child herself would quickly repent. Her life will soon be one long engagement in defense of the integrity of

the individual regardless of color. The fault can best be explained by
the inexperience of the writer.

When the fault is set aside, *Hobomok* as a social history of
seventeenth-century New England is sensitively done. The details of
the Puritan way of life are solidly sketched, the pastimes and anxieties
of the Salem villagers are animatedly described, the characters are
remarkably alive. The pathos is sometimes overwrought, and the
style is often pretentious; yet what novel written in the same period
is free from such affectation.

Mrs. Child clearly makes her point about the excess of religious
zeal, how it warps individuals and erodes the church—a remarkably
liberal view to express in a society not yet aware of Emerson's opinion
of organized religion. In this respect *Hobomok* is seen in sharper
focus by the modern reader, and Mrs. Child herself is seen in a way
typical of her own character. "Nature's noblest mould" is not so much
the primitive savage, already familiar to readers of fiction in her day,
but the man of conscience—capable of rising above forms and
ceremonies, above the restraints imposed by society, and capable of
exercising a freedom which guarantees the happiness of his fellow
human being. Society limits man's nobler nature, often debases him.
Conant is not a free agent because his religion, imposed by society,
will not allow him freedom. Hobomok, "whose nature was unwarped
by the artifices of civilized life," can stoically renounce personal
happiness for the happiness of others. Mrs. Child, too, will defy
forms and ceremonies, forms and ceremonies imposed by society,
and dedicate her life to the service of others. Unwittingly, she is
informing her readers of the course she will soon pursue. And it is
this confidence of conviction, this duty to conscience, that will
sustain her in the dark years ahead.

As important as *Hobomok* is in affirming Mrs. Child's own
principles, the novel when it appeared in 1824—in spite of its flaw—
can safely be compared favorably with any work of fiction which had
been produced in America—no mean accomplishment for a novice.

CHAPTER 3

The Rebels, or Boston
before the Revolution

*T*HE Rebels, or Boston before the Revolution, Mrs. Child's second
effort to create fiction out of New England's past, is largely a
failure for her reader and for the modern reader: a complicated plot.
principal characters who are clearly borrowed from the sentimental
tales in vogue with readers a generation before, token descriptions of
the social pageant, and an inflated style far more precious than that in
Hobomok. Even Mrs. Child confesses in the preface to "many doubts
and fears" about the merit of the novel, and the reviewer in the *North
American* agrees: "The narrative . . . is not so much one story as a
number of separate stories, not interwoven, but loosely tied together."[1] One of the more important "doubts" is that Mrs. Child does
not determine what her emphasis in the novel will be.

I *". . . Incidents . . . [for] Half a Dozen Respectable Novels"*

Unlike *Hobomok*, which is indeed a chapter of New England's
past, *The Rebels* lacks similar structure because Mrs. Child has no
clear focus. The title suggests an historical novel, yet there are only
two scenes—admittedly, dramatically written—that echo the history
of the times: the sacking of the governor's mansion by an unruly mob
angered over the recent imposts levied by the Crown and the fervent
appeals of the patriots Samuel Adams and James Otis to let
conscience and conduct be the guide to the citizens' resistance to the
policies of Parliament. However, the *North American* reviewer was
not impressed with the second of these scenes, reporting that the
incidents were "a mere copy of real history . . . which we find
expressed with far more eloquence in [their own] writings."[2]
    Nor is the novel social history. In the preface Mrs. Child is
confident that the "domestic annals of those times . . . can not fail to

interest every human heart," but the scenes do not present "the truthful picture" she promises. The reader observes the principal characters, the Brahmins of their day, in two social postures: one is during a pleasure cruise around Boston harbor, which serves as the setting for a lively debate on theology; and the other is in a fashionable salon, which provides the backdrop for a monologue on "female" education. They were "eloquent expositions of sentiment," the reviewer in the *Literary Gazette* wryly suggested.[3] There are two cameo scenes: an inspired sermon by the visiting evangelist, Rev. George Whitefield, "an offspring of [Mrs. Child's] own fancy," the *North American* reviewer noted,[4] strikingly executed; and a speech by the patriot Otis, also Mrs. Child's "fancy," which really impressed Thomas Wentworth Higginson.[5] Unlike *Hobomok*, the novel does not catch the spirit of the times.

Although the Puritans were believable, the principals in *The Rebels* are dull—"not original or very interesting," the *Literary Gazette* reviewer pointed out.[6] The minor characters are better: the sprightly spinster aunt Miss Sandford and the appallingly egocentric Rev. Mather Byles drawn from life.[7] The two groups of lovers—with the possible exception of the profligate Mrs. Child may have recalled from reading a novel like *The Coquette*—are inanimate. She showed no "readiness at seizing [their] peculiar characteristics," the *Literary Gazette* reviewer concluded.[8] They deliver set speeches in parlor English, greet calamity with grave composure and good fortune with magnanimous sentiment. They are paragons of propriety who possess, according to the author, "deep wisdom . . . passive courage . . . unyielding firmness." The reader questions their plausibility.

Moreover, the plot is unbelievably complicated by baby-snatchings, concealed identities and clouded ancestries, hidden documents and death-bed confessions which reduce an heiress to pauperism. Individual scenes are badly managed; one in particular, a midnight visit to the tomb of a dead mistress by the bereaved lover, is the kind of grisly horror that better belongs in the verse of the graveyard poets. And none too skillfully does Mrs. Child lead the characters, and the reader, through the morass. As the *North American* reviewer aptly remarked, "The author . . . seems to have been perplexed by the richness of her inventive powers, and has crowded into a short volume, a sufficient quantity of incidents to form the ground work of half a dozen novels."[9] In fact, the burden of a tale like that of *The Power of Sympathy* rests too heavily on *The Rebels*. "It is hardly worthwhile to make [such] American novels," sternly warned the reviewer in the *Literary Gazette*. And he summed up his impression of the novel in candid, even ruthless, language: ". . . Anyone who persists in offering the fruits of literary labour to the public, is willing to assume the profession of authorship, and to discharge the universal debt of usefulness, by making useful books."[10] *Hobomok* may have been flawed, but a second novel ought to show improvement.

The *North American* reviewer commented on the "pure and elegant" style, "free from affectation and carelessness,"[11] but such an opinion is obviously a matter of perspective. It strikes the modern reader as flamboyant and turgid. In all that she writes Mrs. Child could never be called an accomplished stylist, but *The Rebels* suffers more noticeably than any other piece of her writing from an effusive style.

If *The Rebels* is not an historical novel and is not social history, what is it? Perhaps Mrs. Child supplies the only real clue to a satisfactory reading of it, in the vignette which ends the novel. The Revolution is over (which, incidentally, has been fought and won in the last paragraph), and the hero returns home "to his anxious family." His wife welcomes him "to his happy house." As he presses her and his children—"the group of smiling cherubs"—close against him, he says: "The bride was dear; but how much dearer is the wife!" The reader now remembers that there were several domestic scenes played out in parlors or bedchambers or libraries and in strolls on the Common where pride and prejudice alternately play their parts, all faintly reminiscent of a Jane Austen novel. *The Rebels*, which defies close calling, suggests a novel of manners, yet recalls the sentimental tale, and anticipates the domestic romance so popular with women readers in the 1850s. Thus the novel is a vehicle for Mrs. Child's tale of Boston, where the course of true love never runs smoothly, where appearances are deceptive, where sacrifice is the epitome of virtue, and where disappointments are stoically managed. It is a sentimental tale by a young woman who had a gift for "genuine pathos," according to the *North American* reviewer.[12]

II   "*. . . No End to the Wonders . . .*"

The story begins in 1765, just after the late summer riots in protest over the hated Stamp Acts. Frederic Somerville, a nephew of Governor Thomas Hutchinson, has arrived in Boston for a tour of duty in the army. Conveniently, he is immediately introduced to a proper Bostonian, Henry Osborne, son in a highly esteemed family whose father is minister of Boston's first church. The conversation turns to the recent riots and to the burning in effigy of the British officials. "Liberty and property! No stamps!" proclaims Osborne, and Somerville warns that such license will "drive the mother country to severity repugnant to her nature."

With this episode in history presented, Mrs. Child now busies herself with the romantic involvements in the story: the entangled relationships of the young lovers. Somerville is immediately attracted to "the etherial [sic] loveliness" of Grace Osborne, and she in turn responds to him. Osborne prefers Lucretia Fitzherbert, "inelegant [in] form and very plain [of] face" with "a nature bold, impetuous, and unrestrained." Lucretia, however, prefers Somerville; since she and Grace are dear friends, she does not yet declare her own love for Somerville. Osborne and his father do not sympathize with Somerville's "English prejudices and tory predilections," and they question the somewhat capricious nature of the affable soldier who has "a passing pleasing tongue" and "the fascination of a polished manner." They much prefer that Grace accept the marriage proposal of a local rebel, a Dr. Willard, a man of "fixed religious principles and an amicable disposition [which] are of more consequence to domestic happiness than all that wealth, or beauty, or genius can offer." Grace, however, persists in her open admiration of Somerville. Annoyed by his sister's determined effort to win Somerville, Osborne says somewhat petulantly: "A meteor may be dazzling, but we can not calculate its orbit." The father is more direct, accusing Grace of "untruth" because he has assumed that she will accept the doctor's proposal of marriage. "Do not let me go to my pillow," he remonstrates, "with the fear that you have deceived your earthly father, and sinned against your heavenly one." Although "tears fell fast on [her] heaving bosom," Grace dismisses further conversation: "Some other time, dear father, some other time, we will talk of this."

Lucretia is Mrs. Child's curiously proper coquette, substituting for her "plain face" an engaging personality: she is clever, witty, intelligent—too much so, since she is told by one of her acquaintances that "women should only speak when it is necessary." She is a free spirit, combative, impatient with the conventions of society which dictate women's auxiliary role. In some respects she is like Eliza Wharton, the strong-willed coquette in Mrs. Hannah Foster's novel; and in some respects she is like Lydia Maria Child, also "very plain [of] face" and dissatisfied with women's position in society. Since Lucretia is a ward in the governor's household, she has daily contact with Somerville, who is discovering that her candor, her witty conversations, and her obvious learning are nearly as attractive as

Grace's delicate beauty. "What a pity you had not lived in the days of chivalry, Miss Fitzherbert," he remarks after one such display of her charms. "How many lances would have been lowered before the majesty of——mind." She means to win the man from her good friend by a display of brilliance more intoxicating than Grace's loveliness. As it turns out, brilliance is not necessary.

By a quirk of plot Mrs. Child has given Lucretia a mysterious past. The reader is led to believe that the young woman is the daughter of parents now dead, that her father was a man of great fortune, and that her mother at the time of her husband's premature death was misadvised and lost all his money. However, an uncle is suddenly discovered, a British nobleman, who claims his kinswoman and invites her to live with him on his manorial estate. "There is no end to the wonders of your life," Rev. Osborne is moved to say. The news of Lucretia's good fortune comes as a disappointment to Osborne but is greeted with "delightful enthusiasm" by Somerville, who now realizes that it is "mind" and not "etherial loveliness" he is attracted to. Osborne, however, proposes marriage—not in person but by letter:

You do not owe your influence over me to a sudden freak of fancy; it results from a long and intimate knowledge of your character. Yet I will not flatter you, by saying I consider you faultless;—on the contrary, I think you have defects, which may prove very dangerous to yourself and friends, unless timely corrected. But I cannot imagine a character more elevated than might be formed from a mind so vigorous, and a heart so generous and candid as yours.

How largely I think you would contribute to domestic happiness, is proved by the step I have now taken. Whether the lovely garland of hope, that my heart has so long been weaving, is to be scattered to the winds, depends on your answer.

Lucretia, declaring "that it was utterly impossible for her ever to reciprocate his attachment," readies herself to sail for England.

Somerville, meanwhile, is conveniently transferred home, but not before he has given Grace a ring and a rosebush, memorials of their attachment, which the young woman construes as tokens of love and eventual marriage. With Lucretia's wealth and position in baronial society, Somerville with just a twitch of conscience over Grace courts the heiress in a whirlwind romance, encouraged by the uncle who likes the young fortune-seeker. And Lucretia delights in his attention and in her fairy-story reception in London as the darling of polite society, as the special pet of writers and artists.

During the whole of last winter [she writes Grace] we had the finest collection of company in the world. Johnson, Burke, Sir Joshua Reynolds, Garrick, and Goldsmith, spent an evening with us, almost as regularly as they did at the Turk's head, Gerrard-street, Soho. The mere contact of such great minds is enough to inspire one with genius. I have the good fortune to be a favourite with that famous cynic, Samuel Johnson. . . . Johnson sneers about "whig dogs," speaks of America as an uncivilized land, and says it would puzzle any one to tell what good the discovery of it has done the world. Burke contends that our country will eventually be one of the greatest on the globe,—and says that if Britain ever loses her American Colonies, she will part with a jewel worth her whole regalia.

She informs her friend of her impending marriage to Somerville, who, it seems, will take the name Fitzherbert because "the uncle's family pride required this sacrifice." "There seems to be something degrading in the bridegroom's losing his name instead of the bride," she tells Grace. "However, he seems resolved to repay this acquiescence by the most rapid promotion. He is now Colonel of his Majesty's 14th regiment of dragoons."

Mrs. Child now interrupts the story and speaks directly to the reader, in one of those passages of "genuine pathos" reminiscent of similar statements in such novels as *Charlotte Temple.*

As for Colonel Fitzherbert, he might well have envied Tantalus and Ixion their torments. Henry Osborne said truly, "ambition was his guiding star,— the shrine at which he sacrificed both affection and principle." Yet even in this he was inconstant. His feelings, chamelion-like [*sic*], took their colouring from surrounding objects; and whatsoever was present with him, was, for the time, most important. If his heart had ever known genuine affection, Miss Osborne certainly had inspired it, but when he was aware of Lucretia's vast expectations,—when he witnessed the splendour and influence of her high-born uncle,—when he saw her admired in the first literary circles, and daily becoming more polished by intercourse with the fashionable world,—he regretted the tie that bound him to her humble friend. . . .

Could he have seen Grace, wasted as she was by lingering illness, and utterly cheerless in her faithful affection, his better nature would have prevailed; and he would have besought forgiveness with the earnestness of a repentant sinner. But he had resolved to avoid her entirely. His mind was a chaos of fear and conjecture,—and only one hope floated distinctly on its surface; viz, that the impression he had made might be as easily erased as the one he had received; and that pride and delicacy would keep his secret.

Grace dies of a broken heart, "that fatal delusion strong as ever," and is laid to rest in the family tomb just as Lucretia returns to Boston for her marriage to Somerville. Visiting her friend's empty room, she discovers the memorials her fiancé has given Grace, reads a letter in which Grace renounces her lover and with her blessing sends him to her dearest friend—a letter which is never sent. The night before the marriage Lucretia "passed a sleepless miserable night. To love and doubt is torment enough;—but to love, and yet know we are victim of cold, selfish, deceitful policy, is 'anguish unmixed, and agony pure.'" In one of innumerable climactic scenes in the novel, an angry Lucretia at the altar the following morning exposes Somerville and deserts him. The governor, chagrined at the turn of events, turns Lucretia out of his house and sends his scapegrace nephew to the South. Lucretia is given sanctuary at the Osbornes where in time the son, depicted as an eminently sensible man, can once again commence his courtship.

The melodrama can at this point quite logically end, but Mrs. Child has yet a rich store of "inventive powers." Lucretia, it seems, is an impostor, too. This startling information comes from a deathbed confession of a bit-player in the drama: Lucretia and another child were switched as infants, Lucretia becoming the Fitzherbert heiress while the real Fitzherbert heiress, bearing the name of Gertrude Wilson, spends her life in a Catholic orphanage in Canada until she marries a man named Percival. "Many a heroine of romance does not meet with half your reverses," one of Lucretia's acquaintances remarks. Lucretia (née Gertrude) accepts the stroke of ill fortune in appropriate stride; she gives her wealth to the newly discovered Fitzherbert heiress and, marvelously transformed from coquette to docile womanhood, is welcomed still by the Osbornes—the father in his dotage seeing in her his daughter-in-law and the son in his patronlike way seeing in her his wife.

Again, the novel can quite logically end, but Mrs. Child has still more inventions to offer. Returning temporarily to the history of the time, she reminds the reader of the clashes in early 1770 between the Boston citizens and the British troops: "The populace, exasperated beyond further endurance, armed themselves with clubs, and ran to King-street, shouting, 'Drive out the rascals! they are not fit to breathe the air of a free country!'" Osborne joins the zealous patriots as one of the rebels shouts: ". . . The blow is struck; the wound will fester long, before it heals. The rascals say we dare not fight.—By Heaven, I hope I shall die up to my knees in blood." In the rioting Osborne is slightly wounded but returns safely home, where Lucretia-Gertrude ministers to his needs. "The time will come," predicts the nascent rebel. "The land is wide awake, and the good cause gains ground."

And there is a new birth for Lucretia-Gertrude, too. Mrs. Child speaks again to the reader.

Wealth, with all its imposing pageantry, and rank[,] with its embroidered baldrick and blazing star, had been idols before which her imagination had bowed with scarcely inferior homage; and she had proved their utter insufficiency to satisfy the soul in its hour of trial; nay, she had been driven from their sunny paths, and found happiness in more shaded and sequestered walks. All these lessons, severely as they were taught, had produced a good effect. She now began to estimate men and things according to their real value,—to appreciate qualities according to their usefulness, not according to their lustre.

Now the novel can end, but not before Mrs. Child delivers an epilogue: ". . . Gertrude had now devoted all the light of her under-standing, and all the warmth of her affections, to the happiness of her excellent husband. The political horizon soon became more stormy in its aspect; and Henry could not think of leaving America, at a time when she needed all the firmness, the talents, and the courage of her sons. During the whole of the bloody period which followed, he rendered important services in the senate and the field. . . ." Though Mrs. Child's "inventive powers" are indeed fertile, the modern reader agrees with the *North American* reviewer that *The Rebels* suffered from "not a feeble, but a misguided intellect."[13]

III *Characters in the "Imperative Mood . . . [or] Accusative Case . . ."*

In spite of misguidance *The Rebels* is not without some merit. Mrs. Child has on occasion a good choice of incident which provides the characters opportunity to express themselves. One of the better character portrayals is Rev. Mather Byles, whose arrogance, bigotry, and cruelty are sharply revealed during the pleasure cruise around the harbor.

"An excellent though heretical writer hath told us," observed Doctor Byles, "that piety is like certain lamps of old, which maintained their light for ages underground, but as soon as they took air expired. It is a doctrine that the *New* Lights forget, my friend, though it seems the *old* lights acted it out, generation after generation."

"If we are to keep our religion locked up from others, what do you make of the command, 'Let your light so shine before men'?" asked the pilot.

"If I read Scripture aright, that is the light of good works," was the reply.

"Very true," rejoined the [pilot]; "and therefore we should strive to attain to perfect holiness."

"Perfect holiness!" exclaimed the clergyman. "You might as well talk of such a coin as a pound sterling, or a French livre."

"I don't understand what you mean touching the comparison," answered the steersman; "but I will never sell my reason to any man, because he happens to be more *larnt* than I am."

"If you should set it up at auction, it would be a poor pennyworth to him that bought it," observed the reverend doctor. "However, you are made for your place, and I for mine. Some must think, and some must labour; some must rule, and some must be ruled. . . ."

"I tell you what, Doctor Byles," said the pilot, "some folks do say you are a good man; and them who know you, tell that you have more religion than you seem to have. If so be this be true [*sic*], you can't in earnest deny that the New Lights and the Quakers are the only people that have 'put off the old man.'"

"I don't know how far they have put off the old man," rejoined the minister; "but of one thing I am certain,—they keep his deeds. Since New *Lights* are so numerous, it is desirable we should have more new *livers*; and as for the Quakers, 'they come to the gospel not as law, but as a market, cheapen what they like best, and leave the rest for other customers.'"

"The book where you found that, likewise tells you, that 'some people think their zeal lukewarm unless it reduce their charity to ashes,'" retorted Miss Sandford.

"'One man among a thousand have I found; but a woman among all those I have not found,' complains Solomon; and he complains with reason," said Doctor Byles. "What have you to do with subjects above your understanding, Madam San[d]ford?"

"Above my understanding!" echoed the offended maiden; "I can tell you I began the controversy with zeal, and stuck to it with perseverance."

"Aye, no doubt you stuck like a fly in a glue-pot," retorted the Doctor. "Forward you could not stir, by reason of weakness; and the subject matter was too thick for you to dive into."

"Heard ever anybody the like of that?" said Miss Sandford. "There is no use talking with you, Dr. Byles; but tell me in earnest, what can you prove against the Quakers?"

"I know the secret of your taking up in their defence," answered the Doctor. "There was a friend Isaac, or a friend Jacob, that once spoke soft words to thee, and told thee that thy voice was more pleasant to him than the sound of rivulets,—yea, than the voice of spring; and you could never be grateful enough to him for the unexampled favour. . . . What do I know of the Quakers! Haven't I attended their meetings? . . ."

"You seem to be fighting shadows," said Somerville, "since there are no Quakers here."

"Only the ghost of Miss San[d]ford's only lover," answered the doctor. . . .

"You are a master hand for a minister," observed the pilot; "but folks do say you are better than you seem." Then, taking a psalm book from his pocket, he began, "Let us sing a psalm of David."

"No, no," said the Doctor, displaying a piece of writing,—"Let us sing a song of——Mather Byles."

Lucretia, frequently a victim of Byles's acid tongue, complains that "the Doctor sometimes chooses to cut his best friends"; but the portrayal lends support to Mrs. Child's conviction that arrogant churchmen dogmatize their own religion. Byles, like Endicott and Brown, employs specious argument to carry his cause.

The minister's usual foil is Lucretia's aunt, the spinster Miss Sandford, who looks like "an antediluvian image" and speaks in "the squeaking tones of antiquated coquetry." She is an eccentric, frustrated in an early love as Byles knows, abrupt in her manner with Lucretia and Grace, outspoken in her opinion. She is the "antiquated" coquette who delights in gossiping. "Has Aunt Sandford been backbiting her neighbours till her double teeth ache?" Byles asks her one evening. Lucretia gives an account of one of their spats. "Last evening they had some altercation about grammar; at the close of which she told him she thoroughly disliked people that were always in the imperative mood. 'And I for my part,' rejoined the Doctor, 'have no patience with a person who is forever in the accusative case.' It is a pity," Lucretia concludes, "she has not an active verb for an husband."

Osborne is apparently Mrs. Child's moral monitor in the story, and in the role he is pompous and overbearing, talking like a textbook—a dull one at that. "I admire an harmonious, well-adjusted character . . . ," he announces during one of the parlor conversations. "He who gives himself up to the absorbing power of any one single passion, may draw the eyes of all mankind toward him; but qualities of a milder and more consistent cast constitute the chief charm of domestic life." His "well-adjusted" paradigm of appropriate conduct is Benjamin Franklin.

Such a character . . . is solid silver taken from the mine. . . . I remember in the long conversation I had with him the night before he sailed to England, he minutely detailed the process by which he had attained so much self-control. He made a list of the thirteen virtues he thought most necessary, and to each one he paid particular and undivided attention for one week. Thus one week he would refrain from speaking evil of others; another, he would abstain from every thing not absolutely necessary to life and comfort; and so on. At the end of every quarter [year], the circle commenced anew. There was sound philosophy in this,—for as each virtue was successively impressed upon the mind at succeeding intervals, no one had a chance to attain a giant growth at the expense of the others.

The monologue, delivered among friends, is apparently largely intended for Lucretia who, "in the careless gayety of her heart," retorts: "[Y]ou must bear with me just as I am, a few years longer; and then I will promise to be so collected, so prudent." And, of course, with her reversal of fortune she does, bearing out her aunt's prediction: "I said you would marry him that night he gave you such a lecture at our house."

Far more appealing to the reader is Somerville, the soldier of fortune, the villain in this sentimental tale. He has not the evil nature of Belcour in *Charlotte Temple*; but he does share the pride, and later the conscience, of Sanford in *The Coquette*. He is an opportunist, handsome, debonair, likable; even Osborne grudgingly "admired his talents." Like Sanford he is weak willed, "volatile and changeable as the wind"; like Sanford he knows himself: "Confound it! that ever I should place myself in a dilemma, where I can neither take a decided stand, nor retreat with honor." With Grace's death and Lucretia's denunciation of him at the altar, he seems to suffer true remorse. The scene in which he visits Grace's tomb—exaggerated in detail, gothic in description, "revolting" as the *North American* reviewer defined it[14]—is nevertheless a sincere outburst of grief, regret, shame, and despair. Thereafter, he "plunged in every excess of dissipation" and ultimately dies in Baltimore, "in a high fever, and very delirious." In his personal effects is a letter addressed to Osborne. "I am the branded outcast of heaven . . . ," he confesses. "Sense, memory, every thing, lies buried in that cold, distant grave. I wish I could pray,—but my stubborn knee will not bend, and my proud heart rises in defiance of Almighty power. . . . I carry my hell with me." Somerville does create his own hell, and Osborne's estimate is correct: "I never respected [him]." Still, he is a believable character.

IV   *". . . Scenes, Familiar to Every One Who Reads Our History"*

Mrs. Child is equally successful with individual scenes in the novel, some developed with considerable dramatic intensity. One scene takes place in the church where Rev. Whitefield is delivering a sermon. She establishes the scene effectively, first suggesting the personality of the preacher: ". . . His dark blue eyes [were] small and lively: in recovering from the measles, he had contracted a squint with one of them; but this peculiarity rather rendered the expression of his countenance more rememberable. . . . His voice both excelled in melody and compass. . . . To have seen him when he first commenced, one would have thought him any thing but enthusiastic and glowing; but as he proceeded, his heart warmed with his subject, and his manner became impetuous and animated." The time is the "Great Awakening," and the clergyman delivers his sermon in the manner often reputed of Jonathan Edwards with an additional feature— sound effects. A thunderstorm is in progress.

His eye gradually lighted up, as he proceeded, till towards the close, it seemed to sparkle with celestial fire. "Oh, sinners!" he exclaimed, "by all your hopes of happiness, I beseech you to repent. Let not the wrath of God be awakened. Let not the fires of eternity be kindled against you. See there!" said he, pointing to the lightning, which played in the corner of the pulpit—"'Tis a glance from the angry eye of Jehovah! Hark!" continued he, raising his finger in a listening attitude, as the distant thunder grew louder and louder, and broke in one tremendous crash over the building. "It was the voice of the Almighty, as he passed by in his anger!"

As the sound died away, he covered his face with his hands, and knelt beside his pulpit, apparently lost in inward and intense prayer. The storm passed rapidly by, and the sun bursting forth in his might, threw across the heavens a magnificent arch of peace. "Look upon the rainbow; and praise him that made it. Very beautiful it is in the brightness thereof. It compasseth the heavens about with glory; and the hands of the Most High have bended it."

Effective too are the history pieces. As the *North American* reviewer observed, they are not as vivid as history itself, but they summarize the events of the day for readers more familiar with the Revolution than with the period of agitation which came before the first shots at Concord and Lexington. Otis's speech before the British magistrates is one that quickens the patriots' blood.

Some will mistake my zeal for personal resentment; but those who understand me well, will hear, in my voice, the thundering echo of a free people, who can not be silenced, and who will not be mocked. . . .

Arbitrary principles, like those against which we now contend, have cost one king of England his life, another his crown,—and they yet cost a third his most flourishing colonies.

We are two million strong—one fifth fighting men.

We are bold and vigorous,—and we call no man master. . . .

We plunged into the wave with the magna charta of freedom in our teeth, because the faggot and the torch were behind us. We have waked this new world from its savage lethargy; forests have been prostrated in our path; towns and cities have grown up suddenly . . . and the fires in our autumnal woods are scarcely more rapid than the increase of our wealth and population.

And do we owe all this to the kind succor of our mother country? No! we owe it to the tyranny that drove us from her. . . .

But, thanks be to God, there is freedom enough left upon earth to resist such monstrous injustice. The flame of liberty is extinguished in Greece and Rome, but the light of its glowing ambers is still bright and strong in the shine of America. Actuated by its sacred influence, we will resist unto death. But we will not countenance anarchy and misrule. . . . Still, it may be well for some proud men to remember that a fire is lighted in these Colonies, which one breath of theirs may kindle into such fury, that the blood of all England cannot extinguish it.

Although the rhetoric is old-fashioned, it was highly regarded in Mrs. Child's day.[15] It was in the same class as William Wirt's imaginary speech of Patrick Henry.

Although the rebel leaders are fearless in resisting the oppressive measures of the Crown, they do not condone mob violence. Samuel Adams counsels the citizenry: "Be firm. Resist unto death; but . . . be moderate—be prudent. . . . My friends," says Adams, "remember that nothing is to be gained by violence; much by calm and dignified firmness." When the governor's mansion is sacked and he and his family seek refuge with friends, they are threatened by an angry mob. Adams harangues the surly citizens, reminding them, "This is no way to redress our wrongs. . . . Let Governor Hutchinson and his household pass!" The rebel leaders are men of conviction who, though Englishmen abroad, are still protected by the "magna charta of freedom." As Englishmen they are entitled to their natural rights, and "actuated by [their] sacred influence" resist "monstrous injustice." Men of conviction—and conscience—they will not endorse "anarchy and misrule," preferring instead the exercise of reason, sagacious and sound. Conscience controls men of intelligence; only when reason fails are other measures taken.

If the modern reader seeks a theme in Mrs. Child's work—her fiction, her later essays, her devotion to humanitarian causes—it is here in her firm belief that first there is the appeal to conscience: to do what is noble, rational, and right. Americans have that conscience, inbred by the travail of the Revolutionary experience. And it is to this innate strength that she makes her appeal, whether in the youthful heat of *The Rebels* or in the soberer vein of her antislavery tracts and essays on other reforms. Conscience, the large heart, the understanding heart: it is her heritage as it is her fellow Americans' heritage. Only when the heart's valves close are other alternatives conceivable.

V "... A Sad Predicament"

"This much for the period I have chosen," concludes Mrs. Child in the preface to *The Rebels.* "How faithfully it has been portrayed, must be left to critics less merciful than myself." The critics did indeed judge her harshly: "profusion of incidents" and "want of method" and "injudicious choice of subject," the *North American* reviewer summed up, "shackled" her talent. He was disappointed that she had not shown "more concern in the construction of her story, and especially in the unraveling of her plot."[16] The reviewer in the *Literary Gazette* was severer, advising her to forget "novel-making" and "discover [her] proper employment" elsewhere, in some "valuable and honourable works."[17]

To employ one of the comments by a character in the novel, Mrs. Child was in "a sad predicament between new lights and new fires." Was her novelistic talent, obviously better in *Hobomok*, to prove her in time a new light in the American literary scene, or was there another direction—a new fire—for her talent to be channeled in? Perhaps Mrs. Child herself was not sure. She did not publish another novel for ten years, but turned instead to nonfiction writing on avowedly domestic subjects. *The Frugal Housewife*, *The Mother's Book*, and *The Girl's Own Book* made her name a household word. Thereafter, she discovered a greater strength as writer, in an ardent *Appeal in Favor of That Class of Americans Called Africans*, which demanded attention and catapulted her into national prominence. "It is not too much to say," wrote Alexander Cowie, "that she [now] began to *make* history,"[18] not as a novelist but as an humanitarian. She would write two more novels, and one of them, *Philothea*, brought her critical acclaim in her own day and belated appreciation in ours.

CHAPTER 4

Philothea, a Romance

IF the *North American* reviewer was disappointed with *The Rebels*, he was greatly impressed with *Philothea, a Romance:*[1] "... It will take a permanent place in our elegant literature," he predicted. On every page, he proclaimed, there "breathes the inspiration of genius, and [there] shows a highly cultivated taste."[2] "[I]t is certainly the boldest attempt that has yet been made," suggested the reviewer in the *American Monthly Magazine*, "... to paint classic manners in a way to [render] them at once interesting and life-like. ... [S]he has, in a word, attempted that which makes the schoolboy and the sage equally arbiters of her success."[3] Poe—always a disciple of beauty— was more lavish in his praise, declaring that the reader is "overwhelmed" with Mrs. Child's "acquaintance with ... the times, places, and people depicted," marveling as he "turn[s] ... these pure and quiet pages with ... gasping satisfaction."

The novel would become "an effectual aid in the study of Greek antiquity" because the author had presented to the reader so accurately the "manners, habits, and modes of thought" of that Golden Age. He did not quarrel with her novelistic license, her "blunders" in reporting the history of Greece; such "errors" were of no concern to the reader. Indeed, if anything militated against the novel, Poe unhappily concluded, it was the subject matter itself: readers had "little of purely human sumpathy in the distantly antique." Superior to Bulwer-Lytton's *The Last Days of Pompeii*, *Philothea* would not, he felt, have that novel's popular appeal since the story was not nearly as dramatic. A largely intellectual history of the Age of Pericles was simply "at variance with [the] popular interest to-day." Nevertheless, the novel, "a work ... of no common order," should be assured permanence in our literature; and recommending it especially "to the attention of teachers" who might introduce the novel "advantageously into our female academies," Poe reaffirmed the literary success of *Philothea*—"an honor to our country, and a signal triumph for our country-woman."[4]

Subsequent commentators were equally enthusiastic. Griswold called it "the most beautiful of [Mrs. Child's] works," giving life to Athens "in its most glorious age, when Pericles presided over the destinies of the state, Plato taught in the Academy, Phidias built temples and carved statues of the gods, and Aspasia captivated sages by her beauty."[5] The Duyckincks agreed, saying *Philothea* was "the most elaborate and successful of the author's productions, and is in close and artistic keeping with the classic age it portrays."[6] Helene G. Baer, Mrs. Child's present-day biographer, expressed great admiration for the novel, even though she saw the romance largely through its author's eyes:

It told of the days of Pericles, of the indescribable luxury of Aspasia's court and of Maria Child's love of beauty, and it revealed a side of her that the *Frugal Housewife* had denied. It reached toward the purple and fine linen which her life pattern had taken from her. She dwelt lovingly on silver robes, precious vessels, and the glorious sculpture of Phidias; she exulted in the music, gardens, and jewels; she rambled through a complicated plot; but her inmost self called out from every page.[7]

I   "... Romance of the Wildest Kind"

Mrs. Child surely recognized in Poe's concern "the problem" in the novel, its possible lack of popular appeal. "Most readers will consider it romance of the wildest kind," she wrote in the preface. "A few kindred spirits, prone to people space 'with life and mystical predominance,' will perceive a light *within* the Grecian temple." She did not apologize for the potentially limited appeal of the novel, reminding the readers of "the simple fact that I found delight in doing it." But to "kindred spirits" she offered a further explanation: "The work has been four or five years in its progress; for the practical tendencies of the age, and particularly of the country in which I lived, have so continually forced me into the actual, that my mind has seldom obtained freedom to rise into the ideal." With an oblique reference to her nonfiction of the last few years—*The Frugal Housewife* and *An Appeal in Favor of That Class of Americans Called Africans*, among others—she had expended her efforts in "the spirit of the times." "But there have been seasons," she admitted, "when my soul felt restless in this bondage . . . so I, for awhile, bid adieu to the substantial fields of utility, to float in the clouds of romance."

As it turned out, she had no cause to fear the novel's winning the cool reception which *The Rebels* had received. Readers and reviewers alike were pleased with the novel which "brought the era of Plato, and Pericles . . . [so] freshly before us," wrote the *Knickerbocker* reviewer; "and, what is a rare quality with writers who annihilate the past in fiction, she has imparted an air of real life."[8]

Philothea was published in the same year as Emerson's *Nature*. The coincidence does not end here, for there are several transcendental ideas in the novel, most significantly a similar view of nature and a reliance on intuition.[9] There are other influences as well, as the two bits of poetry on the title page suggest—lines from Coleridge and a passage from Wordworth's *The Excursion.* "*Emanations* were perceived," Wordsworth writes, referring to the glory that was Greece; but Mrs. Child's *"emanations"* from the poet are his romantic cult of the child. The novel is dedicated to her brother Convers, who introduced her to Landor's imaginary conversations, in particular the letters between Pericles and Aspasia.[10] Kenneth W. Cameron in his introduction to an edition of *Philothea* acknowledged these "potent" influences, as well as a number of others, which no doubt shaped the substance of the novel. He also made a strong case for the novel as Mrs. Child's answer to Frances Wright's *A Few Days in Athens* (1822), a fictionalized account of a young Athenian who becomes a convert to Epicurus' philosophy of pleasure. "*Enjoy and be happy! . . . Let Epicurus be your guide,*" the philosopher tells his pupil. "The good is—all which can yield you pleasure: the evil—what must bring you pain."[11] The hedonistic philosophy of the senses was a particular anathema to many nineteenth-century New Englanders, and to Mrs. Child and the Concord group especially; and Frances Wright's liberalism—her agnosticism and her views on free love—were obviously offensive to men and women accustomed to "plain living and high thinking." *Philothea* is an antidote to the sensualist's philosophy of life and endorses instead what Mrs. Child read as the nobler sentiments of Plato, more congenial to nineteenth-century New Englanders. And of course nearly all Mrs. Child wrote—fiction and nonfiction—is laced with nineteenth-century New England morality, and *Philothea* clearly demonstrates the value of such morality, supplemented with Christian teachings as well. In one of the notes Mrs. Child supplies in an appendix to the novel, she admits "that the Christian spirit is sometimes infused into a Grecian form; and in nothing is this more conspicuous than the representation of love as a pure sentiment rather than a gross passion." And in this respect, at least—"love as a pure sentiment"—the reader also detects her continuing fascination with the thought of Swedenborg.

Nevertheless, *Philothea* is an exquisite view of the beauties of another world. "Romance of the wildest kind," it truly is. The modern reader as well as her contemporaries can marvel at her knowledge of Greek culture, mythology, and insight into Athenian life. Like many of her fellow New Englanders, Mrs. Child did not read Greek but had to rely on translations of the ancient writers and philosophers.[12] Yet she is familiar with this world, partly historical, largely fanciful for her purposes, in which she introduces her characters—the fictional Philothea and her friend Eudora, who are the intimate companions of the real people of the Age of Pericles: the master statesman himself, Aspasia his wife, the philosophers Anaxagoras and Plato juxtaposed for the purposes of her story, Phidias the sculptor, the sensualist Alcibiades, and the mercurial citizens of Athens. Mrs. Child unfolds the story casually, allowing the characters to work out their lives without her intrusion. For once, she is content to settle for a workable plot.

The main interest in the romance centers on Philothea, but a subordinate interest focuses on Eudora, Philothea's willful companion. Philothea, granddaughter of Anaxagoras, has been educated by him with great care. Eudora, an orphan, is a member of the family of Phidias, who purchased her in early childhood. Paralus, son of Pericles, has also been a pupil of the old philosopher, as was his father before him; although he and Philothea are in love, they do not plan to marry because Pericles does not regard the young woman as a worthy daughter-in-law. She has no dowry to offer and no particular social status to recommend her to the ambitious statesman. Philaemon, a wealthy young Athenian whose mother was born in Corinth, has also been a pupil of Anaxagoras; he has fallen in love with Eudora whom he plans to marry. However, the young couple's plans fall awry when Pericles invokes an ancient law: Philaemon must forfeit his Athenian citizenship and surrender his wealth because his mother was foreign born. The novel opens with a scene in which the two women await the return of their lovers from the court.

Meanwhile Alcibiades, struck by the beauty of Eudora, wishes to add her to his series of conquests. The young woman is vain enough to consider Alcibiades' attentions to her sincere and refuses to heed the warnings of her firmer friend. This is the source of distress in the plot. To carry out his scheme, Alcibiades persuades Aspasia, wife of Pericles, to give a symposium to which Philothea and Eudora are commanded to attend. The most illustrious figures of the age also attend: in addition to Pericles and his wife, there are Anaxagoras, Plato, Phidias, and lesser (fictional) dignitaries. The description of the symposium is the most striking scene in the novel. Eudora is captivated by the splendor of the evening and by Alcibiades, who promises to divorce his wife and marry her. Later Philothea, who cannot dissuade her friend of Alcibiades' perfidy, and Philaemon become observers of a secret meeting the dissembler arranges with Eudora. Philaemon, hurt by Eudora's faithlessness and bitter over the sentence of the court, abruptly leaves Athens, seeking refuge at the Persian court. In time Eudora becomes aware of Alcibiades' stratagem, when she overhears the man's witty account of his successful dupery to Aspasia.

At this juncture in the novel, enemies of the ambitious Pericles, anxious to discredit his popularity with the citizens, provide charges of blasphemy against his friends Anaxagoras and Phidias and his wife Aspasia. The case is heard before an outraged citizens' court which Pericles, to curry favor with the populace, has already established. Anaxagoras is charged with saying that Phoebus, the Sun God, is no more than a huge ball of fire. Phidias is accused of worshiping the gods so that his own statues are more praised. And Aspasia, already under suspicion because she has appeared in public without a veil over her face, is condemned for corrupting the youth of Athens and for wishing to give women greater freedom. The men are sentenced to death, and Aspasia is to be sent into exile. Pericles, however, succeeds in getting the decrees postponed until an oracle can be consulted. A celebrated diviner is sent to Delphi, and in his absence Pericles prepares a defense of the accused. The response of the oracle opportunely declares that the sentences shall be reconsidered. The statesman in masterful oratory persuades the citizens' court to reduce the sentences so that Anaxagoras and Phidias are exiled and Aspasia is acquitted. The trial is the most dramatic scene in the novel.[13]

Soon after, a plague rages throughout Athens, among its victims Paralus who remembers nothing of his past life except his love for Philothea. Subject to deliriums with visions of the land of spirits, he hovers between two worlds. Pericles, his pride shaken by the domestic calamity, sends Plato to bring Philothea, in exile with her grandfather, to marry his son. Even though the lovers are reunited, Paralus' health does not improve; and Hippocrates advises a journey to Olympia, hoping that the excitement of the games and old associates will stimulate the young man's recovery. The experiment is unsuccessful and Paralus dies, having given Philothea insight into the next world by recounting his vision of it just before his death. After Paralus' funeral, with his ashes deposited in the ancestral tomb, Philothea too wastes away and soon dies.

In the coda to the novel Eudora again becomes the victim of

Alcibiades: his hirelings kidnap her and carry her off to his retreat on
the island of Salamis. She is ultimately rescued by devoted servants.
Seeking protection of Phidias' nephew who is at the moment in
Athens, she hides in a grotto until it is safe to approach him. Here she
has a vision of Philothea and Paralus who warn her to seek the help of
Artaphernes the Persian, an ambassador to Athens. It is presently
discovered that she is the lost child of the ambassador. Returning
with her father to Persia, she is presented at court, is wooed by
Xerxes, and is at last reunited with Philaemon who is in high favor
with the king. With their marriage the novel ends.

II   ". . . Politics . . . Ambition . . . Religion and Morality"

With the fictional characters in the novel Mrs. Child works her
fantasy; with the historical personages she exercises the novelist's
prerogative to heighten a trait of character or to ignore another,
selecting in the portrait of the principals their particular idiosyncrasy
which satisfies her demands for the romance. "Wedded to politic
ambition," Pericles wields his power somewhat perilously as disaffection among his followers and plots of his enemies conspire
against him. As Plato reports to Anaxagoras in exile, ". . . this
Peloponessian [sic] war, the noisy feuds in Athens, and afflictions in
his own family, have involved him in continual distractions. He who
gives his mind to politics, sails on a stormy sea, with a giddy pilot." To
win popular favor in the democracy, he has granted new freedoms to
the citizens and has encouraged the support of the fickle populace
with bribes. To fill the depleted treasury of the state, heavily taxed by
the war and by the chicanery of hangers-on, he has invoked the ancient law denying alien residents their wealth and their estates. Although the decree has increased the state's revenues, reducing Philaemon and others to poverty or to slavery, it has disturbed the saner
citizenry and even caused uneasiness among his followers who
remember that the law has been invoked through Aspasia's influence in retaliation against those who have "remonstrated against
[their] shameful marriage." While the rights of the propertied and the
educated are being denied, the rights of the mass of citizens are
being enlarged. "Political assemblies" are encouraged where the
populace like "Cleon the tanner, and Thearion the baker, and
Theophrastus the maker of lyres" debate matters of state they do
not understand, "where one solitary idea [is] rolled over and over in
an ocean of words." Demagoguery is apace, and "every man
boasts of his own freedom, and no man respects the freedom of

his neighbour." As Philaemon puts it: "[Honest] men who love the state and forget themselves . . . are not now found in Athens."

The political gambles of Pericles, his "purchasing the favour" of the rabble which has brought Athens to a near state of anarchy, provides Mrs. Child with a way to charge the plot and emphasize the characters' personal tragedies. Yet is there another purpose as well? By 1836 soberer minds in New England were keenly aware of the excesses of Jacksonian democracy. The story of Jackson's followers who had stood with muddy boots on the White House chairs was history; but the tactics of the kitchen cabinet, the charges of corruption in government, the emphasis on the freedoms of the many with the apparent curbing of the freedoms of the few (the propertied), the bank controversy: all such licenses had disturbing parallels with the situation Mrs. Child is describing in ancient Athens. The conservative mind of New England—Emerson's statement in "The American Scholar" to the contrary—did not approve Jackson's policies. Mrs. Child herself was strongly critical of Jackson's treatment of the Indians and deplored his indifference toward slavery. Where was conscience in Jackson's special brand of democracy, which favored some citizens and denied others? In spite of the liberal thinking, Mrs. Child, like her husband, was conservative, a Whig in politics. The tyranny of the majority exercised through its demagogues—the political appointees, the graft-seekers, the press— seemed to be making a mockery of democracy. Cooper's *Letter to His Countrymen* (1834) and his soon-to-come textbook on democracy, *The American Democrat* (1838), and his novel *Home as Found* (1838) underscored the conservative disaffection. If one changed a word or two, Anaxagoras' comment was perhaps a judgment of Jackson: "Pericles no doubt owes his great popularity to skill in availing himself of existing circumstances; and I am afraid that the same motives for corrupting, and the same willingness to be corrupted, will always be found in democratic institutions."

In fact, the conversation between Anaxagoras and Philaemon, who have suffered under Pericles' policies, reads like a conservative attack on the excesses of democracy in nineteenth-century America:

". . . The real difficulty [Philaemon is speaking] exists in that love of power which hides itself beneath the mask of Democracy, until a corrupted public can endure its undisguised features without execration. No one can believe that Pericles lessened the power of the Areopagus [i.e., Senate] from a sincere conviction that it was for the good of the people. It was done to obtain personal influence, by purchasing the favour of those who had sufficient reasons for desiring a less equitable tribunal. Nor could he have ever supposed that the interests of the republic would be advanced by men whom the gift of an obolus could induce to vote. The Athenians have been spoiled by ambitious demagogues, who now try to surfeit them with flattery. . . ."

"Pericles has indeed obtained unbounded influence," rejoined Anaxagoras; "but he did it by counterfeiting the very principle that needed to be checked; and this is so easily counterfeited, that democracy is always in danger of becoming tyranny in disguise. The Athenians are as servile to their popular idol, as the Persians to their hereditary one; but the popular idol seeks to sustain his power by ministering to that love of change, which allows nothing to remain sacred and established. Hence, two opposite evils are combined in action—the reality of despotism with the form of democracy; the power of a tyrant with the irresponsibility of a multitude. . . ."

"Friendly as I am to a government truly republican," answered Philaemon, "it is indeed difficult to forgive the man who seduces a democracy to the commission of suicide, for his own advancement. His great abilities would receive my admiration, if they were not employed in the service of ambition."[14]

Conscience has again been compromised for ambition, as men in high office ignore their priorities. Mrs. Child herself interjects an aside: "For the great Athenian statesman, like modern politicians, deemed honesty excellent in theory and policy safe in practice. Thus admitting the absurd proposition that principles entirely false and corrupt in the abstract are more salutary, in their practical manifestation, than principles essentially good and true."

It is, as Philaemon says, ambition that nearly destroys Pericles. To please the populace he has diminished the power of the Areopagus, the highest tribunal of Athens, "and a decree had been passed that those who denied the existence of the gods, or introduced new opinions about celestial things, should be tried by the people." Thus the way is opened for Pericles' enemies to bring charges of blasphemy against Anaxagoras and Phidias and Aspasia. In the trial by the people,[15] demagogues now enfranchised by the law to speak deliberately misconstrue testimony offered in behalf of the accused. One such exchange takes place during the trial of the philosopher.

. . . Cleon arose, and said it was well known to the disciples of Anaxagoras, that he taught the existence of but one God. Euripides, Pericles, and others who had been his pupils, were separately called to bear testimony; and all said he taught One Universal Mind, of which all other divinities were the attributes; even as Homer represented deities subordinate to Zeus.

When the philosopher was asked whether he believed in the gods, he answered, "I do: but I believe in them as the representatives of various attributes in One Universal Mind."[16]

For uttering what appears to be blasphemy, the people condemn him to death.

Similar tactics are employed in the trials of Phidias and Aspasia, the clamoring populace demanding Phidias' death and Aspasia's exile. Pericles, frightened by what he has himself encouraged, acts quickly to save his friends. Addressing the belligerent "multitude," who nevertheless attach "something of sacredness . . . to his person," he asks a "public favour"—that an oracle be consulted before the citizens carry out their will. Confidently, he adds, "If it please you, let a vote be taken who shall be the messenger." The request is granted.

"Anaxagoras and Phidias," writes Mrs. Child in a subsequent paragraph, "being under sentence of death, were placed in prison, until the people should finally decide upon their fate. The old philosopher cheerfully employed his hours in attempts to square the circle. The sculptor carved a wooden image, with many hands and feet, and without a head; upon the pedestal of which he inscribed Demos, and secretly reserved it as a parting gift to the Athenian people."

The sentences temporarily upheld until the judgment of the oracle can be heard, Pericles uses the interim cunningly. "[H]is emissaries [were] busy in softening the minds of the people." Aspasia offers sacrifices to the gods, "during the continuance of which, the citizens would be publicly feasted at her expense." Pericles convinces a wealthy Athenian, a close friend of Anaxagoras and Phidias, "and a munificent patron of the arts," to offer in exchange for his friends' lives "a golden lamp to Pallas Parthenia" and to place "in each of the agoras any statue or painting the people thought fit to propose." And a petition signed by Pericles, Euripides, Socrates, Plato, "and many other distinguished citizens" is sent to the people requesting a retrial. The petition is granted, and when the trials are again heard "strong efforts were made to fill the [assembly] at a very early hour with friends of Pericles." The sentences of death for Anaxagoras and Phidias are reduced to sentences of exile, but the charges against Aspasia still stand.

When Pericles replied to the charges against Aspasia, his countenance became more pale, and his voice was agitated: "You all know," said he, "that Aspasia is of Miletus. That city which the poets call the laughing daughter of Earth and Heaven: where even the river smiles, as it winds along in graceful wanderings, eager to kiss every new blossom, and court the dalliance of every breeze. Do ye not find it easy to forgive a woman, born under those joyful skies, where beauty rests on the earth in a robe of sunbeams, and inspires the gayety which pours itself forth in playful words? Can ye harshly judge of one, who from her very childhood has received willing homage, as the favourite of Aphrodite, Phoebus, and the Muses? If she spoke irreverently, it was done in thoughtless mirth; and she has sought to atone for it by sacrifices and tears. . . ."

He paused for a moment, and held his hand over Aspasia's head, as he continued: "In the midst of perplexities and cares, here I have ever found a solace and a guide. Here are treasured up the affections of my heart. It is not for Aspasia, the gifted daughter of Axiochus, that I plead. It is for Aspasia, the beloved wife of Pericles. . . ."

As he spoke, he raised Aspasia's veil. Her drapery had been studiously arranged to display her loveliness to the utmost advantage; and as she stood forth radiant in beauty, the building rung with the acclamations that were sent forth, peal after peal, by the multitude.

Pericles had not in vain calculated on the sympathies of a volatile and ardent people, passionately fond of the beautiful, in all its forms. Aspasia remained in Athens, triumphant over the laws of religion and morality.

There follows a dramatic reversal in the character of Pericles, terrified apparently by what he has so narrowly averted, the loss of his wife. He becomes a shadow of his former self: Mrs. Child does not really account for the change because Pericles ceases to figure significantly in the romance hereafter. When the plague comes, he is restored to health by the skill of Hippocrates, but his son falls victim to it. The leader, broken in spirit, gradually shifts the power of state to his loyal and trusted advisers and devotes his attention to Paralus, "the best beloved of his children." These "visitation[s] of the gods"— the phrase is Anaxagoras'—have "softened and subdued his ambitious soul"—the phrase is Plato's. Pericles' transformation is indeed miraculous, a twist of plot Mrs. Child, like so many of her contemporaries who write novels in the nineteenth century, is always capable of executing. However, Pericles the demagogue and the fickle Athenian populace have provided her the means as a cautionary critic to comment obliquely on the American political arena.

Perhaps the parallel with the American political arena does not end yet. Aspasia is, in the eyes of many high-born Athenians, an usurper—"an elegant and voluptuous [woman]" whom Pericles became so enamored of that he divorced his wife and married her, even though his friends "earnestly remonstrated against this union . . . disgraceful to Pericles and injurious to public morals." It is Mrs. Child who controls the impression the reader makes of the beguiling, dark-haired woman.

The celebrated Aspasia . . . succeeded admirably in pleasing the good taste of the Athenians, while she ministered to their vanity and their vices. The wise and good lamented the universal depravity of manners, sanctioned by her influence; but a people so gay, so ardent, so intensely enamoured of the beautiful, readily acknowledge the sway of an eloquent and fascinating woman, who carefully preserved the appearance of decorum. Like the Gabrielles and Pompadours of modern times, Aspasia obtained present admiration and future fame, while hundreds of better women were neglected and forgotten.

She holds symposiums where evenings are spent in conversation and in feasting and drinking marked on occasion by decadent revelries. Eudora, Philothea's impressionable friend, is entranced with Aspasia and delights in attending the galas. When Philothea protests the infatuation, Eudora bridles in her defense: "I think women should judge kindly of Aspasia's faults, and remember that they are greatly exaggerated . . . for she proves that [women] are fit for something better than mere domestic slaves. Her house is the only one in all Greece where women are allowed to be present at entertainments."

Although Aspasia may appear to some of Mrs. Child's readers as the liberated woman, she is by no means Mrs. Child's candidate for a nineteenth-century feminist.[17] Aspasia's appeal is simply sensual: she uses her beauty to command attention. She cares nothing for principles but courts flattery from Pericles and his friends. Her view is Philothea's, when she tells Eudora that Aspasia is no more than a strumpet, a "siren . . . luring you to destruction." Such a woman has no appeal, not even envy, to Mrs. Child reared in a New England environment where plain living was more often than not the standard.

But is not Aspasia somewhat like the notorious Margaret Eaton, the Washington belle—some called her hussy—and the center of a social scandal in Jackson's administration? Willful, impetuous, apparently indiscreet, the widow of a luckless naval officer, she married John H. Eaton of Tennessee, Jackson's friend and cabinet secretary, the President frankly insisting on the marriage to save the woman's already shady reputation. Snubbed by "proper" Washington society, Margaret Eaton was installed by Jackson as mistress of the White House, usurping, it was felt, the role Mrs. Jackson before her death had asked her niece to fill. Washington society and conservative matrons in New England were on the side of the niece. The President's levees, the lavish entertainments, were the gossip in Washington parlors and in country kitchens. Such extravagance seemed at variance with the announced aims of Jacksonian democracy.

With "earnest cordiality and graceful self-possession," Mrs. Eaton, like Aspasia in the novel, triumphed for a time over her critics, "her features . . . well-trained to conceal her sentiments." And just as Jackson's defense of Mrs. Eaton had caused a near-crisis in the cabinet, so Pericles risked his office protecting Aspasia. An angry, defiant Jackson rode out the Eaton affair, even though social conventions were ignored. And Pericles, in "melodious voice and fluent tongue," won the day for Aspasia.[18] If *Philothea* is in part a commentary on the American political arena, it is as successful, in a soberer way, admittedly, as Washington Irving's *History of New York*.

Although the parallels drawn between conscience and conduct in government and scandal in Washington society may be implicit in the novel, far more explicit are the comments on slavery in ancient Greece, more humane, perhaps, in Athens than in America, but slavery nonetheless. Eudora is herself a slave, having been purchased by Phidias in her youth and raised in his house with "all the privileges of a daughter." Even so, Eudora complains to Philothea: ". . . The very circumstance that I was bought with his money embitters it all. . . . I can never be an Athenian. The spirit and the gifts of freedom ill assort with the condition of a slave." Aspasia, whom Eudora openly admires, never fails to "remind me of being a slave." Anaxagoras vehemently denounces the system, his dying request to Plato and Philothea that he "be buried after the ancient manner, with the least possible trouble and expense. The money you would expend for a monument may be given to some captive sighing in bondage." By Athenian law, however, slaves can be freed and cannot be abused; if they are, they have the right to take refuge in the Temple of Theseus and "to make complaint to the magistrates, and demand another master," as two of Alcibiades' slaves do after they have been beaten. Mrs. Child in her notes in the appendix remarks that "the Athenian slave laws were much more mild than modern codes."

However, Spartan slave law is much stricter. Philaemon, disenfranchised and exiled, is himself in a position little better than that of slave. He condemns the Spartan law "forbidding masters to bestow freedom on their slaves" and "the custom which permits boys to whip them, merely to remind them of their bondage." He scorns the Spartans for their smug belief that "the sun of liberty shines brighter with the dark atmosphere of slavery around it"; Spartans forget "that the passions are the same in every human breast." Such treatment of the helots will provoke an uprising: "it is never wise in any state to create natural enemies at [one's] own doors." Again Mrs. Child in the appendix supplies in reference to Sparta's slave laws a parallel, in her mind, at least, with the evils of American slavery:

. . . No pains were spared to render [the helots] servile and degraded. Once a year they publicly received a severe flagellation, merely to remind them that they were slaves. They were never allowed to learn any liberal art, or to sing manly songs. In order to expose them to greater contempt, they were often obliged to perform indecent dances, and to get brutally drunk, that their master's children might learn to despise such uncomely things.

Whatever distortion appeared in the character of Pericles and Aspasia, for whatever reason Mrs. Child had in mind, no readers seriously questioned. Nor did they resent the attack on the evils of slavery. Yet some readers and reviewers did take issue with the partial portrait of Plato. The Duyckincks, for instance, objected to her "dwelling on the mystical doctrines of the philosopher to the exclusion of his practical traits."[19] Mrs. Child chose to refer to only a few of the philosopher's ideas, thus presenting him only through their medium.

The reader sees him first at Aspasia's symposium where Pericles, in presenting Plato to the assembled guests, describes him thus: "He walks with his head among the stars,—and, by a magic influence, we rise to his elevation, until we perceive the shadows of majestic worlds, known in their reality only to the gods. As the approach of Phoebus fills the priestess with prophecy, so does this son of Phoebus impart something of his own eloquence to all who come within its power." "You speak truly," adds a guest, "but it is a truth felt only by those who are in some measure worthy to receive it. . . . The gods are ever with us, but few feel the presence of the gods." Philothea completes the impression: "And Plato rejoices in their glorious presence, not only because he walks with his head among the stars, but because he carries in his heart a blessing for every little child." "These words," Mrs. Child breaks in to say, ". . . reached the ear of the philosopher himself; and he turned toward [Philothea] . . . with a beaming glance, which distinctly told that his choicest blessings were bestowed upon spirits pure and gentle as her own." Thus Plato is seen not as a man but as a demi-god. The portrait is deliberate because he is set distinctly apart from the ambitious Pericles, the voluptuous Aspasia, the sensualist Alcibiades. He is a mystic and a sentimentalist. At the banquet table he eats only olives and bread and water "scarcely tinged with Lesbian wine." When Alcibiades twits him about his abstemiousness and Pericles reminds him that Socrates "gave Dionysus his dues," Plato responds, "I can worship the fiery God of Vintage only when married with Nymphs of the Fountain." He is a Pythagorean and a poet. During the ensuing conversation he expresses ideas closest to Mrs. Child's heart. At one point he rhapsodizes, responding to a comment about the architecture of Athens' temples:

The very spirit of harmony is embodied in the proportions of the Parthenon. It is marble music. I sometimes think the whole visible beauty of creation is formed from the music of the Infinite; and that the various joys we feel are but the union of accordant notes in the great chorus of the universe. There is music in airy dance; music in poetry; music in the glance of a beautiful woman; music in the involutions and inflexions of numbers; above all, there is music in light! And what *Light* is in this world, *Truth* is in that glorious world to which the mind of man returns after its long exile. . . .

Again, he speaks another idea which romantic Hellenists—the "hyper-Attic" like Mrs. Child—cherish:

. . . Anaxagoras said wisely that material forms lead the contemplative mind to the worship of ideal good, which is in its nature immortal and divine. Homer tells us that the golden chain resting upon Olympus reaches even to the earth. Here we see but a few of the last links, and those imperfectly. We are like men in a subterranean cave, so chained that they can look only forward to the entrance. Far above and behind us is a glowing fire: and beautiful beings, of every form, are moving between the light and us poor fettered mortals. Some of these bright beings are speaking, and others are silent. We see only the shadows cast on the opposite wall of the cavern, by the reflection of the fire above; and if we hear the echo of voices, we suppose it belongs to those passing shadows. The soul, in its present condition, is in exile from the orb of light; its ignorance is forgetfulness; and whatever we can perceive of truth, or imagine of beauty, is but a reminiscence of our former more glorious state of being. He who reverences the gods, and subdues his own passions, returns at last to the blest condition from which he fell. But to talk, or think, about these things with proud impatience, or polluted morals, is like pouring pure water into a miry trench; he who does it disturbs the mud, and thus causes the clear waters to become defiled. . . .

He is always aesthetic and other-worldly. When the conversation at the symposium turns to affairs in Athens, Plato is disturbed. Whether he discourses at the symposium, or with Philothea and her friends, or with Anaxagoras in exile, he always declaims: fanciful analogies, mystic intimations, poetical rhapsodies. He never appears as a man engaged in the actual business of life. When he says that "philosophy has wrought in me a dislike of conversing with many persons" and that he "cannot go into the Prytanaeum, the agoras, and the workshops, and jest, like Socrates, to captivate the attention of young men," the reader with some knowledge of Plato is abashed. Plato, after all, was a teacher. He continues, "I feel the breath of life taken away from me by the multitude. Their praises cause me to fear . . . I should offend the gods, [and] acquire glory among men." He, after all, did establish a school. Mrs. Child deliberately provides the reader with only a partial view of the philosopher's character, true perhaps as far as it goes but false as a general impression.

The ideas Plato presents he did discuss occasionally. They are a part but not the whole of his philosophy. The doctrine of preexistence is voiced several times. "At times, I have thought glimpses of . . . eternal truths were revealed to me," he remarks to Anaxagoras,

but I lost them almost as soon as they were perceived, because my soul dwelt so much with the images of things. Thus have I stood before the thick veil which conceals the shrine of Isis, while the narrow streak of brilliant light around its edges gave indication of unrevealed glories, and inspired eager but fruitless hope that the massive folds would float away, like a cloud before the sun. There are indeed times when I lose the light entirely, and cannot even perceive the veil that hides it from me. This is because my soul, like Psyche bending over the sleeping Eros, is too curious to examine, by its own feeble taper, the lineaments of the divinity whereby it hath been blessed.

Yet for the reader this sentiment has a more modern ring—in the poetry of Wordsworth or in the essays of Swedenborg. Plato, like Swedenborg centuries later, speculated on an ideal world; but he was more often the logician, a dealer in hard facts. He created beautiful visions, yet he discussed questions about the destiny of man. Only brief mention is made of *The Republic*,[20] which so clearly demonstrates Plato's awareness of policies of state. He often suggested in his writing a common sense; no doubt his conversations with men and with his students had the same authority. However, Mrs. Child has been deliberately selective: "this is the teacher . . . this is the divine Plato; this is the soaring swan, whose melodious notes allure all that hear him."

In Mrs. Child's romance, her tale of history and fantasy, the history is reflected in the character of Pericles and Aspasia; the fantasy is seen largely in the character of Plato, exclusively in the character of Philothea.

III   *". . . Strange, Unearthly Language"*

Philothea is a lovely creation, carved with "sculpture-like distinctness."[21] She is a young woman of unsurpassed beauty, with "a complexion fair even to transparency." Modest and unprepossessing, she wears an "expression [that] had the innocence of infancy," yet "tinged with something elevated and holy, which made it seem like infancy in Heaven." Ethereal, contemplative, sublime. Like her "grandfather" Anaxagoras, she too prefers "wisdom to gold" and has been given "an education seldom bestowed on daughters," often in the company of the best genius Athenian society can provide. She is deliberately contrasted to the sensual Aspasia, who seems quite attracted to her. Through Pericles, Aspasia commands Philothea to attend one of the evening symposiums, and reluctantly the young woman appears.

The interview between the two women may well be one of the portions of the book Poe had in mind when he recommended it for the "female academies," for Philothea under pressure is a model of conduct.

[Aspasia's] own face was uncovered, contrary to the custom of Grecian women; and after a few of those casual remarks which everywhere serve to fill up the pauses in conversation, she playfully seized Eudora's veil, and threw it back over her shoulders. She would have done the same to Philothea; but the maiden placed her hand on the half transparent covering, and said, "With your leave, lady, I remain veiled."

"But I cannot give my leave," rejoined Aspasia, playfully, still keeping her hold upon the veil: "I must see this tyrannical custom done away in the free commonwealth of Athens. All the matrons who visit my house agree with me in this point; all are willing to renounce the absurd fashion."

"But in a maiden it would be less seemly," answered Philothea. . . .

Aspasia continued, "From what I had heard of you, Philothea, I expected to find you above the narrow prejudices of Grecian women. In *you*, I was sure of a mind strong enough to break the fetters of habit. Tell me, bashful maiden, why is beauty given us, unless it be like sunlight to bless and gladden the world?"

"Lady," replied the gentle recluse, "beauty is given to remind us that the soul should be kept as fair and perfect in its proportions, as the temple in which it dwells."

"You *are* above ordinary women," said Aspasia; "for you hear me allude to your beauty without affecting to contradict me, and apparently without pleasure."

Philothea firmly resists Aspasia's request; the conversation turns to other matters, among them "future existence." "[T]he simple fact that the human soul has ever *thought* of another world," suggests Philothea, "is sufficient proof that there is one; for how can an idea be formed by mortals, unless it has first existed in the divine mind?"

"You utter nonsense," Aspasia retorts. "There is no immortality but fame. . . . To the remotest period of time, the world . . . will hear of Aspasia, the beautiful and the gifted!" And she adds arrogantly, "In history, the star of my existence will never set."

What to you seem idle dreams [Philothea continues], are to me sublime realities, for which I would gladly exchange all that you prize in existence. You live for immortality in this world; I live for immortality in another. The public voice is your oracle; I listen to the whisperings of the gods in the stillness of my own heart. . . . Listen to the voice that tries to win you back to innocence and truth! Give your heart up to it, as a little child led by its mother's hand!

Aspasia, gazing "intently" at the young woman, responds: "Philothea, you have moved me strangely. There is about you an influence that cannot be resisted. It is like what Pindar says of music; if it does not give delight, it is sure to agitate and oppress the heart." Mrs. Child thus establishes the character of the other-worldly Philothea, perhaps too obviously for the modern reader, in the interview between the two women—this within the first twenty pages of the romance. Idealism shapes Philothea's character and governs the romance as well. Aspasia, wedded to this world, provides appropriate counterpoint. The interview over, the women join the guests at the symposium. Before a mirror of polished steel, Aspasia pauses to adjust her robe. "As she passed, she continued to look back at the reflection of her own fair form, with a proud glance which seemed to say, 'Aspasia is herself again!'"

However, the interview serves Mrs. Child another purpose; it enables her to introduce through Philothea certain philosophical speculations close to her heart: the sentiments of Swedenborg, regarded by some of her contemporaries—among them, her brother Convers—as near-charlatan, but by others, including Mrs. Child, as divinely inspired. Although she assured Convers some years before that he need not be concerned about her "stranding on the shoals of [Swedenborg's] fanaticism," it is nevertheless his thought that often sets the tone for the romance: it is found in Plato's dialogs, in Anaxagoras' wisdom, and in Philothea's other-worldliness.

Philothea is deeply imbued with the life of the spirit, listening "to the whisperings of the gods in the stillness of my own heart." Like her friend Plato, there is the mystic and the sentimentalist in her; yet she is more the daughter of Swedenborg, as Mrs. Child reads that writer's thought. "Mortals," Philothea tells Eudora, "without the aid of experience would always be aware of the presence of evil, if they sought to put away the love of it in their own hearts, and in silent obedience listened to the voice of their guiding spirit. Flowers feel the approach of storms, and birds need none to teach them the enmity of serpents. This knowledge is given to them as perpetually as the sunshine; and they receive it fully, because their little lives are all obedience and love." With "a spirit receiving the gift of prophecy," Philothea comes before the reader not as a woman of this world but as a child of the skies. As a novitiate in the temple on the Acropolis, she has had visions of immortality.

Her love for Paralus is spiritual: they are kindred souls. "The liberty of loving Paralus," she tells Eudora, "no power can take from me; and in that I find sufficient happiness. I am bound to him by ties stronger than usually bind the hearts of women."

... From our childhood, Paralus and I have shared the same books, the same music, and the same thoughts, until our souls seem to be one. When I am very happy, I always see a peculiar brightness on his countenance; and when I am powerfully impressed by any of the fair sights of this beautiful world, or by those radiant deities who live among the stars, often, before I can speak my thoughts, he utters my very words. I sometimes think the gods have united human beings by some mysterious principle, like the according notes of music. Or is it as Plato has supposed, that souls originally one have been divided, and each seeks the half it has lost?

Wooed later by a wealthy prince struck by her beauty who promises her "more grandeur than Penelope could boast in her proudest days," Philothea quietly replies, "I have never learned to value riches; nor could I do so, without danger of being exiled far from my divine home." (The rejected suitor, in melodramatic fashion, declares, "Curse on the folly which philosophers dignify with the name of wisdom!") And Plato, hearing her response, reaffirms: "Maiden, your own spirit has always remained near its early glories."

Mrs. Child has patiently and lovingly drawn the character of the young woman, this other-worldly creature who embodies the sentiments she and a number of her contemporaries in nineteenth-century New England are attracted to: Plato's speculations regarding pre-existence, Wordsworth's cult of the child, the romantics' view of nature, Emerson's doctrine of correspondences, the Quakers' belief in the inner light, Swedenborg's concept of immortality, Eastern mysticism, and even a bit of New England morality.[22]

Greeted by Pericles on her return to Athens, after he has struck the decree preventing her marriage to Paralus, he praises her devotion: "Your presence . . . has a blessed influence; but oh, my daughter, what a sacrifice you are making—young and beautiful as you are!" "Nay, Pericles," she answers, "I deem it a privilege once more to hear the sound of his voice; though it speaks a strange, unearthly language." For Paralus, already hovering at the entrance to the spiritual world, has visions which only Philothea can interpret. At the wedding ceremony he is "so unconscious of the scene he was acting" that Pericles performs some of the customary rites. "The ceremonies being finished . . . two doves alighted on the altar; but one immediately rose, and floated above the other. . . . Its mate looked upward for a moment; and then both of them rose high in the air, and disappeared."

Spring becomes summer, and Paralus' condition remains unchanged; yet Philothea is watchful, having "faith only in the healing power of perfect quiet, and the free communion of congenial souls." Reluctantly, she submits to Pericles' desire to take Paralus to the Olympic games, the father thinking that the excitement may kindle life in his son. "It is partly for your sake that I wish it, my poor child," he tells her. "If it may be avoided, I will not see the whole of your youth consumed in anxious watchings." "Nay, my father," Philothea responds, "you have never seen me anxious, or troubled. I have known most perfect contentment since my union with your son." Oblivious to all around him, Paralus speaks of "things unrecognized by those of earthly mould," yet Philothea finds in his visionary wanderings "a strange and marvellous beauty that seemed not altogether new to the soul, but was seen in a dim and pleasing light, like the recollections of infant years." When Eudora sees her friend again after some years of separation, she is struck by a subtle change in the young woman: ". . . You have ever seemed to live in a region above darkness and storms. Earth has left no shadow on your countenance. It expresses the same transparent innocence, the same mild love. A light not of this world is gleaming there; and it has grown brighter and clearer since we parted."

The excitement of the games does not stir Paralus from his comatose state, and out of a heavy sleep he rouses once more to recite to Philothea the vision of his death—a vision not unlike Swedenborg's as Mrs. Child understood it.

". . . I was in the temple of the most ancient god. The roof was of heaven's pure gold, which seemed to have a light within it, like the splendour of the sun. . . . Anaxagoras stood beside me; and he said we were living in the age

of innocence, when mortals could gaze on divine beings unveiled, and yet
preserve their reason. They spoke another language than the Greeks; but we
had no need to learn it; we seemed to breathe it in the air. . . . Many other
things I saw and heard, but was forbidden to relate. The gate of the temple
was an arch, supported by two figures with heavy drapery, eyes closed, and
arms folded. They told me these were Sleep and Death. Over the gate was
written in large letters, 'The Entrance of Mortals.' Beyond it, I saw you
standing with outstretched arms, as if you sought to come to me, but could
not. . . . I tried to meet you; but as I passed through the gate, a cold air blew
upon me, and all beyond was in the glimmering darkness of twilight. I would
have returned, but the gate had closed; and I heard behind me the sound of
harps and of voices, singing:

> 'Come hither, kindred spirits, come!
> Hail to the mystic two in one!'"

Philothea kissed his hand, and her face beamed with joy. She had earnestly
desired some promise of their future union; and now she felt the prayer was
answered.

"Could it be a dream?" said Paralus: "Methinks I hear the music now."

Philothea smiled affectionately, as she replied: "When sleep hath passed,
thy dreams remain."

The "light not of this world" which Eudora sees in her friend gleams
brighter after Paralus' death; silent and composed, "in this perfect
stillness of resignation," she awaits reunion with her husband. She
remembers the legend of the wood nymph Erato, who implored the
assistance of Arcus when a raging flood threatened to carry away the
tree over which she presided. The tree was lost, and the Dryad
perished with it. "There is a deep and hidden reason why the heart
loves to invest every hill, and stream, and tree, with a mysterious
principle of life," Philothea tells Eudora. "All earthly forms are but
the clothing of some divine ideal; and this truth we *feel*, though we
know it not. But when I spoke of Arcus and [Erato], I was thinking
that Paralus had been the tree, on whose existence my own depended;
and that now he was removed, I should not long remain."

She does not, and Eudora witnesses her death: a sudden radiant
light, the unearthly beauty of the young woman, the sound of music
in the air—"the tune Paralus had learned from the celestial harps,"
and the scarcely audible "well-remembered words." The souls
"originally one [having] been divided" have now won "the half it
[had] lost." Mrs. Child's reading of Swedenborg's mystic insights
governs the final scenes devoted to Paralus and Philothea.

Philothea's character is delicately, sensitively, wrought; nothing
discordant interrupts the harmony of her being—no harsh sentiment,

no wild passion, no unlovely thing. She is the ideal. She is not Greek, and she is not human; she is the dream-creation of Mrs. Child's rich imagination. Nevertheless, she seems far more sensitive a character of fiction than Mary Conant or Grace Osborne and Lucretia Fitzherbert.

The romance was dedicated to her brother Convers as a tribute to him for the love of literature he had instilled in his sister. It was he who had inspired in her an admiration for Greek life and culture. Philothea herself was a tribute to the woman who created her, suffused with the glow of life it was said Phidias worked into his marble.

IV   *". . . Mellow the Lights and . . . Enrich the Shadows . . ."*

Philothea is sheer romance, gossamerlike. The pages of the book unfold the glory of the age Mrs. Child is so imaginatively creating. Athens—its temples and villas, its altars and statues—glows in refulgent light. Its history, customs, legends, and routine of daily life come alive before the reader. The style complements the story, musical and metaphorical, glittering like the radiant forms of art which fill the ancient city. The imagery, the allusions, the associations she awakens, and the scenes she paints all invoke the glorious age.

It was obviously "romance of the wildest kind," which some reviewers complained about. ". . . Laboriously classical in minute details," wrote the *North American* reviewer; "in her Atticism, she is hyper-Attic."[23] Although "classical in minute details," she was far less exact in historical fact.[24] Carl Van Doren referred to the book as "a gentle, ignorant romance . . . the fruit of real desire to escape the clang of current life,"[25] a charge Mrs. Child would readily admit. *Philothea* was finished in the dark days when her husband was in Europe pursuing his sugar-beet dream and she was living in near pauperism in an older brother's home. Far more insightful perhaps was Van Wyck Brooks's comment that the romance was "a virginal vision,"[26] if one wishes to look at the ideal love of Philothea and Paralus as a thinly veiled allusion to what may have been the innocent love of Maria and David Child.[27] Higginson remembered with what "admiration . . . this romance was hailed," however, when it first appeared, with sales brisk enough to call for three printings. "Personally," he recalled, "it was one of those delights . . . which the criticism of maturity cannot disturb. What mattered it if she brought Anaxagoras and Plato on stage together . . . ? What mattered it if in her book the classic themes were treated in a romantic spirit?"[28] Only Sarah J. Hale, editor of the *Boston Ladies' Magazine*, worried that the bitter feelings Mrs. Child had raised because of her antislavery writings might prevent "the merits of this remarkable book from being appreciated as they deserve."[29] And Thoreau was sufficiently impressed with the romance to make several pages of extracts from the novel in his journal during his senior year at Harvard.[30]

Mrs. Child has provided her estimate of the novel in the preface, calling it a romance that hopefully would appeal to the reader's imagination as much as it did to the author's. Admittedly, it is an escape novel, "for awhile," she writes in the preface, "[to] bid adieu to the substantial fields of utility, [and] to float on the clouds of romance." As a novel it is far more skillfully composed than *Hobomok* and *The Rebels*. Some years hence Hawthorne will write a definition of the romance, yet Mrs. Child has written a romance largely along the lines Hawthorne will suggest, "to present truth under circumstances, to a great extent, of the writer's own choosing or creation . . . so [to] manage his atmospherical medium as to bring out or mellow the lights and deepen and enrich the shadows of the picture." The plot of *Philothea* is simple, the structure is tight, the style is rich, the background is carefully sketched in, the characters are substantial, and the themes are artfully worked out. If it is true, as Mark Van Doren said of Hawthorne, that a writer's genius is reflected in one book, then *Philothea* is Mrs. Child's. She never equaled her accomplishment again. "The flowers of the field are unlike," Philothea tells Eudora, "but each has a beauty of its own." *Philothea* has its unique beauty.

CHAPTER 5

Letters from New York

THOUGH *Philothea* was "a pleasant ramble into classic lands," Mrs. Child acknowledged to a friend that some of her readers might "deem [it] utterly useless."[1] The workaday world was the arena where service to others was to be performed, where *The Frugal Housewife*, *The Mother's Book*, and *The Girl's Own Book* had provided useful instruction to her readers. Thus, it was to the workaday world she turned her attention once again, writing a series of articles for the *National Anti-Slavery Standard*, when she was editor, on her impressions of New York. The articles also appeared in the *Boston Courier* by contractual arrangement and were widely printed in other newspapers throughout the country. Of all Mrs. Child's nonfiction, these articles had the greatest appeal to readers of her day, perhaps to readers today as well. They were the kind of personal journalism that was becoming popular—informal "essays" which allowed the writer to focus on whatever subject he chose. Since the articles had been so well approved, she wished to publish them; unable to find a publisher willing to take the risk, she borrowed money from a friend and paid for an edition herself. *Letters from New York* quickly sold out,[2] and now several publishers urged her to plan a second series which they would gladly print. She saw the *Letters* not only as a contribution to social reform but as a means of affirming her continuing interest in literature. On both counts she was successful: reviewers praised the book, here and abroad; and Poe among other editors asked for articles. Emerson thought that the *Letters* were "really a contribution to *American* literature, recording in generous spirit, and with lively truth, the pulsations of one great center of national existence."[3] The reviewer in the *Democratic Review* was even more generous: ". . . a refreshing book . . . com[ing] so straight from her own heart—a heart overflowing with all love and tender kindness—that it cannot fail to go straight to that of her reader. It is truly delightful to . . . note how beautifully she can shed

the light of her own shining spirit upon all surrounding objects."[4]
Of course, there were those reviewers who carped—the antireformers
to whom Mrs. Child's causes were an anathema and those
who complained about the "bizarre . . . and mawkish . . . ultra-
sentimentalities" in some of the more romantic essays whose appeal
was largely to "*the woman's heart.*"[5]

I   ". . . The Toiling Age of Reform . . ."

There is certainly in the *Letters* something for every reader: the
casual browser and the romanticist, the reformer and the housewife.
She provides "a panorama of passing scenes, then child-like prattle
about birds or mosses . . . a serious exposition of facts, for the
reformer's use, then the poet's path . . . far up into the blue." For the
reader today the description of the Battery "in the silence of
midnight"; a visit to the site of Hamilton's duel with Burr, "as lovely
as a nook of Paradise, before Satan entered its garden"; the country
estate of an eccentric Scotsman who "fashioned such a flowery
fortune from the barren sands" along the East River; or a ferry trip up
the Hudson on a scorching August day to sightsee the Dutch country
appear as mere "rhapsodies," so said too the reviewer in the London
Athenaeum, "displaying sentiments and notions . . . [in] eloquent
effusions."[6] But such essays are only a small part of the *Letters*,
interludes when for the moment she turns "aside from the dusty
road of reforming duty, to gather flowers in sheltered nooks, or play
with gems in hidden grottoes."

It is her impressions of the "great Babylon" of nineteenth-century
America which dominate the book: "The din of crowded life, and the
eager chase for gain, still run through its streets, like the perpetual
murmur of a hive. . . . In Wall Street, and elsewhere, Mammon, as
usual, coolly calculates his chance of extracting a penny from war,
pestilence, and famine; and Commerce, with her loaded drays, and
jaded skeletons of horses, is busy as ever fulfilling the 'World's
contract with the Devil.' The noisy discord of the street-cries gives the
ear no rest." There was a time, she admits just after she first arrived
in the city, when the contrasting scenes of New York—"where Wealth
dozes on French couches . . . while Poverty camps on the dirty
pavement," where "amid the splendour of Broadway, sits the blind
negro beggar . . . while opposite to him stands . . . the slave trader,
still plying his bloody trade"—were a source of wonderment, passing
by her "like the flitting figures of the magic lantern, or the changing
scenery of a theatre." Now, however, "magnificence and mud, finery

and filth, diamonds and dirt" anger her: "I have lost the power of looking merely on the surface." Instead of kaleidoscopic impressions of city life by a disinterested passerby, she sees in "the vast emporium of poverty and crime" scenes of degradation and despair, loneliness and heartache; and "straightway my mind is filled with thoughts about mutual helpfulness, human sympathy, [and] the common bond of brotherhood." The Battery "in the silence of midnight" may still have its illusory charm, and the street hawkers and wandering musicians may "cheer this weary world" with their wares and their songs, but "this world has passed from its youthful Troubadour Age, into the thinking, toiling Age of Reform." She is "cutting the lines deep," she informs the reader in her first letter, and the memory of "sheltered nooks" recedes before the pressing problems of "poverty and crime."

With priorities established, she turns to the good work of temperance societies. Viewing a passing parade, a procession of the Washington Temperance Society "two miles long," she is reminded of the activities of its members—returning erring husbands to wives and children. "I used to say," she remarks, "I knew not where were the righteous men to save the city; but I have found them now." She recounts an incident of a man rescued by the temperance workers, now "comfortably clothed" and "kindly encouraged" by a job in a printing office which they had procured for him, "work[ing] steadily all day, and preach[ing] temperance in the evening." She tells of other work of the temperance members with drunkards, destitutes, and potential criminals, where "human sympathy [and] the common bond of brotherhood" minister directly to the social ills of the city.[7] She conjectures: Are there not enough men and women like the temperance workers, multiplied a hundred fold, to save the city? Are there not other agencies, other concerned citizens, whose help to their fellows can alleviate despair and poverty? Is not the work of such benevolent organizations, of such interested citizens, really the business of society at large? If the "Law of Love," which the temperance workers practice, can reform habits of drunkards and destitutes, cannot society through similar efforts root out its social ills and bring about its own rejuvenation? Her conclusion offers insight, apparent today perhaps, but not so readily acknowledged in nineteenth-century America: "This [Washington Temperance] Society is one among several powerful agencies now at work, to teach society that it *makes its own criminals*." If society, as guardian of the public welfare, has ignored through circumstance or indifference the destitute among its members, then is it not society's responsibility to rectify the problem, to eliminate the social diseases infecting its members? How can the drunkard whom society puts in debtors' prison, she argues, become a useful member when the work he can do is denied him? Society injures itself with the wrongs it tolerates, and "at prodigious loss of time, money, and morals" inflicts the criminals' disease upon itself.

The account of the Washington Temperance Society and its work in eliminating one kind of social disease establishes the major thesis of the *Letters*. In the "toiling Age of Reform" removal of social ills as Mrs. Child observes them in New York—the cancer most injurious to the nation's health—is her real work, the "destined mission," she writes in the preface, "of helping human souls to be truthful and free."

Of course, there are passages in these reform essays in which "*the woman's heart*" controls her pen, as she imagines how the "polluted city" will treat the "ragged urchin" whom she meets in the street—a newsboy who looks "blue, cold, and disconsolate on a bleak February day."

How I wanted to warm him in my heart. . . . Imagination followed him to the miserable cellar where he probably slept on dirty straw; I saw him flogged after his day of cheerless toil, because he had failed to bring home pence enough for his parents' grog; I saw wicked ones come muttering and beckoning between his young soul and heaven; they tempted him to steal to avoid the dreaded beating. I saw him, years after, bewildered and frightened, in the police-office, surrounded by hard faces. . . . [He] drew the inference that they were his enemies. . . .

Yet the reader may grant the reformer's concern when she draws less forlorn conclusions, as in the case of the inmates of a sailors' home on Staten Island. Society, she writes, has erected through the munificence of a benefactor "a noble stone edifice . . . large, airy, and convenient." The grounds of the home are attractively laid out; "and the whole aspect of things is extremely pleasant—with the exception of the sailors themselves," who show "a sort of torpid resignation in countenance and movement, painful to witness."

I have always thought too little provision was made for this lassitude of the mind, in most benevolent institutions. Men accustomed to excitement, cannot do altogether without it. . . . Those poor old tars should have sea-songs and instrumental music, once in a while, to stir their sluggish blood; and a feast might be given on great occasions, [by] younger sailors from temperance boarding-houses, that the Past might have a chance to hear from the Present. We perform but half a charity, when we comfort the body and leave the soul desolate.

Even when society does attempt to ameliorate the condition of its "most neglected" and "most abused" citizens—in this case, disabled sailors, it ministers only to their physical needs. No provision is made for their spiritual needs, worse nothing is done for their psychological health.[8] Indifference on the part of society—the minimum effort to provide security for the disabled sailors—is as baleful to Mrs. Child as its irresponsibility toward the drunkards and destitutes the temperance workers care for. The sailors' home is not a home when no consideration is given its inmates, when the body is looked after but the mind is left in ignorance or despair. Will society get "right side up, by and by"? Will it assume its commitments? Although she sees so little in her impressions of New York to encourage her, she is not deterred, still seeking—as one editor put it—"[to strike] a chord to which the heart of some reader will vibrate in unison."[9]

In another essay she writes about the prison, the mad house, and the hospital on the "quiet loveliness" of Blackwell's Island: an anachronism assuredly because society has placed its criminals here "in the midst of green hills, and flowing streams . . . after the heart is petrified against the genial influence of all such sights and sounds." The sight of the prisoners rouses "into great activity," reports Mrs. Child, "the organ of justice (which phrenologists say is unusually developed in my head)," and she deplores society's "manifold injustice" and "cold neglect" of these unfortunate men and women. "Would you have them prey on society?" asks one of her companions who is touring the compound with her. "I am troubled that society has preyed upon *them*," she retorts. "I will not enter into an argument about the right of society to punish these sinners; but I say she *made* them sinners." More than half the inmates of the prison are women, many of them prostitutes who became "street-walkers" because men have "made them such" by perverting "love [in] a human heart" into "sensuality and crime." A similar charge Margaret Fuller levels as well in *Woman in the Nineteenth Century*. Yet those same men, Mrs. Child charges, sit in council chambers and pass ordinances "to clear the streets they have filled with sin." Is it any wonder, she asks, that the women made "vicious" by society's indifference have no respect for laws? "Their whole being cries out that it is a mockery; all their experience proves that society is a game of chance, where the cunning slip through [the laws] and the strong leap over [them]." In fact, the prevailing sentiment among the prisoners, she points out, is that they "*feel* . . . they are *wronged*." What society labels justice, they regard as "unlucky *chance*." And, she concludes, "whosoever looks calmly and wisely into the foundations on which society rolls and tumbles, (I cannot say on which it *rests*, for its foundations heave like the sea,) will perceive that they *are* victims of chance."

Society, she maintains, is built on the policy that what is good by its standards is good, that what is wrong by its standards is wrong—an echo of Emerson's sentiment in "Self-Reliance." What it does not condone, it condemns. "Animal instincts" not "higher powers of the soul" govern the conduct of men in society: "everything in school-books, social remarks, domestic conversation, literature, public festivals, legislative proceedings, and popular honours, all teach the young soul that it is noble to retaliate, mean to forgive an insult, and unmanly not to resent a wrong." And in no area of life, Mrs. Child insists, is the hypocrisy of society more apparent, where man's "animal instincts" are more strongly exercised, than in making money:

. . . The maxims of trade, the customs of society, and the general unreflecting tone of public conversation, all tend to promote it. The man who has made "good bargains," is wealthy and honoured; yet the details of those bargains few would dare to pronounce good. Of two young men nurtured under such influences, one becomes a successful merchant; five thousand dollars are borrowed of him; he takes a mortgage on a house worth twenty thousand dollars; in the absence of the owner, when sales are very dull, he offers the house for sale, to pay his mortgage; he bids it in himself, for four thousand dollars; and afterwards persecutes and imprisons his debtor for the remaining thousand. Society calls him a shrewd businessman, and pronounces his dinners excellent; the chance is, he will be a magistrate before he dies. The other young man is unsuccessful; his necessities are great; he borrows some money from his employer's drawer, perhaps resolving to restore the same; the loss is discovered before he has a chance to refund it; and society sends him to Blackwell's island, to hammer stone with highway robbers. Society made both these men thieves; but punished the one, while she rewarded the other.

Perhaps "*the woman's heart*" is aroused; perhaps these "ultra-sentimentalities" are, as the *Knickerbocker* reviewer said, the exaggerations of a mind not always "*intellectually* feminine";[10] perhaps the charges leveled against society are for immediate effect—she is bitten by reforming zeal. But the reader can hardly deny the sincerity of such sentiments "com[ing] so evidently from her own heart," as the reviewer in the *Democratic Review* realized.[11] When the destitute is rehabilitated through honest labor, when the prostitute is provided through honest employment her self-esteem, when the embezzler is given a second chance, then society will have played its appropriate role of protector, not prosecutor. Money, since it is society's criterion for success, and the means of making it, since it is man's criterion for self-respect, must somehow be guaranteed. "If we can abolish *poverty*, we shall have taken the greatest step towards the abolition of crime," Mrs. Child is convinced. Although she does not submit a formula, a plan, to effect this change (other than "the gospel of Christ"), she has arrived at a sound premise.

What is wanted is, that no human being should grow up without deep and friendly interest from the society round him; and that none should feel himself the victim of injustice, because society punishes the very sins which it teaches, nay drives men to commit. The world would be in a happier condition if legislators spent half as much time and labour to *prevent* crime, as they do to *punish* it. The poor need houses of *encouragement*; and society gives them houses of *correction*.

Society's obligation is to encourage, not to frustrate, man's efforts to win self-respect. Is such an "idea of *reconstruction*" folly? Let one "reflect a moment upon the immense changes that have already come over society. In the middle ages, both noble and peasant would have laughed loud and long at the prophecy of such a state of society as now exists in the free States of America; yet here we are!"

Mrs. Child has a large heart, her earnest idealism and her Yankee stamina are strong; otherwise, she would have long since turned "aside from the dusty road of reforming duty." Her "highest wisdom" tells her that society is capable of the revolution she envisions, that men once motivated will want to do what is right. The line separating criminal and prostitute and embezzler from herself and her reader is thin indeed: ". . . You will perceive that there have been periods in your own life when a hair's-breadth further in the wrong would have rendered you amenable to human laws. . . ." "Put away from thy soul all desire of retaliation," she implores her reader, "all angry thoughts, all disposition to overcome or humiliate an adversary, and be assured thou hast done much to abolish gallows, chains, and prisons, though thou hast never written or spoken a word on the criminal code." An apathetic society will be moved when its members resist tyrannies of mind and work for "Law of Love." Such commitment is the program of peaceable revolution Thoreau will ask for a few years later. This essay, one of the longest in *Letters*, is the most sensitively written. Deep conviction marks every line: a "*woman's heart*" and Mrs. Child's "destined mission . . . helping human souls to be truthful and free."[12]

Another essay exposes the "savagery" of capital punishment. She begins by recounting the preparations for a much-publicized hanging of a murderer: "The gallows had been erected for several hours, and with a cool refinement of cruelty, was hoisted before the window of the condemned; the hangman was all ready to cut the cord; marshals paced back and forth, smoking and whistling; spectators were waiting impatiently to see whether he would 'die game.' Printed circulars had been handed abroad to summon the number of witnesses required by law:—'You are respectfully invited to witness the execution of John C. Colt.'" However, the prisoner escapes the gallows by suicide, and the news is received by the assembled witnesses "with fierce mutterings of disappointed rage." Mrs. Child is not concerned with right or wrong, whether the convicted murderer is guilty of the crime or whether the witnesses themselves are guilty of fratricide; instead, "over all thought and feeling flowed impulsive joy that this 'Christian' community was cheated of a hanging." With heavy irony she ponders the circumstances of the case.

To me [she writes], human life seems so sacred a thing, that its violent termination always fills me with horror, whether perpetrated by an individual or a crowd; whether done contrary to law and custom, or according to law and custom. Why John C. Colt should be condemned to an ignominious death for an act of resentment altogether unpremeditated, while men, who deliberately, and with malice aforethought, go out to murder another for some insulting word, are judges and senators in the land, and favourite candidates for the President's chair, is more than I can comprehend. There is, to say the least, a strange inconsistency in our customs.[13]

What frightens Mrs. Child is that "hearts of men were filled with murder; they gloated over the thoughts of vengeance, and were rabid to witness a fellow-creature's agony." She deplores the demoralizing influence of capital punishment, castigating the society that tolerates such a practice and that rationalizes it as an "instrument of *law*." This relic of barbarism, she protests, must be done away with, in spite of society's argument that "it will not do to abolish these salutary restraints" and that "it will break up the foundations of society." With capital punishment society makes its members equally guilty of the crime: hangman, judge, jurors, legislators, citizens; "for every criminal [society] execute[s], you make a hundred murderers *outside* the prison." "Executions," she implies, "always excite a universal shudder among the innocent, the humane, and the wise-hearted. It is the voice of God, crying aloud within us against the wickedness of this savage custom." In an enlightened age, the Old Testament precept of "an eye for an eye" must be counterbalanced by the New Testament precepts of the Sermon on the Mount.

A society which promotes violence and revenge and animosity and hate makes "me ashamed of belonging to the human species," she declares. The only recourse for offended humanity is the homilies of the New Testament, which in our doubting age may sound somewhat shallow. However, given Mrs. Child's times and her temperament—her basic optimism and her ingenuous faith—the words carry conviction.

> Believe me, the great panacea for all the disorders of the universe, is Love. For thousands of years the world has gone on perversely, trying to overcome evil *with* evil; with the worst results, as the condition of things plainly testifies. Nearly two thousand years ago, the prophet of the Highest proclaimed that evil could be overcome only with *good*. . . . Write it on thine own life: and men . . . shall say, lo, something greater than vengeance is here; a power mightier than coercion. And thus the individual faith shall become a social faith.

With "social faith" men and women—members of society—correct errors and become responsive to the needs of all. A "*woman's heart*" may prompt the pen, yet a romantic vision born of her age inspires the confidence she has in people.[14]

Only one "custom" of society does Mrs. Child view with some amusement in *Letters*—moving day in New York:

> . . . All New-York *moves* on the first of May; not only moves about, as usual, in the everlasting hurry-scurry of business, but one house empties itself into another, all over the city. The streets are full of loaded drays, on which tables are dancing, and carpets rolling to and fro. Small chairs . . . go ricketing along on the tops of beds and bureaus, and not unfrequently pitch into the street, and so fall asunder. Children are driving hither and yon, one with a flower-pot in his hand, another with work-box, band-box, or oil-canakin. . . .

The pastime, she observes, is an analog of the times, the rootlessness of American society and the willingness of Americans to "change politics, and move from sect to sect, and from theory to theory" as inclination, or public opinion, dictates. Yet even this "volition," she wittily notes, does not match the alacrity of "Rev. O[restes] A. Brownson, who seems to stay in any spiritual habitation a much shorter time than the New-Yorkers do in their houses."

It is "custom" too for the New Yorkers who move to leave the accumulated dust and dirt of the year for the new occupants to clean up. "I apprehend," she remarks wryly, "it is somewhat so with all the ecclesiastical and civil establishments, which have so long been let out to tenants in rotation." Society seems, even in its milder sway, to dictate the conduct of men. Yet below the surface humor of New Yorkers' pastime, Mrs. Child sees still another pernicious effect of society on its members. It is Mammon and Commerce in Babylon— the insatiable greed for the material which society fosters—that is largely responsible: "aspirations after the infinite, lead [New Yorkers] to perpetual change, in the restless hope of finding something better and better still." Society never ceases pressuring its members, she ironically maintains, in matters as serious as disregard for the welfare of its constituents or in matters as inconsequential as moving every first of May. "Human beings are such creatures of habit and imitation . . . each one wish[ing] to do what everybody else is doing." Society, recognizing the mercurial nature of its members, takes the opportunity of promoting its own vagaries. She shrewdly concludes: "One could not well imagine a fact [i.e., moving day] more characteristic of the despotic sway of custom and public opinion, in the United States and [in] the nineteenth century."

The injuries that society aggrieves the heart of man with, the wrongs that society overlooks in the action of its members: these form a large part of the *Letters*. But there are essays which speak out against Protestant sectarianism and prejudice against Catholics and Jews, and there are character sketches of men and women whose humanity demonstrates the verities of the human heart. There are descriptions of flowers and birds, even an essay on animal magnetism (a current phenomenon Mrs. Child was much taken with, a subject of some interest to her in *Philothea* as well), and nature walks which define the delights of "God's world." And there are essays so popular with women readers in her day on old age and sorrow, love and universal education. Interspersed throughout the *Letters* are her own New England biases, perhaps an admission of her own penury during the New York sojourn, certainly her delight in the simplest pleasures and always the urgent need for work to do and tasks to perform— echoes of the Puritan ethic and the New England creed of plain living and high thinking. Her response to New Year customs in New York makes her sentiments clear.

[New Yorkers] observe this festival after the old Dutch fashion; and the Dutch, you know, were famous lovers of good eating. No lady, that *is* a lady, will be out in the streets on the first of January. Every woman, that *is* "anybody," stays at home, dressed in her best, and by her side is a table covered with cakes, preserves, wines, oysters, hot coffee, etc.; and as every gentleman is in honour bound to call on every lady, whose acquaintance he does not intend to cut, the amount of eating and drinking done by some fashionable beaux must of course be very considerable. The number of calls is a matter of pride and boasting among ladies, and there is, of course, considerable rivalry in the magnificence and variety of the eating tables. This custom is eminently Dutch in its character, and will pass away before a higher civilization. . . .

But I will not moralize. . . .

Lastly, there are two essays on specific reforms she herself worked for: better treatment of the Indians and greater freedom for women.

She discounts immediately, in the essay on the Indian, the notion of racial inferiority believed by many of her contemporaries. It is simply that the white man "through a succession of ages, has been exposed to influences eminently calculated to develop [his] moral and intellectual faculties" which the Indian has not yet had the opportunity to refine. It is therefore the white man's responsibility as the redman's "brother" to introduce him to the benefits of civilization; the white man has also, Mrs. Child adds, a similar responsibility to "the African savage." Since the white man has largely ignored this responsibility, his relationship with the Indian and the Negro from the outset has been lamentable. That the races of mankind are different there is obviously no doubt; but "it is a difference between trees of the same forest, not as between trees and animals." Although she probably knows little about the theory of evolution, she recognizes a scientific fact that races are biologically the same. She imputes so-called superiority not to genes but to civilization and to circumstances—the "effects of spiritual influences" long operating on the character of the white man and as yet largely undeveloped in the Indian and the Negro. "Similar influences brought to bear on the Indians or the Africans, as a race, would gradually . . . enlarge their perceptions of moral and intellectual truth." She does not suggest, however, that the white man's civilization be imposed on the Indian and the Negro, because "*their* Past is not *our* Past." Yet they can learn from civilization so that the white man's culture can "mingle with theirs, and you will find the result variety, without inferiority." As perceptive as Mrs. Child is, many of her contemporaries could not tolerate such a truth. She intuits no distinction among races, just a series of fortunate "influences" which give the white man for the present a superiority. Each race has its "gifts," as Deerslayer also recognized.

Her deep concern is how to bring about the "elevation" of the

Indian and the Negro, and she sees its accomplishment, once again, "in the name of Jesus—the LAW OF LOVE." The white man must not "teach as superiors; [he] must *love as brothers.*" To date, the white man's "great deficiency" is that he has not recognized what, many years later, the old woman in Frost's poem instinctively felt:

> White was the only race she ever knew.
> Black she had scarcely seen, and yellow never.
> But how could they be made so very unlike
> By the same hand working in the same stuff?

"We," observes Mrs. Child, "stand apart from them, and expect them to feel grateful for our condescension in noticing them at all. We do not embrace them warmly with our sympathies, and put our souls into their soul's stead." Even under such disadvantages and in spite of our treatment of the Indian—"our smooth, deceitful talk, when we want their lands . . . the cool villany [*sic*] with which we break treaties when our purposes are gained . . . cheated by knavish agents, cajoled by government"—he has demonstrated, if we but accept it, his own civilization.[15]

> . . . The Choctaws and Cherokees are admirable proofs. Both these tribes have a regularly-organized, systematic government, in the democratic form, and a printed constitution. The right of trial by jury, and other principles of a free government, are established on a permanent basis. They have good farms, cotton-gins, saw-mills, schools, and churches. Their dwellings are generally comfortable, and some of them are handsome. The last annual message of the chief of the Cherokees is a highly interesting document, which would not compare disadvantageously with any of our governors' messages. It states that more than $2,500,000 are due to them from the United States; and recommends that this sum be obtained, and in part distributed among the people; but that the interest of the school fund be devoted to the maintenance of schools, and the diffusion of knowledge.

The inspiration for the essay on the Indian had been a recent visit to New York by representatives of midwestern tribes, who had placed themselves "on exhibition" at a museum to satisfy the "eager curiosity of the crowd" who thronged to see them. For these men and women Mrs. Child felt great compassion, wondering if "they understood our modes of society well enough to be aware of their degraded position"; they, however, displayed "the most philosophic indifference," although she thought that "in their imperturbable countenances" once or twice she "detect[ed] a slight expression of scorn." As she stood there herself looking at them, she admitted that she "would suffer almost anything, if my soul could be transmigrated into [Do-Hum-Me, one of the Indian women] . . . that I might experience the fashion of [her] thoughts and feelings."

In that other world [she speculated], shall we be able to know exactly how heaven, and earth and hell, appear to other persons, nations, and tribes? I would it might be so; for I have an intense desire for such revelations. I do not care to travel to Rome, or St. Petersburg, because I can only look *at* people; and I want to look *into* them, and *through* them; to know how things appear to *their* spiritual eyes, and sound to *their* spiritual ears.

Later, she watched a war dance performed for the spectators. "Their gestures were as furious as wild-cats, they howled like wolves, screamed like prairie dogs, and tramped like buffaloes. Their faces were painted fiery red . . . and they were decorated with all sorts of uncouth trappings of hair, and bones, and teeth." It was for her an unforgettable experience, "terrific both to eye and ear." As a white woman she for the first time fully conceived the sacrifices and the perils of the New England settlers. And then, remembering her own convictions, as a sister human being, "I felt I was wronging them in my thought."

Mrs. Child's perception, her insight, is as remarkable today as it must have astounded the more serious reader in her own day. Not many of her race could acknowledge the charity of her thoughts, let alone admit the truth of her observations. She adds a postscript to the essay, in its matter-of-factness an appropriate comment on what the white man has done to the Indian.

Alas, poor Do-Hum-Me is dead . . . and several of the chiefs are indisposed. Sleeping by hot anthracite fires, and then exposed to the keen encounters of the wintry wind; one hour, half stifled in the close atmosphere of theatres and crowded saloons, and the next driving through snowy streets and the midnight air; this is a process which kills civilized people by inches, but savages at a few strokes.

She applies the principle of equality of the races to the relationship between men and women as well. She begins the essay on "women's rights" by confessing a strong distaste for the subject as it is usually treated because both "advocates" and "opponents" have expressed so much "false, mawkish sentiment, shallow philosophy, and sputtering, farthing-candle wit" that she wonders if any statement sensibly written will win the attention of the impartial reader. She does resent deeply the inferior role women in society are expected to play. For one thing, she resents the advice that is always directed toward women. Men, she reminds her readers, are ever willing to give the "gentle" sex "the exclusive benefit of [their] gospel-teaching."

For another, she resents men who are so often condescending toward women, as if they require special protection or special consideration. She quotes from Hazlitt a sentiment too many men espouse, one she has too often been keenly aware of: "[I]t is not easy to keep up a conversation with women in company. It is thought a piece of rudeness to differ from them; it is not quite fair to ask them a *reason* for what they say." This sort of social "politeness"—what men "call gallantry"—is odious to all sensible women; it no way indicates "sincere esteem because it suggests that women are incapable of intellectual discussion."

What is even more irritating is the fact that women accept this subordination as "good behaviour." It is at this point she announces her thesis: "I consider prevalent opinions and customs highly unfavourable to the moral and intellectual development of women; and I need not say, that, in proportion to their true culture, women will be more useful and happy, and domestic life more perfected. True culture, in them, as in men, consists in the full and free development of individual character, regulated by their *own* perceptions of what is true, and their *own* love of what is good."

She recalls a lecture she heard Emerson give on Being and Seeming. In the course of his remarks, Emerson urged women to *be*, rather than to *seem*. He told them that women's concern for the social conventions—the "genteel etiquette" and the acceptable proprieties—were not as important as *being* "truly what God made them; that earnest simplicity [and] sincerity of nature, would kindle the eye, light up the countenance, and give an inexpressible charm to the plainest features." Men, on the other hand, were exhorted to *be* rather than to *seem* that they might "in God's freedom, grow up into the full stature of spiritual manhood; but women were urged to simplicity and truthfulness, that they might become more *pleasing*." Although the advice was excellent, Mrs. Child remarks, the motive brought "a flush of indignation over my face."

Are we not all immortal beings? Is not each one responsible for himself and herself? There is no measuring the mischief done by the prevailing tendency to teach women to be virtuous as a duty to *man* rather than to *God*—for the sake of pleasing the creature, rather than the Creator. "*God* is thy law, *thou* mine," said Eve to Adam. May Milton be forgiven for sending that thought "out into everlasting time" in such a jewelled setting. What weakness, vanity, frivolity, infirmity of moral purpose, sinful flexibility of principle—in a word, what soul-stifling, has been the result of thus putting man in the place of God!

She does quote approvingly the idea, if not the context, she read in a book by Alexander Kinmont, *Twelve Lectures on the Natural History of Man* (1839). Kinmont, in defending the warlike courage of women in ancient times, argued that although women were not made for war, neither were men. "But since the fashion of the times had made it so, and settled it that war was a necessary element of greatness, and that no safety was to be procured without it, I argue that it shows a healthful state of feeling in other respects, that the feelings of both sexes were *equally* enlisted in the cause; that there was no *division* in the house, or the state; and that the serious pursuits and objects of the one were the serious pursuits and objects of the other."

For the reader today Mrs. Child may blunt a highly persuasive statement with her conclusion, because she finds perfect equality between the sexes demonstrated within the confines of the home.

Women will . . . [share] the care and education of their children, [and] men will find themselves ennobled and refined by sharing those duties with them; and will receive, in return, co-operation and sympathy in the discharge of various other duties, now deemed inappropriate to women. The more women become rational companions, partners in business and in thought, as well as in affection and amusement, the more highly will men appreciate *home*—that blessed word. . . .

A far more effective example of her gentle but firm militancy, her sincere conviction that men and women together do the world's work, is an anecdote associated with her abolitionist activities in Boston. After a particularly emotional meeting at the Tremont Temple in January 1861, one where Wendell Phillips was addressing a hostile audience on the urgent need to end slavery, it seemed, as Phillips was concluding his appeal, that he would be mobbed by the angry throng. Mrs. Child and her abolitionist friend Maria Chapman went to the podium, linked arms with Phillips, and escorted him from the hall amid the hisses and snarls of the assembled audience. Thereafter, they accompanied him home, Mrs. Child at one point striking out at an angry heckler who stepped in their path. Higginson recalled Mrs. Child's account of the incident.

Mrs. Child describes her collaring and pulling away a man who was shaking his fist in Mr. Phillips's face . . . and her surprise when he tumbled down. When [another dinner guest] Jonas H. Frank said, "This is no place for women," she answered, "They are needed here to teach civilization to men."[16]

The anecdote bears out the final comment in the essay, pale by comparison, that ". . . men will perceive more and more that there is no separation or discord in their [i.e., men and women's] mutual duties. They will be one; but it will be as affection and thought are one; the treble and the bass of the same harmonious tune."

II ". . . My Own Views and Impressions"

Letters from New York, Second Series, is a potpourri, articles "miscellaneous and incongruous in their character." A number of them had been published in newspapers and in various periodicals. The claim Mrs. Child makes for them is modest—"an honest record of my own views and impressions." Writing "nothing from affectation, sectarian prejudice, or partisan zeal," she hopes to give the reader "an image of my soul." Perhaps, she concludes, the reader will forgive deficiencies "for the sake of my kind intentions, and sincere love of truth." The reviewers by and large ignored the book, the *Knickerbocker* reviewer saying at the end of a brief notice that "the great popularity . . . of [*Letters from New York*] renders it unnecessary for us to comment on the present series. . . . The work will make its own way to the public heart."[17] Poe was much more generous, suggesting that the appeal of the second series was attributable "to the fact that they treat of human beings and things that interest humanity. . . . Mrs. Child instructively seizes upon subjects which are interesting to all classes, to men and women rather than to statesmen, or ladies and gentlemen . . . delightful heart-touching subjects."[18] The essays are indeed so miscellaneous that it is difficult to associate them to a theme, such as the errors of society which commanded so large a part of the reader's attention in the first series. She explores no new areas in her "fragments" but contents herself with "subjects which interest me most." Thus Christmas invokes religious sentiments and concern for the poor and the oppressed; "New Year's Festivities" in "this city of turmoil and traffic" where pursuit of the material predominates becomes a plea for renewed dedication to pressing reforms: "how crime can be prevented, poverty abolished, and the meanest of abominations, Slavery, swept from the face of a loathing earth." Valentine's Day, after a paragraph or two devoted to the "rose-coloured dreams of unsuspecting youth," offers her the opportunity to write about the special benevolence of Isaac Hopper, the Quaker "missionary of humanity." A concert by Ole Bull leads to an essay of "excessive enthusiasm" on the skill of the famed violinist and provides her with a chance to cite her special love of music. A lengthy description of Mammoth Cave in Kentucky is one reconstructed from a "vivid account . . . from a young friend who spent several days there." "I will try," she writes, "to transfer to your mind, as well as I can, the picture he gave me." She does detail minutely the special beauty of the subterranean world: its cataracts and vaulted chambers, its chasms and labyrinths, its brilliant rock formations. Perhaps she is most impressed, however, by her friend's recollection of Stephen, "the presiding genius of Mammoth Cave," a slave whose knowledge of the "strange region" is so "ample and accurate" as to make him "an extremely useful and agreeable guide." "May his last breath be a free one," she asks.

There are speculative essays on preexistence (she quotes Words-worth's lines from "Intimations of Immortality") and on a new system of mnemonics urged by a popular lecturer (she is unimpressed with a mind that remembers only statistics and charts, "convenient in the details of business"). She finds stimulation in the lectures on anatomy she recently attended and suggests for her day a very advanced point of view: "I know nothing so well calculated to diminish vice and vulgarity, as universal and rational information. But the impure state of society has so perverted nature, and blinded common sense, that intelligent women, though eagerly studying the structure of the earth, the attraction of the planets, and the reproduction of plants, seem ashamed to know anything of the structure of the human body, and of those physiological facts most intimately connected with their own health, and that of their children." She theorizes on the doctrine of correspondences between the natural and the spiritual worlds where she discovers in such things as music, numbers, optics, colors, water, and garments analogs with spiritual qualities in man. She quotes Plato, alludes to Swedenborg, and concludes: "That there must be immense complication in science, you will perceive if you reflect that the good and the true mirror themselves in all the varieties of creation, and all have a reversed image in the evil and the false."

She explains in another essay what she believes to be Swedenborg's "teachings concerning future life," an essay prompted by a friend who had lost her child, but motivated as well by Mrs. Child's strong attraction to the thinking of the Swedish mystic. "The information," she writes, ". . . will not soothe the grief of mere natural affection, or

satisfy any selfish craving of the heart. But if all thoughts of self are
merged in the wish for your child's spiritual welfare, a belief in
Swedenborg's testimony would make you happy. He does not say
that we shall be united in the other world, on account either of natural
relationship, or natural affection, however strong these may have
been on earth. *Spiritual* consanguinity, or similar states of the *Soul*,
alone can produce companionship there. Strangers, who never saw
each other in body, may be very near together as spirits; while natural
brothers and sisters, or legal husbands and wives, may be very far
apart." Swedenborg, she continues, discovers the joys of heaven to
rest in love of others. By progressive degrees love of others becomes
so perfect "that the highest angels love their neighbours *better* than
themselves, and each is active in ministering delight to all." Swedenborg's doctrine of correspondences, Mrs. Child believes, is not found
on mere "fancied resemblances." He lays it down as an exact science,
declaring that everything in the universe is the form of some variation
of thought or affection: ". . . Ideas and feelings are the souls, of which
animals, vegetables, and minerals, are the bodies. These feelings and
ideas are in their elements few and simple; but as musical sounds
produce infinitely varying harmonies by their ever-changing relations
and combinations, so from these sentiments and ideas are evolved all
the manifold forms of beauty and order in creation."

Mrs. Child apparently read Swedenborg's thought as she read
Plato's in *Philothea*, extracting from it that which was most agreeable
or meaningful to her. "Thus the large sentiment of human brotherhood takes manifested form in various truths," she avers. "In one
form, it seeks to break the fetters of the slave; in another, to throw
down the walls of sect; in another, to abolish national antipathies.
The holy sentiment of forgiveness of enemies takes to itself form in
doctrines opposed to capital punishment, and in favour of increased
kindness toward prisoners. The pure sentiment of real marriage
manifests itself in theories, which acknowledge women as the equal,
the friend, the partner of man in all his pursuits. Each of these is a
melody from the central heart of love; and because the various
modifications of utterances are coming more and more into accord
with each other, therefore the science of harmony approves." The
essay provided textbook analysis for reading passages in *Philothea*.

Endeavoring to give her friend "as clearly and concisely as possible,
an outline of what I understand to be Swedenborg's statements," she
admits that many of her contemporaries regard him "insane"
and his theological writings "the mere absurd ravings and grotesque
visions of a crazy man." And she quotes Swedenborg himself on the

truth of his teachings: "The things which are in the heavens cannot be seen by the eyes of man's body, but only by the eyes of his spirit. When it pleases the Lord, these interior eyes are opened, while man is withdrawn from the natural light, in which he is from the senses of the body, and is elevated into spiritual light, in which he is from his spirit. In that light, the things which are in the heavens have been seen by me. It has been given me thus to pass through the dwellings of the angels, in full wakefulness, when my interior sight was opened." He always declared, Mrs. Child goes on to say, that his doctrines were not a product of his own intellect, but were imparted to him by express revelation, in a state of divine illumination. "So strong and sincere is this belief, that he habitually proves one part of his writings by another; repeatedly saying, with the most child-like *naiveté*, 'That this is true, is proved by what I have written in another volume.'"

His ideas generally were regarded as "improbable or ridiculous fictions," Mrs. Child tells her friend, until "these very peculiar writings spread into various languages, found a place in the libraries of scholars, mixed with theological studies in colleges, modified the preaching of various sects, and became more or less infused into literature. He who had been contemptuously styled the crazy prophet, at last came to be most respectfully mentioned in public lectures, as a man remarkable for scientific learning and depth of spiritual insight. He was ranked with Kant and Goethe, as one of the three minds that would permanently affect the coming ages." His followers, she adds, thought that it was wrong to criticize or explain or reject any portion of his teachings "because they believe them to be an especial revelation to him, for the establishment of a new church on earth, so perfect that no further dispensation will ever be needed." And there is "a class of thinkers," not his disciples, who believed that his child-like, reverential spirit, his learning, and "the singular power of abstracting his soul from the senses" fitted him to be the medium of profound spiritual truths. Whether Swedenborg had "clairvoyant perception" or remarkable insight—"whatever may be the solution of the mystery"—the thinker is for Mrs. Child at least a writer whose ideas she can transfer immediately to the work of this world. He is for her "unquestionably the most remarkable phenomenon of the age."[19]

Other essays are character sketches of remarkable women she has known—Hannah Adams, literary recluse, historian of religious sects, Mrs. Child's compeer as a card-holding member of the Boston Athenaeum, whose spiritual visitation by a deceased sister intrigued Mrs. Child; and Charity Brown, a free black woman who tried unsuccessfully to buy freedom for her children. "In the course of my conversation with this interesting woman," she writes, "she told me much about the patrols, who, armed with arbitrary power, and frequently intoxicated, [would] break into houses of the coloured people at the south, and subject them to all manner of outrages."

Among her contemporary readers were the Millerites, who in the fall of 1844 were predicting that God in his wrath was about to burn the world. Followers were preaching with "enthusiasm and earnestness of conviction" Rev. William Miller's belief, and apparently a number of proselytes were being welcomed to the ranks "as brands plucked from immediate burning." Although "thousands of minds are in a state of intense alarm," reports Mrs. Child, "I have heard of very few instances of stolen money restored, or falsehoods acknowledged, as a preparation for the dreaded event." And she records with some amusement that a merchant in selling her some cloth took two cents a yard less for the material, telling her, "If we are all to come to an end so soon, it is best to be pretty moderate and fair in our dealings." Several Millerites had written her letters, entreating her "to make haste to escape from the wrath that is impending over all unbelievers," one of them seeing her "in a vision, radiating light, and consider[ing] this a special indication that I was to be summoned to ascend with the saints. I feel sincerely grateful to these kind, well-meaning persons, for their anxiety to save me. But if there has been no preparation in my previous life, the effort to make ready in a few days could avail but little." The furor caused by the Millerites, whom she does not ridicule for their beliefs ("All sincere convictions should be treated respectfully."), nevertheless motivates her to express briefly her own particular creed, strongly influenced by Swedenborg's philosophy.

My belief in spirit is so strong, that to me matter appears the illusion. My body never seems to me to be myself. Death never seems to me an end of life, but a beginning. I suppose it is owing to this vivid and realizing sense of spiritual existence, that the destruction of the visible world would have so little power to affect me, even if I foresaw its approach. It would be but a new mode of passing into life. For the earth I have the same sort of affection that I have for a house in which I have dwelt; but it matters not to me whether I pass away from it, or we pass away together. If I live a true and humble life, I shall carry with me all its forms of love and beauty, safe from the touch of material fire.

The stern warning of the Millerites reminds her of "the old Puritan days of spontaneous zeal" and of "good old President Edwards."

Implied in her thinking is a similarity between Edwards's manifested piety and that of the Millerites, both of whom were alarmed at the state of the world and at the liberties men were assuming. "Alas for President Edwards . . . if [he] should reappear in the midst of times like these," God's vice-gerent who "conceived his station worthy of so much respect that his own children were in the habit of rising, in token of reverence, whenever he entered the family sitting-room."

But given her choice, Mrs. Child certainly prefers "times like these," in which God's work is being done by men and women devoted to ameliorating the ills of the world. "The very uproar of evil, at the present time, is full of promise," she writes in an earlier letter; "for all evil must be made *manifest*, that it may be cured. . . . [T]he *manifestation* is ever healthy, the precursor of restored harmony. Welcome then to such books as Oliver Twist and [*Les Miserables*]; welcome to all the painful unfolding of Anti-Slavery, Temperance, and Prison Associations; to all that, in a spirit friendly to man, lays open the crimes, the vices, and the harshness of society."

Rather than look at the world as the Millerites did and fear God's wrath because of man's sinfulness, she sees the challenge given to men as the "joyful omen" that precedes change for the better. The world "*has* made progress[.] Consider well the great fact of British emancipation in the West Indies. Show me another instance in the world's history, where the heart of a whole nation was kindled, as it were by a divine flame, to right the wrongs of a distant and helpless people." And she is confident that emancipation will come to the United States as well. She sees progress too in the improved condition of women, particularly in the area of education. "A woman as well educated as half the mechanics' daughters in our country [today], would have been pointed at as a prodigy, a century ago. It is astonishing what a moderate knowledge of science or literature, then passed for prodigious learning. A woman who had written a book was wondered at, and feared; and judicious mothers cautioned their daughters not to follow such an eccentric example, lest they should lose all chance of getting husbands. Now, books from the pens of women, and some of them excellent books too, are poured forth by hundreds, and no one considers the fact a remarkable one."

She sees progress too in the enlightened public opinion regarding capital punishment which had encouraged legislators to abolish the practice, and in prison reform where society was beginning to recognize that its role was not primarily "to punish, or restrain . . . [but] prevent" crime. She points to the work of Dorothea Dix, "the God-appointed missionary to prisons and alms-houses," and her successful work with inmates of insane asylums; to the work of the Quakers, among them Isaac Hopper, with prisoner rehabilitation; and to the public acceptance of the reformed criminals. She recalls the work of Charles Fourier who "patiently investigate[d], for thirty years, the causes of social evils and their remedy." Not in vain are "communities starting up all around us, varied in plan, but all born of one idea." She sees evidence of "Christian principles" more visibly at work in the world than at any other time in the history of man, and she is incautiously confident. "Away with your scepticism! . . . God does not thus mock with false hopes the beings He has made in his own image. He has taught us to pray that his kingdom may come on earth, as it is in heaven; and He will answer the prayer in glorious fulfilment [sic]." Although such exuberant faith—one might say, pollyannaism—may sound hollow to the reader today, he is left to reflect on Mrs. Child's modest claim to the sincerity of her convictions; in response to a correspondent's request for her opinion, she wrote that ". . . since you are pleased to say that you value my impressions, because they are always my own, and not another person's; because they are spontaneous, disinterested, and genuine; I will give [them] to you . . . as they breathed through my soul."

This romantic conviction is due in large part to "times like these," to the spirit of change Emerson too proclaimed with such confidence in "The American Scholar": "If there is any period one would desire to be born in, is it not the age of Revolution . . . when the energies of all men are searched by fear and by hope; when the historic glories of the old can be compensated by the rich possibilities of the new era?"

A final essay in *Letters* deserves consideration. Mrs. Child's explanation of transcendentalism to an inquiring correspondent underscores her particular awareness. "The German school of metaphysics, with the celebrated Kant at its head," writes Mrs. Child, rejecting the philosophy of John Locke ("All knowledge is received into the soul through the medium of the senses.") ". . . maintains that the highest, and therefore most universal truths, are revealed within the soul to a faculty *transcending* the understanding. This faculty they call pure Reason; it being peculiar to them to use that word in contradistinction to the Understanding. To this pure Reason, which some of their writers call 'The God within,' they believe that all perceptions of the Good, the True, and the Beautiful, are revealed, in its unconscious quietude." Though this "doctrine of inspiration" is important to Mrs. Child as the source of confidence in herself and in the rightness of her work in the world, she does not endorse the more passive doctrines of transcendentalism. She is not content with "theories . . . so expansive and indefinite," with reverie and contemplation. She cannot, for instance, accept Emerson's statement in the ode to William Henry Channing: "I cannot leave/My honied thought/For the priest's cant/Or the statesmen's rant./If I refuse/ My study for their politique . . . /The angry Muse/Puts confusion in my brain." Rather than "lie still in the spiritual sunshine," she pursues the active life which Emerson at least advocated in "The American Scholar" when he wrote: "Life is our dictionary." The "hurry-scurry" of living—involvement in the world's work—gives Mrs. Child's philosophical conviction its practical application. The "activity of reform" gives her life meaning and purpose. Although she says that she is "sometimes called a transcendentalist," she abjures the reluctance "to analyze, compare, and prove." How else is the world's work to be done? The esoteric she rejects as well, recounting with some amusement a particular incident:

I did once, out of pure mischief, send a politician and an active man of business to a house, where I knew they would encounter three or four of these disciples [of transcendentalism], who occasionally ride a pretty high horse. When they came back, I asked with a sober face, what they had talked about. They said they did not know. . . .

I then asked the man of business how he had been edified. "My head aches," said he; "they have put my mind and body both in a confounded muss."

". . . I acknowledge considerable sympathy with the perplexed politician and man of business," Mrs. Child confides. "For there are people, very intellectual ones too, who mystify me in the strangest fashion. After talking with them, my spirt always has to bite its finger, to know whether it exists or not."[20]

III *Service to Others*

In conclusion, it is the final paragraphs of *Letters* which best summarize Mrs. Child's conviction about herself and her role in society.

The laws of our being are such that we must perform some degree of use in the world, whether we intend it, or not; but we can deprive ourselves of its indwelling joy, by acting entirely from the love of self. The manufacturer benefits others somewhat by the cloth he makes, and the baker by his bread. But if they seek to enrich themselves only, by the use of poor materials, and the payment of prices that oppress their workmen, they take out of the use that divine life, which imparts to the soul perpetual youth and bloom. Money thus acquired never satisfies the possessor; for in the process of making it, he parts with the state of mind, which is alone capable of enjoying happiness. The stories of men selling their souls to the devil, for treasures which merely tantalize them, are not mere fables. Thousands of poor rich men feel the truth in their daily experience.

To obtain unfailing spiritual wealth by cheerfully imparting of what we have, does not require this world's riches, or genius like Beethoven's. The poorest and least endowed can secure the treasure, by a loving readiness to serve others, according to their gifts. The lady who plants bulbs, and gathers garden-seeds, and tries curious horticultural experiments, has gained much by the mere innocent occupation of her time and thoughts. But if she is unwilling to give away rare seeds and plants, if she cultivates them only for the sake of having something handsomer than her neighbours can have, she takes the heart out of her beautiful employment, and renders it a spectral pleasure. But if she gives a portion of vegetables to a poor widow, who has no land, if she invites the aged, and destitute invalids, into her pleasant walks, if she gives boquets [sic] to poor children, and strives to make all the neighbouring gardens as beautiful as her own, why then she really possesses her garden, and makes it an avenue of paradise. . . .

Some may think these theories sound well, and might work admirably if this world were heaven; yet they too utter the prayer, "May thy kingdom come on *earth*, as it is in heaven." This wide distance between our practical life and the religion we profess, teaches, too plainly to be misunderstood, that men really do *not* believe that it would be wise or safe to practise [sic] the maxims of Christ in a world like this. I remember a wealthy family, who scrupulously observed all the outward forms of Christianity, and inculcated the utmost reverence for its precepts. The children were trained to attend church regularly, and read the bible every morning. But when one of the sons took it into his head that the teachings of the New Testament were to be applied to daily life, and public affairs, they were in the utmost consternation at the ungentility of his views, and the oddity of his proceedings.

But I am preaching a sermon instead of writing a letter. If one ever falls into a moralizing vein, they are likely to do it on the last day of the year. I bid you an affectionate farewell, with this New Year's wish for you and myself:

> "So may we live, that every hour
> May die, as dies the natural flower,
> A self-reviving thing of power;
> That every thought, and every deed,
> May hold within itself the seed
> Of future good and future meed."

Mrs. Child's remark about "preaching a sermon" is no doubt pertinent, and *Letters* may impress the reader today in the same way that the writings of the transcendentalists often affected her:

"oracular and mystical . . . because they rather *announce*, than argue, what seems to them truth." It is, however, always earnestness that governs her pen and her thought, and it is always conviction that prompts her commentary. The reader is impressed by her prodigious industry, the curious mind, the mental vigor, the practical sense, the gentle humor. So often homely metaphor, drawn frequently from the real world around her, punctuates the prose, giving it freshness and originality. She writes in one of the essays, in connection with her fellow Americans' celebrating the Fourth of July, that ". . . with all the hurly-burly . . . there is doubtless mixed a genuine reverence for man, and noble aspirations for a world-wide freedom. If the bells and the rockets, the guns and the orations, add one particle to the love of liberty, or a sincere appreciation of its blessings, they are not expended in vain." The reader today also grants that Mrs. Child's *Letters from New York* are not "in vain."

CHAPTER 6

Literary Ephemera

M RS. CHILD was a prolific writer, but aside from the novels and *Letters from New York*, much of the material was ephemeral. She compiled books of stories and verse for children and young people; she published domestic manuals primarily for women readers; she argued the slavery issue in a significant number of articles, pamphlets, and book-length treatises; she wrote on religion and history; and like many women writers of her day, she prepared gift books for the seasonal trade—collections of her work and that of her contemporaries. The material, quasi-literary or topical, was usually didactic in tone; and, like the second series of *Letters*, many of the essays—informal and chatty—and much of the verse had appeared previously in magazines and periodicals. In composing any one volume she frequently culled for reprinting the best of what she had already written and supplemented the book with newly drafted material. The books and pamphlets were written in response to special demands or particular interests; prominent in her mind as she assembled the material was the personal dictum: service to others. A sampling of the volumes, indicating their content and suggesting their subject matter, provides the reader with some awareness of Mrs. Child's varied interests.

I *Books for Young People*

After publishing *Hobomok* and *The Rebels*, she turned to *The Juvenile Miscellany* (1826–1834), the first periodical for children to appear in the United States. Childless herself, she had a mother's love, a woman's compassion, and a teacher's concern for the education of children and young people. She wrote much of the material for the *Miscellany* herself, some ninety pages for each issue, which appeared every other month. She included her own teaching aids, supplementing them with imaginary dialogs, bits of history, and pieces of legend that had impressed her as a girl; digests of articles she had read; short biographies; original stories; quizzes and acrostics. The magazine was hugely successful; she wrote her sister Mary Preston: "The Miscellany has been very kindly received. It seems as if the public was resolved to give me a flourish of trumpets, let me write what I will."[1]

Many years later she put together materials for three more volumes for children, ages eight to twelve. The preface to the first volume announced her plan: "Several years ago I published a little periodical called The Juvenile Miscellany. It found favor in the eyes of parents and children; and . . . I have had frequent requests to republish it. I did not think it advisable to do this. But I have concluded to publish a series of small books, under the title Flowers for Children [1844–1846]. About half of each of these volumes will consist of new articles expressly written for the occasion; and the other half will be a selection of what seem to me the best of my articles, formerly published in the Juvenile Miscellany." In the second volume there appeared a poem, "A Boy's Thanksgiving Song," a nostalgic backward glance at her own childhood, written in a singsong fashion; children in subsequent years remembered it for the first two lines:

> Over the river and through the wood
> To grandmother's house we go.[2]

Another collection, *The Girl's Own Book* (1831), was addressed to teenagers. In the preface she informed mothers that the book "contain[ed] nothing to corrupt or mislead" and admonished daughters that they "should know how to be *useful*; amid the universal dissemination of knowledge, *every mind should seek to improve itself to the utmost*; and in this land of equality, as much time should be devoted to *elegant accomplishments, refined tastes,* and *gracefulness of manner,* as can possibly be spared from the holier and more important duties. In this country it is peculiarly necessary that daughters should be so educated as to enable them to fulfil [*sic*] the duties of a humble station, or to dignify and adorn the highest." Still, she included in the book the kind of material which her younger readers had so enjoyed—rules for games,[3] arithmetical puzzles and conundrums, charades and exercises; but she incorporated material of particular interest to older girls—directions for sewing and knitting, embroidery and needlework, cooking and baking; and instructions for simple art projects like laying mezzotinto prints on glass and preserving roses.[4] And there were lessons in conduct and propriety, in gracefulness and elegance.[5]

II   *Domestic Manuals*

Her interest in writing books of "improvement" was a very practical one; when *The Rebels* was so unfavorably reviewed, she turned to writing the kind of instructive essays which had sold well. Additionally, she needed the money these domestic manuals brought in. Two of the most popular of these manuals were *The Frugal Housewife* (1830) and *The Mother's Book* (1831). *The Frugal Housewife* was a manual well calculated to appeal to women "who are not ashamed of economy," like Mrs. Child herself. In severe, matter-of-fact style she provided "odd scraps for the economical"; no book, one scholar wrote later, "was more representative of the practical and prosaic aspects of New England character."[6] "It is wise," she told the housewives, "to keep an exact account of all you expend—even of a paper of pins."

This answers two purposes: it makes you more careful in spending money, and it enables your husband to judge precisely whether his family live within his income. No false pride, or foolish ambition . . . should ever induce a person to live one cent beyond the income of which he is certain. If you have two dollars a day, let nothing but sickness induce you to spend more than nine shillings; if you have one dollar a day, do not spend but seventy-five cents; if you have half a dollar a day, be satisfied to spend forty cents. . . .

She supplied household hints that even a sober, frugal Poor Richard had not thought of.

Look frequently to the pails, to see nothing is thrown to the pigs which should have been in the grease-pot.

Look to the grease-pot, and see nothing is there which might have served to nourish your own family, or a poorer one. . . .

Spirits of turpentine is good to take grease-spots out of woollen clothes; to take spots of paint, etc., from mahogany furniture; and to cleanse white kid gloves. Cockroaches, and all vermin have an aversion to spirits of turpentine. . . .

After old coats, pantaloons, etc. have been cut up for boys, and are no longer capable of being converted into garments, cut them in strips, and employ the leisure moments of children, or domestics, in sewing and braiding them for door-mats.

The first young leaves of the common currant-bush, gathered as soon as they put out, and dried on tin, can hardly be distinguished from green tea.

Save vials and bottles. Apothecaries and grocers will give something for them. If the bottles are of good thick glass, they will always be useful for bottling cider or beer; but if they are thin French glass, like claret bottles, they will not answer.

It is poor economy to buy vinegar by the gallon. Buy a barrel, or half a barrel, of really strong vinegar, when you begin house-keeping. As you use it, fill the barrel with old cider, sour beer, or wine-settlings, etc., left in pitchers, decanters or tumblers; weak tea is likewise said to be good: nothing is hurtful, which has a tolerable portion of spirit, or acidity.

. . . Paper brings a cent a pound, and if you have plenty of room, it is well to save it. "A penny saved is a penny got."

Keep a coarse broom for the cellar stairs, wood-shed, yard, etc. No good housekeeper allows her carpet broom to be used for such things.

Run the heels of stockings faithfully; and mend thin places, as well as holes. "A stitch in time saves nine."

A little salt sprinkled in starch while it is boiling, tends to prevent it from sticking; it is likewise good to stir it with a clean spermaceti [*sic*] candle.

A bit of isinglass dissolved in gin, or boiled in spirits of wine, is said to make strong cement for broken glass, china, and sea-shells.

Page after page of household hints informed the housewife how to extend the family budget, along with comforting reassurances and stern reproofs: "We shall never be free from embarrassment until we cease to be ashamed of industry and economy. . . . Let [housewives] prove, by the exertion of ingenuity and economy, that neatness, good taste, and gentility, are attainable without great expense. . . . In early childhood, you lay the foundation of poverty or riches, in the habits you give your children. Teach them to save everything,—not for their *own* use; for that would make them selfish—but for *some* use. Teach them to *share* everything with their playmates; but never allow them to *destroy* anything." She remembered her own childhood experience in the home in Medford, when each year the Francis family had shared Thanksgiving Eve with the poorer villagers. There was no reason, even with limited income, Mrs. Child advised, not to share with less fortunate neighbors, not to be generous and unselfish. "True economy," she advocated, "is a careful treasurer in the service of benevolence; and where they are united, respectability, prosperity and peace will follow."

The rigid nature of *The Frugal Housewife* said something about Mrs. Child's own straitened circumstances, but she made no apology in "offer[ing] . . . this cheap little book of economical hints, except her deep conviction that such a book [was] needed." "The information conveyed is of a common kind," she continued; "but is such as the majority of young housekeepers do not possess, and such as they cannot obtain from cookery books. Books of this kind have usually been written for the wealthy: I have written for the poor. . . . I have attempted to teach how money can be *saved*, not how it can be *enjoyed*." The book was, in the words of another frugal housewife, and woman editor, Sarah J. Hale, "the most approved work for these 'hard times.'"[7] Not only was the book a guide through "hard times," but it was an "harangue," not unlike *The Way to Wealth*, addressed to the industrious and the thrifty among the readers. "If any person thinks some of the maxims too rigidly economical, let them inquire how the largest fortunes among us have been made. They will find thousands and millions have been accumulated by a scrupulous attention to sums 'infinitely more minute than sixty cents.'"

Not only household hints but cheap and wholesome recipes were included, as well as directions for preparing vegetables and herbs and buying inexpensive cuts of meat and poultry. "General maxims for health" appeared, too.[8] Nothing was omitted that would teach housewives "how money can be *saved*." Although there were a number of cookbooks and household manuals available to readers at the time, *The Frugal Housewife* more than any other book caught the public mind.[9]

Not only the Childs' precarious finances but New England practicality and the Puritan ethic dictated the tone of the pages, as "hints to persons of moderate fortune" amply conveyed. "The prevailing evil of the present day is extravagance. . . ," she noted; "it is too plain that our present expensive habits are productive of much domestic unhappiness, and injurious to public prosperity." As she looked about her, she saw people in New England succumbing to vice and extravagance, departing "from the simplicity and industry of our forefathers." "A republic without industry, economy, and integrity," she warned, "is Samson shorn of his locks."

To her readers in more moderate circumstances, she also gave advice about the education of their daughters, "to contribute to their own ultimate happiness, [and] to the welfare of the country." She counseled mothers to be concerned about the "*domestic* education" of their daughters: "I do not mean the sending daughters into the kitchen some half dozen times, to weary the patience of the cook, and to boast of it the next day in the parlor." Remembering her own training in the kitchen in Medford under the watchful supervision of her mother and sisters, she continued: "I mean two or three years spent with a mother, assisting her in her duties, instructing brothers and sisters, and taking care of their own clothes. This is the way to make them happy, as well as good wives; for, being early accustomed to the duties of life, they will sit lightly as well as gracefully upon them." With attention to a practical education ("young ladies should be taught that usefulness is happiness, and that all other things are but incidental"), daughters were prepared for marriage and family responsibilities. The greatest cause of "domestic disquiet" was, Mrs. Child believed, the *"mismanagement of education."* For how could young men and women brought up to consider frugality contemptible and industry degrading become "prudent and useful, when the cares of life press heavily upon them." Too often mothers excused their daughters' indifference to household chores with the statement, *"Let her enjoy herself all she can, while she is [young and] single."* It was "a false and dangerous theory," she flatly declared and mentioned a young woman, married to a promising young lawyer, who had been brought up to be "perfectly useless; a rag baby would, to all intents and purposes, have been as efficient a [marriage] partner." Having no practical skills to run the household, she soon involved her husband heavily in debt. ". . . When I lived at home," she complained, "mother always took care of everything." When poverty came, they moved to a remote village in the West where he taught school, then came home and cooked and cared for the children. "His patience," Mrs. Child dryly remarked, "and her real love for him" ultimately impelled the wife to change. "She promised to learn to be useful, if he would teach her. And she did learn! And the change in her habits gradually wrought such a change in her husband's fortune, that she might bring her daughters up in idleness, had not experience taught her that economy, like grammar, is a very hard and tiresome study, after we are twenty years old."

The last half of *The Frugal Housewife* was no less decidedly "utilitarian" than the first, as a reviewer in the *North American* several years later observed, but she shifted her emphasis from the purely domestic routine to the general "deficiency in the [nation's] system of housekeeping."[10] Education for the country's pursuit of industry, frugality, and integrity was a logical extension of home and fireside rules. Franklin's special virtues—his chart for national well-being—was Mrs. Child's remedy as well. The reviewer was perceptive when he called *The Frugal Housewife* "a more revolutionary book than any other that Mrs. Child has written,—more so even than the Rebels; for the revolution with which this busies itself, extends . . . over [all] our houses. It operates like a health committee, or a committee of vigilance."[11] "Some will think," Mrs. Child wrote in conclusion, "the evils of whch I have been speaking are confined principally to the rich; but I am convinced they extend to all classes of people." Ironically, her "plainness in telling the truth" about the nation's health went largely unnoticed by the housewives who discovered among the other useful hints that beer was "a good family drink, and its constant use a preservative against fevers." The soberer message was greeted in much the same way as Father Abraham's harangue, as Poor Richard reported it: "The People heard it, and approved the Doctrine and immediately practiced the contrary, just as if it had been a common Sermon. . . ."

However, if Mrs. Child needed reassurance as to the success of her hints on economy for the home, the *North American* reviewer once again provided it, remarking on the book's "tone of healthy morality . . . and good sense" and finding in Mrs. Child herself "just the woman we want for the mothers and daughters of the present generation." He ended the review by hoping that she would "continue her useful labors" but recommended that she not forsake fiction altogether: "high and beautiful lessons may be inculcated by a good story, and as good a rule in morals *deduced, as laid down.*"[12]

But remembering the reviewers' criticism of *The Rebels*, she preferred to repeat her success with another manual, *The Mother's Book* (1831), dedicated to American mothers, "on whose intelligence and discretion the safety and prosperity of our Republic so much depend." The itch to instruct the nation in respect to its moral health, however, was subordinated to the more immediate task of advising mothers on matters of rearing their daughters. Confessing that the book owed a great deal to frequent conversations she had had with "an intelligent and judicious mother," she was offering her readers as well "the result of my own reading and observation in maxims of plain practical good-sense, written with earnestness and simplicity of style."

The "simplicity of style" was not as severe as that in *The Frugal Housewife*; homely, yet genial, with metaphor frequently drawn from the domestic routine, *The Mother's Book* was a homily devoted to the education of young women from babyhood to marriageable age. Some of the advice was already a matter of record, the hints on domestic education having been dealt with in the earlier manual. She cautioned once again about the seriousness of marriage, reminding her readers and perhaps members of her own family as well (who had been critical of her marriage) that "the great difficulty at the present day is, that matrimony is made a subject of pride, vanity, or expediency; whereas it ought to be a matter of free choice and honest preference." Neither mothers nor daughters should precipitantly plan for the daughters' marriage, and she asked them to consider three questions to determine a "suitable and desirable union: 1st, Has the person good principles? 2d, Has he, or she, a good disposition? 3d, Is there a strong, decided, deeply-founded preference? . . . [W]here there is deep, well-founded love, and an humble reliance on Divine

Providence, all things will work right in the end." This last piece of advice was no doubt not the "judicious mother['s]" but Mrs. Child's own. With her husband's bent for impractical ventures, she was already thrust into the position of breadwinner and manager of the household, where "well-founded love," if not "reliance on Divine Providence," was being heavily taxed.

Of the twelve chapters devoted to discipline, dress, politeness, gentility, and teenage years, perhaps the chapter on education, specifically on the reading of books, is most immediately interesting to the modern reader. Again the advice was practical, combining "amusement with instruction." Reading, particularly for women, "cheers so many hours of illness and seclusion; it gives the mind something to interest itself about, instead of the concerns of one's neighbors, and the change of fashion; it enlarges the heart, by giving extensive views of the world; it every day increases the points of sympathy with an intelligent husband; and it gives a mother materials for furnishing the minds of her children." She suggested that serious reading—"History, Voyages, Travels, Biography, etc."—be systematically encouraged and that novel-reading be for "the *recreation* rather than the *employment* of the mind . . . a sort of literary confection . . . [which] if eaten too plentifully . . . tend[s] to destroy our appetite for more solid and nourishing food." Although she cautioned them against prohibiting their daughters from reading novels altogether, there were certain fictions and poetry, too, which ought not to be read until the daughters' taste for "wiser and better molds" had been carefully formed: "works of Byron, Bulwer, Eugene Sue, etc."[13] "[H]ighest" in the category of appropriate fiction were the works of Frederika Bremer, Mary Howitt, Maria Edgeworth, and Mrs. Child's compatriot, Catharine M. Sedgwick, "whose name alone is a sufficient guarantee that the book is safe for young people." Scott's novels should be "read in connection with history, presenting, as they do, a lively picture gallery of the manners, costumes [*sic*], and superstitions of the past." Yet her final advice was to promote the "more solid" reading, such as Plutarch's lives, essays on Christian morality, and one of Mrs. Child's own favorites, Jean Jacques Barthélemy's *Voyage du jeune Anacharsis en Grèce. . . .* She included a list of books acceptable for various age groups, many of the titles unfamiliar to the modern reader, yet *Robinson Crusoe* and *Swiss Family Robinson* were recommended for children, ages eleven and twelve. *The Mother's Book* and *The Girl's Own Book* were companion manuals, part of "the general plan" which she "laid out," one reviewer believed, identifying "the reciprocal duties of parent and child, and . . .

showing to both, by example and precept, the importance of the . . .
relations in which they stand to each other."[14]

She followed these popular manuals with two other volumes which
would have appeal, she hoped, to men. *Biographies of Good Wives*
(1833), dedicated to her husband who had shown Mrs. Child "her
purest happiness and most constant incentives to duty," were brief
sketches of eminent women in history.[15] In each of the sketches
through anecdotes and illustrations, she stressed the wives' moral
character; they were their husbands' "help-mates," who through
implanting the household virtues in their children made their nation
strong. ". . . She knows how to teach the art of living well," wrote the
reviewer in the *Southern Quarterly Review*, "which is certainly the
highest wisdom."[16]

History of the Condition of Women in Various Ages and Nations
(1835), in two volumes, as the title suggests, traced the influence of
women through the ages, concentrating on changing social customs
and household responsibilities. Mrs. Child made it clear in the
preface that the volumes "are not an essay upon woman's rights, or a
philosophical investigation of what is or ought to be the relation of
the sexes. . . . I have simply endeavored to give an accurate history of
the condition of women." It was by no standard, however, the
remarkable study Margaret Fuller would write some years later,
Women in the Nineteenth Century (1844).

At the end of the introductory essay in *Good Wives*, before she
turned to the sketches, Mrs. Child admitted that the book would
perhaps do little to alter public opinion or improve the present state
of women in nineteenth-century American society. "My efforts
remind me," she wrote, "of a story often repeated by a valued friend.
'When I was a small boy,' says he, 'I often plunged my little hoe into a
rushing and tumbling brook, on the borders of my father's farm,—
thinking, in the childish simplicity of my heart, that I could stop the
course of its impetuous waters.' Gentle readers, I have put my little
garden hoe into a mighty stream—and perchance the current will
sweep it to oblivion." Mrs. Child spoke prophetically. These
ephemeral books, with the possible exception of *The Frugal Housewife*, now gather dust on the shelves in library annexes and university
stacks.

III   *Antislavery Writings and* The Freedmen's Book

Mrs. Child's appeal as a writer of popular nonfiction works was
certainly secure in the early 1830s. More important, perhaps, enough

money was being realized from sales to give her and her husband a financial base they had not had since their marriage. Readers and reviewers looked "with constantly increasing favor" on all she wrote.[17] Then she published *An Appeal in Favor of That Class of Americans Called Africans* (1833), and overnight her name became an anathema in Boston society.[18] The *Appeal* shocked, then angered, her contemporaries whose prejudices she so wrongfully exposed; yet the modern reader is impressed by her good sense, her objectivity, and her fervor. What William Lloyd Garrison had already written in *Thoughts on African Colonization* (1832) and what Whittier had achieved in *Justice and Expediency* (1833) was nothing compared to the attention Mrs. Child commanded when the hard-hitting *Appeal* was published. She had anticipated the storm of resentment as she wrote the preface: "I am fully aware of the unpopularity of the task I have undertaken; but though I *expect* ridicule and censure, I cannot *fear* them. A few years hence, the opinion of the world will be a matter in which I have not even the most transient interest; but this book will be abroad on its mission of humanity, long after the hand that wrote it is mingling with the dust. Should it be the means of advancing, even one single hour, the inevitable progress of truth and justice, I would not exchange the consciousness for all Rothchild's [*sic*] wealth, or Sir Walter's fame."

The statement was made, the position was taken. She had prepared herself well for the assignment; and she had gathered the facts upon which to build her case, having read in the Athenaeum library the various newspapers—*Niles' Weekly Register*, among others—which reported accounts of the barbarous treatment of slaves, as well as countless tracts on slavery in the West Indies and in the American South. The *Appeal* began with a history of slavery, from the time when Prince Henry of Portugal had exchanged ten Moorish prisoners of war for ten African Negroes and then sold them for profit. Thus, the African slave trade commenced. Tracing its expansion to the New World, she drew on firsthand accounts, citing statistics and figures, using whatever data were available to her to relate the horrors of slavery: the transportation on slaveships when thumbscrews and shackles and pressure bars were used to confine the slaves to their rude beds; the scant rations which hardly kept them alive; the stench which permeated the holds of the ships, when the odor of confined bodies and the excrement built up in the close quarters; the selling of slaves often to insensitive and cruel owners; and the breaking-up of family units and friends. Patiently and explicitly she detailed the brutal inhumanity of slavery.

Had she ended the essay with the simple history of slavery's atrocities, readers might have accepted it as an emotional curiosity written by a compassionate woman and let it go at that. However, she did not, but appealed to readers on the grounds of the injustice of slavery and the denial of human rights. The style, which had heretofore been highly charged and emotionally tense, changed as well; it became terse, unsentimental, accusatory. She described the effects of slavery on masters who too often repaid service of their slaves with negligence and death. She taunted slaveholders for believing that anyone preferred to be owned rather than to be free. She accused New Englanders of a predilection for slavery and a prejudice against Negroes, perhaps more inveterate than it was in the South. While the planter was sometimes attached to his Negroes and "lavish[ed] caresses and kind words upon them, as he would on a favorite hound," New Englanders' antipathy of Negroes was "cold-hearted, ignoble prejudice admit[ting] of no exception—no inter-mission." She itemized the specific injustices against Negroes in the state of Massachusetts: the law prohibiting mixed marriages and the law prohibiting Negroes unless slaves to remain in the state more than two months; the denial of free education, of access to many churches, of public transportation; particularly, the prejudice against mulat-toes.

She showed that morally and economically slavery weakened the United States. Free men, not slaves, became useful citizens. Free men, white and black, worked together for the mutual strength of the Union. Free men, white and black, were brothers in God's eyes. Free labor, not slave labor, would bring prosperity to the Union. Free labor, not slave labor, erased the feeling of inferiority among men. She called on God to condemn as criminals any man who owned another. The Union, under the condition which it now existed, half slave and half free, was worthless, a mockery among nations, she proclaimed. "If the Union cannot be preserved without crime, it is eternal truth that nothing good can be preserved by crime." Blind, selfish material interests alone perpetuated slavery. Prejudice, ugly and cruel, perpetuated feeling against the Negroes. Blame fell on both Northerner and Southerner for the despicable, inhumane practices slavery fostered. "An error often and urgently repeated is apt to receive the sanction of truth," Mrs. Child charged; "and so it is in this case. The public take it for granted that slavery is a 'lamentable necessity.' Nevertheless[,] there *is* a way to effect its cure, if we all join sincerely, earnestly, and kindly in the work; but if we expend our energies in palliating the evil, or mourning over its hopelessness, or quarreling about who is most to blame for it, the vessel,—crew, passengers, and all,—will go down together."

The only way—the right way, the safe way—was immediate emancipation, the very way to address the wrongs of slavery. She did not advocate colonization, a pet project of many of her New England contemporaries. Instead, she announced the bold plan for freedom of the Negroes in America, where all men—white and black—could "live together in mutual good will, and perform a mutual use to each other." She then turned in the *Appeal* to that most alarming declaration—a truth implied in the title of the essay itself—that since Negroes were in fact Americans by birth or circumstance, they were the equal of their fellow white Americans. Since God saw no distinction among men, why should His creatures impose one? The Negroes were entitled as Americans to a free public education. And in a statement that would give any honest man with distinct insight a challenge to write, she exposed mercilessly Americans' bigotry: "With our firm belief in the natural inferiority of negroes, it is strange we should be so much afraid that knowledge will elevate them quite too high for our convenience. In the march of improvement, we are several centuries in advance; and if, with this obstacle at the very beginning, they can outstrip us, why then, in the name of justice, let them go ahead! Nay, give them three cheers as they pass. If any nation, or any class of men, can obtain intellectual preeminence, it is a sure sign they deserve it; and by this republican rule the condition of the world will be regulated as surely as the waters find their level."

Having introduced the popular shibboleth of racial inferiority— that notion upon which the South based its argument for slavery and the North took grim satisfaction in promulgating, she addressed herself to the task of refuting the superstition. "The intellectual inferiority of the negroes is a common, though most absurd[,] apology for personal prejudice, and the oppressive inequality of the laws; for this reason, I shall take some pains to prove that the present degraded condition of that unfortunate race is produced by artificial causes, not by the laws of nature." She then submitted a number of case histories, among them a sketch of "Phillis Wheatly," to prove the Negroes' native intelligence and moral character.

She went even further, mentioning what for even the most enlightened of her readers was the basic, often unspoken, canker in the relationship between whites and blacks in America: "In regard to marrying your daughter, I believe the feeling in opposition to such unions is quite as strong among the colored class as it is among white people. While the prejudice exists, such instances must be exceedingly rare because the consequence is degradation in society. Believe me, you may safely trust to anything that depends on the pride and selfishness of unregenerated human nature." The threat implied by her severe comment, though denied by it, could not be ignored.

In conclusion, she wrote: "By publishing this book I have put my mite into the treasury. The expectation of displeasing all classes has not been unaccompanied with pain. But it has been strongly impressed upon my mind that it was a duty to fulfil [sic] this task; and earthly considerations should never stifle the voice of conscience." Had Mrs. Child anticipated the vehement protests the *Appeal* created in Boston and elsewhere in the country, she would not have changed a word in the essay. Her friend Mrs. Hale, meeting a deadline, regretted that she could not give the work the kind of review she felt it merited: "This is a most extraordinary work. We cannot now notice it, as it deserves; but we extract the preface, and entreat our readers—our sex to comply with the request of the gifted author—*read the book!*"[19] Garrison gave notice of the essay front-page coverage in *The Liberator*, reprinting a review from another antislavery newssheet. "We admire the moral courage of this lady risking her literary name by taking the stand which she does in this volume," the reviewer wrote in part.[20]

The more conservative reviews apparently ignored the *Appeal* altogether, the *Knickerbocker* referring to it only in the "Editor's Table" column as "An Appeal in Favor of the Africans, by Mrs. Child."[21] Although the *North American* listed it as a new publication when it first appeared,[22] it was nearly two years later before a reviewer assessed the argument Mrs. Child had presented. By this time Boston had become somewhat accustomed to the antislavery agitators. Even so, the reviewer "regret[ted] that a writer capable of being so agreeable, and at the same time so useful, should have departed from that line of authorship in which she [had] justly acquired a high reputation." It was the reviewer's assignment in the article "to correct impressions upon the subject" and to underline the "danger" in such appeals as Mrs. Child's, where "passion . . . rather [than] . . . judgment" prevailed. Citing Biblical and historical precedents for slavery, he traced the development of the institution to its present condition in the South. Admitting the fact that slavery must be abolished, he nevertheless questioned Mrs. Child's solution of immediate emancipation and with alarm rejected her proposal that Negroes be absorbed into American society. Apparently there lurked in his mind, and in the minds of many white Americans, the awesome possibility that Negroes might indeed be intellectual equals, given the opportunity for education Mrs. Child demanded. He voiced a frightening thought: ". . . If the truth of this doctrine be admitted, where is the progress of this improvement to stop?" Rather than entertain the "doctrine," he evaded the issue, saying that he was "approaching almost dangerous ground," and fell back on the argument men of easy conscience in New England were now espousing: "If in a struggle for this end [i.e., the abolition of slavery] the Union should be dissolved, it needs not the gift of prophecy to foresee that our country will be plunged into that gulf which . . . is full at once of the fire and the blood of Civil war, and of the thick darkness of general political disgrace, ignominy and ruin." The conservative argument—preserve the Union because slavery, sanctioned by the Constitution, was part of the original compact—became the reviewer's ultimate defense; yet he could not forgive Mrs. Child for her impropriety: "It is, therefore, we repeat, with regret that we see intellects like that of Mrs. Child, and pens like hers, which may be otherwise so agreeably and beneficially employed, diverted from their legitimate spheres of action, and employed in urging on a cause so dangerous to the Union, domestic peace, and civil liberty, as the immediate emancipation of the slaves at the South."[23] The reviewer—in fact, Boston—could not excuse the clear logic that she set forth in the *Appeal*, any more than many New Englanders could accept the charges Thoreau leveled some fifteen years later that legislators endorsed social expediency rather than moral justice in condoning slavery. In a dialog as iconoclastic as Thoreau's in "Civil Disobedience," Mrs. Child had set down in the *Appeal* a statement of principle memorable for its clarity and remarkable for its vision.

Nevertheless, she was hurt by the public response. Old friends turned from her; reviewers were silent; editors refused her work; subscriptions to *The Juvenile Miscellany*, that labor of love for her "little readers," nearly ceased. Although she had prepared herself for the abuse and the criticism for the sake of her belief, the end of the *Miscellany* affected her deeply, as the editorial in the final issue of the magazine revealed:

After conducting the Miscellany for eight years, I am now compelled to bid a reluctant and most affectionate farewell to my little readers. May God bless you, my young friends, and impress deeply upon your hearts the conviction that all true excellence and happiness consist in living for *others*, not for *yourselves*.[24]

With these words Mrs. Child established the credo by which she would live—"for *others*," not for herself. On the credit side, however, the *Appeal* won notable converts to the antislavery cause: William Ellery Channing and Thomas Wentworth Higginson,[25] and Wendell Phillips, the abolitionists' most effective speaker.

She was to write a great number of antislavery tracts in the years ahead, but none equaled the earnest conviction of the *Appeal*. The notoriety she earned led in a few years to her becoming editor of the *National Anti-Slavery Standard* for two years (1841–1843), the New York–based newspaper of the New England abolitionists and the American Anti-Slavery Society. Some who had objected to naming a woman as editor were convinced that their reservations were well-founded when they read her cool, sensible declaration of editorial policy: ". . . I am here," she announced, "ready to work according to my conscience and my ability, providing nothing but diligence and fidelity, refusing the shadow of a fetter on my free expression of opinion from any man or body of men, equally careful to respect the freedom of others, whether as individuals or societies."[26] Unlike the aggressive editorial tone Garrison had taken in *The Liberator*, the tone in the *Standard* under her editorship was firm but conciliatory—Mrs. Child believing that a rational exposition of the wrongs of slavery would lead more converts to the cause than violent outbursts of wrath and indignation. "I often attack bigotry," she wrote a friend, "with 'a troop of horse shod with felt,' that is, I try to enter the wedge of general principles, letting inferences unfold themselves very gradually."[27] Certainly a rational exposition of facts in the *Appeal* had rallied three influential Bostonians to the cause. Then, too, the *Standard*, as she conceived its policy, was a newspaper that appealed to women readers with articles on family life and temperate discussions of women's rights. Friends, among them Maria Chapman in Boston, herself an advocate of more aggressive abolitionism, urged her to a more petulant tone in the paper; but Mrs. Child demurred, insisting that the *Standard* under her editorship was not "a controversial and agitating newspaper."[28] She demanded the moderate approach, not intrigue or harassment or duplicity engaged in by the "veteran abolitionists." When she found the pressure of the more militant antislavers "to co-erce [her] individual freedom"[29] intolerable, she resigned the post—reiterating in her last editorial that she was "too distinctly an individual"[30] to compromise her own beliefs or to jeopardize the respect she had for others to believe as they believed.

She wrote several more antislavery tracts, typical of the hundreds of such appeals that were published in the country during the decades before the Civil War, urging emancipation as "a measure of plain, practical good sense, and sound policy" and "entreat[ing] all who wish well to their country to aid me in this work."[31] She also edited *Incidents in the Life of a Slave Girl* (1861), written by a young woman, Harriet Brent Jacobs, which was still another attempt to reveal the "monstrous features" of slavery. "I do this for the sake of my sisters in bondage," she said in the introduction, "who are suffering wrongs so foul, that our ears are too delicate to listen to them. I do it with the hope of arousing conscientious and reflecting women in the North to a sense of duty in the exertion of moral influence on the question of Slavery, on all possible occasions. I do it with the hope that every man who reads this narrative will swear solemnly before God that, so far as he has power to prevent it, no fugitive from Slavery shall ever be sent back to suffer in that loathsome den of corruption and cruelty." The narrative described in "language . . . her own" Mrs. Jacobs's experiences in reaching New York by the Underground Railway to win her freedom.[32]

When emancipation came, she prepared another manual, *The Freedmen's Book* (1865), prefacing her "advice from an old friend" with biographies of ex-slaves, poetry of Phillis Wheatley and Frederick Douglass, as well as verse by Whittier, Harriet Beecher Stowe, and herself. She asked freedmen to read aloud to their friends who could not selections from the manual to derive "fresh courage and strength." The "advice" was encouraging, reassuring, and perhaps to the modern reader somewhat patronizing. "For many years," she began, "I have felt great sympathy for you, my brethren and sisters, and I have tried to do what I could to help you to freedom. And now that you have at last received the long-desired blessing, I most earnestly wish that you should make the best possible use of it." Then, in manner and style similar to that in *The Frugal Housewife*, she exhorted the blacks to become useful citizens. "It is not the *greatness* of the thing a man does which makes him worthy of respect," she informed them; "it is the doing *well* whatsoever he hath to do. In many respects, your opportunities for usefulness are more limited than those of others; but you have one great opportunity peculiar to yourselves. You can do a vast amount of good to people in various parts of the world, and through successive generations, by simply being sober, industrious, and honest."

She spoke of their personal appearance, echoing, perhaps, experiences of the Childs' lean years: "Working-clothes that are clean and nicely patched always look respectable; and they make a very favorable impression, because they indicate that the wearer is neat and economical." She talked about the appearance of their homes, remembering, perhaps, the shabby dwellings she had made comfortable: "Whitewash is not expensive; and it takes but little time to transplant . . . shrubs and vines, that make the poorest cabin look beautiful; and, once planted, they will be growing while you are working and sleeping."

She asked the blacks not to bear ill will against their former masters who might be provoked "to see those who were once their slaves acting like freemen." In fact, she advised them to work for their former masters "if they treat you well, and pay you as much as you could earn elsewhere." Should they, however, be oppressive, "quit their service, and work for somebody who will treat you like freemen." She underscored the fact that as free men they had rights which were now protected under the laws of the land: "It is one of the noblest privileges of freemen to be able to respect the law, and to rely upon it always for redress of grievances, instead of revenging one wrong by another wrong."

You will have much to put up with before the new order of things can become settled on a permanent foundation [she concludes]. . . . [W]hatever wrongs you may endure, comfort yourselves with two reflections: first, that there is the beginning of a better state of things, from which your children will derive much more benefit than you can; secondly, that a great majority of the American people are sincerely determined that you shall be protected in your rights as freemen.

The "advice," however condescending in tone, was sincerely given; and it was not unlike the sentiment Booker T. Washington advocated in his work with his "people" at Tuskegee Institute a few years later.

IV   *Religion and History*

The same desire—that people could be helped to better understanding through enlightenment—impelled Mrs. Child to undertake what, in her day, at least, was a monumental task: recording in two volumes the *Progress of Religious Ideas through Successive Ages* (1855). Eight years of reading and research, often interrupted by more pressing concerns, went into the preparation of the book she wanted to write more than any other. The preface announced its intent and provided a warning: "I would candidly advise persons who are conscious of bigoted attachment to any creed, or theory, not to purchase this book. Whether they are bigoted Christians, or bigoted infidels, its tone will be likely to displease them." Written for the "popular mind," not the learned, Mrs. Child in clear prose and with remarkable facility to summarize and digest complex tenets of faith set forth "impartially the beauties and the blemishes" of the world's religions. "To write with the unbiassed justice at which I aimed," she continued, "I was obliged to trample under my feet the theological underbrush, which always tangles and obstructs the path, when the soul strives to be guided only by the mild bright star of religious sentiment." Realizing that she might well offend some of her readers, she justified the history by reminding them that "plain statements of truth can never eventually prove injurious, on *any* subject"; if the book succeeded in bringing about better understanding among people, she was amply rewarded.

The history met with mixed reviews, the comments either highly flattering or openly hostile. "A work like this of Mrs. Child's has long been needed . . . by the mass of thoughtful readers, whose craving for knowledge exceeds their opportunities," said the reviewer in the *Democratic Review*; "to all such it will be a handbook of curious religious lore." He admired the candor of her approach, "without bias or prejudice: giv[ing] the facts of religious history calmly and dispassionately. . . . And after all, this seems to us, the only way of writing history properly. . . . If Mrs. Child has any fault, it is that she is *too fair*."[33] The reviewer in the *Christian Examiner* was also pleased but acknowledged, as Mrs. Child herself had done, that the undertaking was indeed a large one—perhaps an impossible one. He wondered whether "any one who has been educated as a Christian" could without "bias" write about the world's religions; "Christian training," he went on to say, "has resulted in the firm conviction that Christianity is a direct and special revelation from God. . . ."

Was it possible, then, "for one who is a Christian . . . to present with perfect fidelity, the conceptions and convictions" of ancient Greece and Rome, China, India and the East or of Jews and those peoples who subscribe to "the religion of Mahomet"? Voicing perhaps his own skepticism, or the conservative Christian view of the recent phenomenon, transcendentalism, the reviewer asked: Was it possible, specifically, "for a New England Christian to enter into the dreamy pietism and the genealogical divinity of a Brahmin of India"? Although he had great reliance on Mrs. Child's integrity because she "wisely sought to make . . . allowances" for her Christian training, would there not be still "an unconscious influence"? To emphasize his point, he concluded the notice: "We ought not to close without recognizing the beautiful tribute of affection and gratitude which Mrs. Child renders to the blessed faith of Jesus of Nazareth."[34] The question was in Mrs. Child's mind, too, as letters to family and friends reveal,[35] yet the question no doubt defied an answer.

It was assuredly "one who [had] been educated as a Christian," a reviewer for the conservative *New England Magazine*, who was sharply critical of the book: "[S]he would have done infinitely better if she had not written it at all." The history was blasphemous because there was "a vein of malicious skepticism respecting the divine origin and authority of [Christianity's] sacred scriptures, which creeps out so often in disingenuous interpretation and misstatements, in innuendos and suggestions." And unforgiveable was her deliberate misrepresentation of God "as [His] Divine character and conduct [were] delineated in the Old Testament" as well as her ill regard for the Old Testament prophets who made, she averred, "their communications in a state of religious frenzy, because the same word in Hebrew means to prophesy and to be mad." "We might as well say," retorted the reviewer, "that Mrs. Child's work on the Progress of Religious Ideas is stuffed with infantile babblings, because the name of the distinguished authoress means both a marriageable lady and an infant."

What was most reprehensible in the history was Mrs. Child's speaking of Christ "as *a* son of God," regarding him "only as one of many wise men who have from time to time appeared in the world." Even the Bible was referred to "as having no higher authority than the Vedas of the Hindoos and the Zend-Avistas of the Persians." And in a final salvo directed against the book, he smugly informed his readers: "We do not regard these volumes as reliable for accurate and just representations of religious history. They exhibit too great partiality for Paganism, and too great prejudice against the sacred Books of the Christians."[36] The reviewer's opinion was shared by the writer in the *Methodist Quarterly Review* as well, who chose also to belittle the history: "The whole book . . . is one of the most marvellous instances of toil misspent and talent misapplied that the history of literature affords."[37]

Mrs. Child told her friend Lucy Osgood that she knew she had "marched into the enemy's camp" when she published the history.[38] The conservatives in religion were outraged, even her brother Convers was "not *altogether* pleased."[39] The *Progress of Religious Ideas* struck at the sacrosanct convictions of some of her contemporaries even more deeply than the *Appeal* had hit at their prejudices. Nevertheless, she was to have satisfaction some years later; she wrote Whittier that the history had apparently been "endorsed by a very learned Professor at Oxford, the gold had received the stamp of the Mint, and will pass current in the world."[40]

Ever anxious to provide "food for heart and mind,"[41] Mrs. Child wrote *The First Settlers of New England* (1829), an account of the conquest of the Indian tribes in colonial Massachusetts—inspired in part by the work done in writing *Hobomok* and, more immediately, by the recent removal of the Cherokees to lands in the West, one of Jackson's administrative decisions which she and Child had denounced in articles sent to newspapers. Often referred to as a novel, it was hardly more than an extended conversation carried on between a mother and her daughters. It had no plot, little characterization, no specified setting; it was a narrative of stilted dialog, the daughters asking questions which the mother occupied several pages of the book in answering. Wholly sympathetic to the plight of the Indians, Mrs. Child drew on a number of sources, among others Irving's "Philip of Pokonocket" in *The Sketch Book*.[42]

The fate of the Pequod, Narragansett, and Pokanocket tribes at the hands of seventeenth-century Puritans is well known to the modern reader, although doubtless many of the details were not known, or not believed, by Mrs. Child's contemporaries. This defense, the first of her books to advocate a cause, inaugurated the reform programs she championed throughout her life.

She was largely sympathetic in her portrait of the Puritans in *Hobomok*, but here she was particularly harsh, condemning them for their hypocrisy. "The Indians [in New England] have been strangely misrepresented," the mother informed her daughters, "either through ignorance or design, or both; and men have given themselves little trouble to investigate the subject. People seldom forgive those whom they have wronged, and the first settlers appear to have fostered a mortal aversion to the Indians, whom they had barbarously destroyed." Over and over she reiterated that it was the Puritans, not the Indians, who precipitated the violence and bloodshed in colonial Massachusetts; even the sources she employed obliquely informed the reader that the atrocities committed in God's name were Puritan-motivated. "I have been unable," the mother said in one dialog, "to detect any hostility on the part of the Pequods, but what was justifiable in self-defence."

A daughter asked about intermarriage, and for the reader who had read *Hobomok* and was curious why Mrs. Child never fully explained the Indian chief's union with Mary Conant, the answer the mother gave supplied an insight into Mrs. Child's liberal humanity: "Whatever objections there may be for people of different colours to unite, it would doubtless abundantly diminish the amount of crime, and we might thus testify our obedience to the will of our heavenly

Father, who has made of one blood all the nations of men, that they may dwell together."

Although Mrs. Child did not condone the Puritans' treatment of the Indians, she understood why they acted as they did, given the particular tenets of their faith: ". . . If it be admitted that God had chosen a people who were commanded to punish and exterminate a portion of His creatures who had been blinded and kept in ignorance of the truth, then is the doctrine of election firmly established, and the elect may sin with impunity, for, of course, men are not responsible for what they are unable to resist." Yet there was a sardonic note: "It becomes us, however, who acknowledge and feel our accountability as followers of Jesus, earnestly to insist, that a being who authorizes injustice, revenge, and cruelty, cannot be the God and Father of our lord Jesus Christ." But she was much severer on nineteenth-century Americans who deliberately mistreated the Indians, not out of superstition or religious error but for purposes of selfishness and greed: "To what purpose is 'the multitide of our sacrifices, and vain oblations,' our sabbaths, and calling of assemblies, and solemn meetings, whilst we omit to 'do justice and show mercy' to the oppressed, whose relief has become to us a most sacred duty."

V *Gift Books*

Among the gift books Mrs. Child compiled are *The Coronal*, *Autumnal Leaves*, and *Looking Toward Sunset. The Coronal* (1832), an early anthology, contained the best of her previously published verse and stories. Even though she did not have much enthusiasm for her own verse, undisciplined reviewers in the early years often praised it; so in the anthology she satisfied their tastes. One of the verses is mildly interesting to the modern reader. "To the Fringed Gentian" was a poem with a Wordsworthian sentiment and on the same subject as one written by her acquaintance William Cullen Bryant.

> Purple flower, pale autumn's child,
> Blooming in beauty lone and wild—
> Slowly matured by sun and shower,
> To reign awhile in fleeting power;
> Yet bashfully in that brief space
> Hiding from view thy lovely face,
> Veiling thy imperial tinge
> Beneath a modest robe of fringe.
> When summer-days are long and bright,
> Thy lovely form ne'er meets the sight;

> But when October guides the year,
> And points to seasons cold and drear,
> It gracefully his path-way strews,
> And smiles beneath his shiv'ring dews.
> Thus buds of virtue often bloom
> The fairest, mid the deepest gloom.
> Thus latent loveliness conceal'd,
> And not one embryo tint reveal'd;
> Till left by fortune's sunny beam,
> To ripen in affliction's gleam.

She may have had the foresight to know that, while her piece was graceful, Bryant's would fare better in anthologies of literature.

Aware of the popular appeal of Indian material in the periodicals, Mrs. Child included several of hers. "The Lone Indian" was a lament over the destruction of the redman's natural world through the rapacity and the indifference of the white man—a working out of the *ubi sunt* theme which Cooper had employed with far greater effect in the Leatherstocking tales. The Indian's hunting grounds were destroyed; his wife and child were dead, their graves desecrated by the white man's need for progress. The Indian sadly reflected: "The leaves are falling, and the clouds are scattering, like my people." Alone, he headed west to escape for the time at least the crash of falling trees.

"The Indian Wife" was calculated for the teary-eyed readers. An indolent Frenchman married an Indian princess for her inheritance, lands on the Missouri. Two children were born—a son and a daughter. Not long after, the husband sold his wife's lands and left for Quebec, taking the daughter with him. The Indian wife, bereft and angry, nursed in herself and in her son a "deadly hatred of whitemen." The husband returned after some three years and won back his son's affection. The mother, alarmed and desperate at the turn of events, glided with her son in a canoe over a mountain waterfall to their death.

There were some thirty-odd pieces of Mrs. Child's verse and stories in *The Coronal*, undistinguished yet representative of the popular taste. Pleasant enough reading to occupy her readers' leisure time, yet insignificant when placed alongside her better work. One other story, "The Young West-Indian," suggested that Mrs. Child might have had in mind the germ of her later novel, *A Romance of the Republic*, years before she wrote that fiction. It was a tale of a lost brother and sister ultimately reunited through the good services of a benefactor.

Autumnal Leaves (1856) is another collection of her articles; as the title hints, they are sober pieces—homilies on self-improvement and the conduct of life—"characterized by great simplicity and vigor of language, much picturesqueness of description, and abundant natural feeling," so wrote the *Knickerbocker* reviewer.[43]

"The Eglantine" describes a young woman who aspires to be a teacher "of the highest class." She succeeds, marries, and has a family. Her husband is an idealist: it is a fixed principle with him that no man has a right to live in the world without doing his share of its work. "My fruits and vegetables will soon command a ready sale in the city market," he says at one point in the story; "but the proceeds shall go toward a school-fund, and the establishment of a Lyceum. . . . The wisest and kindest thing we can do for [our children] is to educate equally themselves and the people among whom we are to live." In so many ways it is an autobiographical sketch of the Childs who selflessly devoted their lives to the service of others.

"The Juryman" is a lesson in forgiveness and temperance, containing, Mrs. Child suggests, "a few good ideas concerning the culture of an immortal soul." An irascible, vindictive man, the foreman of a jury, persuades his fellow jurors to ask for the death of a young man who has killed in a drunken rage. Justice is, however, often retributive; and the man's son, some years later, is on trial for the same crime. He realizes too late that his son's conduct was the result of his own "violent words and actions." ". . . It was wrong, wrong, all wrong," he laments.

"Home and Politics" is the story of a young couple whose happy life together is ruined because of the husband's involvement in politics: ". . . In [an] evil hour a disturbing influence crossed their threshold. It came in the form of political excitement; that pestilence which is forever racing through our land, seeking whom it may devour; destroying happy homes, turning aside our intellectual strength from the calm and healthy pursuits of literature or science, blinding consciences, embittering hearts, rasping the tempers of men and blighting half the talent of our country with its feverish breath." George Franklin puts aspirations for public office above love for his family. Their child dies, the wife loses her mind in grief, all his worldly possessions are taken from him when he gambled on the outcome of an election and lost. "Thus," Mrs. Child warns, "left adrift on the dark ocean of life, George Franklin hesitated whether to trust the chances of politics for another office, or to start again in his [law] profession, and slowly rebuild his shattered fortunes from the ruins of the past. Having wisely determined in favor of the latter," she approvingly concludes, "he works diligently and lives economically, cheered by the hope that reason will again dawn in the beautiful soul that loved him so truly." Highly melodramatic, the story is not so much a homily on self-improvement or the conduct of life as it is Mrs. Child's attack on the caprice of politics. The modern reader smiles.

However, another story is better calculated for a lesson in tolerance, "The Catholic and the Quaker"—a tale of a Quaker family caught in the middle of warring Protestants and Catholics in Ireland. The story turns on the love of a young Catholic for a Quaker girl, to the dismay of both families. The girl is referred to as a black Protestant by the Catholic mother; "[n]ot a black Protestant, dear mother, only a dove-colored one," rejoins her lover. Eventually the families accept their children's wishes to marry. "And so Catholic and Quaker are married, according to the forms of both their churches. The Society of Friends mostly withdraw from the companionship of Alice, though they greet her kindly at their meetings. The Catholics shake their heads and complain that Camillo Campbell is already half a Quaker. Both prognosticate evil consequences from such a union. But the worst that happens is, Alice learns that there may be superstition in the cut of a garment, as well as in veneration of an image; and Camillo becomes convinced that hatred and violence are much greater sins than eating meat on Fridays." An insightful story, no doubt somewhat disturbing to many of her contemporary readers, "The Catholic and the Quaker" has a message even today when one remembers the bitterness alien faiths create.

"Brother and Sister" underscores the value of education, for men *and* women. Esther and John Golding "had the good fortune to be born in New England where the moral atmosphere stimulates intellect, and the stream of knowledge flows free and full to all the people. Esther was as eager for information, as her more vivacious brother; and though, as a woman, her pathway of life was more obstructed, and all its growth more stinted, she helped to lead him into broader avenues than she herself was allowed to enter." It is Esther's dream as she grows older to earn enough money to send her brother to college. "Why don't *women* go to college?" John asks; Esther replies "that women never *had* done such things."

The boy [Mrs. Child interjects] . . . had started ideas which he was too ignorant to follow. But in his simple question lies the germ of thoughts that will revolutionize the world. For as surely as there is a God of harmony in the universe, so surely will woman one day become the acknowledged equal and co-worker of man, in *every* department of life; and yet be more truly gentle and affectionate than she now is.

Yet in Mrs. Child's day women didn't go to college, so Esther's determination to educate her brother succeeds, at the expense of her own health. She wastes away and dies; and John, many years later when he is able, and the times are more propitious, establishes a female seminary. For Mrs. Child the story was perhaps significant, since she owed so much of her intellectual growth to the patient instruction of her brother and her husband who had supplied what no college in her younger years would provide. Fictional as it is, it is an eloquent plea for education for women.

One of the stories, "The Kansas Emigrants," was written expressly for the anthology. The story was topical and timely, since news of the bloodshed in Kansas and the plight of the emigrants from the North to the territory were so much in the papers. Young New Englanders— John and Kate Bradford and William and Alice Bruce—descendants of "those heroic pilgrims, who left comfortable homes in England and came to a howling wilderness to establish a principle of freedom," set out for the Kansas territory to assist in the "glorious privilege . . . [of] laying the foundation of states on a basis of justice and freedom." With their friends they settle the town of Lawrence, where mere survival is placed in jeopardy when an influx of Missourians comes to the village.

> . . . In the little shops [Kate] often found . . . these ruffians, half-tipsy, with hair unkempt, and beards like cotton-cards, squirting tobacco-juice in every direction, and interlarding their conversation with oaths and curses. Every one that entered was hailed with the interrogatory, "Stranger, whar ar yer from?" If their answer indicated any place north of the Ohio, and east of the Mississippi, the response was, "Damn yer, holler-hearted Yankees! What business have you in these diggens? You'd better clar out, I tell yer."

The incident, the product of Mrs. Child's active indignation, is nevertheless prelude to the ensuing history of the territory. With the proslavers' systematic infiltration of the territory, the Bradfords and the Bruces become targets for the ruffians' violence; their homes are entered and pillaged, frightening wives and children. The husbands committed to nonviolence refuse to strike back. In the holocaust which ensues Bruce loses his life, shot in the back during a foray; subsequently the village is "wiped out."

> . . . [Thus] at the close of one of their darkest days . . . a messenger . . . was seen riding across the prairie. Through various perils, he had brought [newspapers] to Lawrence. . . . A crowd of men and women assembled . . . to hear the news. Mr. Bradford was reading aloud to them, when his

countenance suddenly fell. "Go on! Go on!" cried the anxious listeners. He gasped out, "The Legislature of Texas has voted to give fifty thousand dollars to make Kansas a Slave State."

"And Massachusetts? What has Massachusetts done?" asked Kate, with nervous eagerness.

He lowered his eyes, as one ashamed of his mother, while he answered, "The Legislature of Massachusetts has voted not to give one dollar to make Kansas a Free State."

In the midst of all the sufferings that had harrowed her soul, [Kate] had always remained calm and collected. Now, for the first time, she groaned aloud . . . exclaim[ing] in tones of bitter anguish, "Oh, Massachusetts! How I have *loved* thee! How I have *trusted* in thee!" Then bowing her head in her hands, she sobbed out, "I *could* not have believed it." But Massachusetts was far off. The Governor and Legislature of her native state did not hear her appeal. They were busy with other things that came home to their *business*, not to their *bosoms*.

When assistance from the North is not forthcoming, when the government refuses to intervene and "President Pierce issue[s] a proclamation which made it treason for the citizens [i.e., the free-staters] to defend themselves," when the rigged elections are held, the "Missouri rabble, with bowie-knives and revolvers," succeed in making Kansas a slave state. "What cared New England that *her* six stars were looking down upon the scene, in shameful 'Union' with that blood-red flag?" heatedly concludes Mrs. Child. The story, dramatic, tense, feverish in the telling, has the emotional power to move the reader even today, as he relives a particularly lurid episode in America's past.

Autumnal Leaves is well titled; "The Kansas Emigrants" is the final story in the anthology. It states that America has lost its healthy promise—a circumstance Mrs. Child feared years before when she questioned the country's moral health in *The Frugal Housewife*. Even the verse in the volume echoes the "sad lessons." With resignation, yet with characteristic defiance, she views "The World That I Am Passing Through."

> Few, in the days of early youth,
> Trusted like me in love and truth.
> I've learned sad lessons from the years;
> But slowly, and with many tears;
> For God made me to kindly view
> The world that I am passing through. . . .

And though I've learned some souls are base,
I would not, therefore, hate the race;
I still would bless my fellow men,
And trust them, though deceived again.
God help me still to kindly view
The world that I am passing through! . . .

Looking Toward Sunset (1864) was remarkably successful, some 4,000 copies selling in the first few days.[44] Perhaps one of the reasons for the "unexpected good luck"[45]—considering it was a gift book for the Christmas trade—was due to the fact that Mrs. Child was at last being regarded in a more kindly light by many of her contemporaries. The long battle for the abolition of slavery, which she had fought so eloquently with her pen and had worked so tirelessly for in her daily life, had been won with the Emancipation Proclamation. Many of the reforms she had called for in *Letters from New York* and in editorials and essays were being enacted; the country's conscience had been awakened. Now an advocate of disunion, even war, if the recalcitrant South did not realize its error, she and her countrymen and country-women were presently experiencing the war to make America free. Her contemporaries no longer remembered her as the gadfly who stabbed their consciences over moral guilt, but as a compassionate humanitarian dedicated as she so often said to the service of others— a prophetess not of doom but of better tidings. She too recognized the change in public attitude: the readers who "acknowledge me as the household friend of two generations." With *Looking Toward Sunset* she hoped to give elderly people "some words of consolation and cheer." As she compiled the book, she and her husband were severely crippled with rheumatism, Child having to make hot poultices to put on his wife's swollen fingers so that the pain in her hands subsided enough for her to do her editorial work.

Unlike the other gift books she prepared, *Looking Toward Sunset* was not solely an anthology of Mrs. Child's work. Of the seventy-odd pieces—prose and poetry—only nine were hers; selections by Bryant, Holmes, and Whittier; her brother Convers, Theodore Parker, and Mrs. Stowe; Burns, Wordsworth, Dickens, and Tennyson; Alice Cary and Frederika Bremer, as well as less well known writers, provided the material for the anthology. Her pieces were genial and warm, confident and inspirational—the kind of writing she was best able to control for her reader's pleasure.

The sentiment of "The Mysterious Pilgrimage" was intended to comfort those who like herself were in their sunset years. It was an

abbreviated version of Pilgrim's progress to the celestial city, without
the worldly temptations and distractions which had plagued Bunyan's
Christian. A "traveller" and his life's companion, Mary, embarked
upon the road of life. When Mary reached her destination before her
traveling companion, he "patiently" journeyed on, "leading [other]
children" until he reached a narrow bridge over a dark river. In a
passage that echoed Paralus' vision of the next world in *Philothea*, the
traveler saw "a flowery arch, bearing the motto, 'The Gate of Life.'
Within it stood Mary . . . shining in transfigured light . . . [her]
welcoming smile . . . more beautiful than it had ever been in the
happy old time of roses and rainbows. 'This is only one more of the
magical transformations, my beloved,' she said. 'It is as I told thee.
The beautiful, mysterious road leads to something far more beautiful
than itself. Come and see!'"

Another essay was a tribute—"Unmarried Women." She supplied
brief sketches of noteworthy women and alluded in passing to those
who had "employed their lives usefully and agreeably as authors,"
among them Mary Russell Mitford, Frederika Bremer, Maria Edgeworth, and Catharine M. Sedgwick. She wrote gracefully about these
women whom society would have married, indicating that their
character was in many respects deepened and mellowed as a result of
"inward sources" which had allowed them to adjust to their single
state. Since "the human soul is placed here for development and
progress," she continues, ". . . it is capable of converting all circumstances into means of growth and advancement."

In "Moral Hints" she cautioned against two of the frequent habits of
old age: fretfulness and despondency. "Both then ought to be resisted
with constant vigilance, as we would resist a disease." As an antidote
to these senile despairs, she advised an active life and "not . . . become
indifferent to the affairs of the world." She catalogued again the
contributions of men and women in their sunset years who defied
depression by involvement in the world. "It is salutary," she advised,
"both for mind and heart, to take an interest in some of the great
questions of the age; whether it be slavery or war, or intemperance, or
the elevation of women, or righting the wrongs of the Indians, or the
progress of education, or the regulation of prisons, or improvements
in architecture, or investigation into the natural sciences, from which
proceed results so important to the daily comfort and occupations of
mankind. It is for each one to choose his object of special interest."
The projects were, of course, frequently those which she herself had
espoused. She ended the essay with reference to a habit of elderly
people particularly annoying to her: "love of gossiping." No good

comes from it, she warned, "and a great deal of trouble is made in neighborhoods."

The messages in the homilies, like those in *The Mother's Book* and in *The Freedmen's Book*, were simple, even pedestrian, yet sincere and optimistic. They were household hints for men and women in their sunset years.

VI   *Coda*

She told a friend, "My Sunset book has brought me a flood of letters to be answered": from old friends and well-wishers, from readers of *The Juvenile Miscellany* and the domestic manuals. "How many letters do you think I have written since New Year's? This is the twentieth."[46] However, the comments of two friends who had always stood by her during the tempestuous reform years were perhaps more treasured than the soberer after-thoughts of readers and reviewers who had carped and ridiculed in the past. "Thy beautiful work," Whittier wrote, ". . . reached me a few days ago and my heart has been thanking thee ever since. It was an exceedingly happy thought of thine to send out these words of cheer to those of us who are beginning to pass down life's sunset declivities. I do not like, however, to have thee call thyself old. I never think of thee as such. Where the heart and fancy are still young, why should we recur to family registers?"[47] And Bryant wrote a tasteful, even touching, acknowledgment—a tribute to the woman who had given so much of her life in service to others. ". . . You are like some artists, who excel in *sunset* views. You give the closing stage of human life an atmosphere of the richest lights and warmest hues, and make even its clouds add to its glory. My wife and I have read your book with great delight."[48] The friends expressed the readers' sentiment, an appreciation not only for the latest anthology but for all the books that had made her "the household friend for two generations."

CHAPTER 7

A Romance of the Republic

A Romance of the Republic (1867) was drawn from real-life incidents "which [grew] out of slavery"; yet in the words of one of the characters in the novel, Mrs. Child's "too fertile imagination" made that reality "strange and romantic." Not content with telling a simple story, she improved upon real life with an elaborate tale of intrigue. Such a mixture was no doubt agreeable to readers of *The Rebels* some forty years before, even to readers a decade earlier when, in Hawthorne's words, the "d——d mob of scribbling women" glutted the book market in the 1850s with their tales of domestic woes; but the appeal of such stories in the late 1860s was lost, a casualty of soberer judgment brought about by the war. Writers, and readers, now preferred novels of real life—stories that revealed the harsher realism of American life, even the uglier aspects of American character— such a novel as John W. DeForest's *Miss Ravenel's Conversion from Secession to Loyalty*, which was published in the same year as *A Romance of the Republic*.

It is somewhat surprising that a woman of Mrs. Child's intellect did not adapt her "novel-making" to the current literary tastes. The material for a realistic story was present in Mrs. Child's novel; however, she chose to package it in sentiment and suspense. Apparently friends warned her, suggesting that she tell her story squarely; the plight of mulattoes in American society was real enough for truly dramatic effort. But she preferred to embellish real life, thereby magnifying the story out of proportion. In spite of misgivings she went ahead with the plan, promising the royalties she received from sales to the Freedmen's Association. The reviewers ignored the novel, so did the reading public. The readers who did pick it up were faced with a literary anachronism, as are readers today. Given this situation, they decide how well she carries the novel off.

I   *". . . When There Is Both the Will and the Means . . .*
    It Will Be Strange If a Way Cannot Be Found . . ."

The long novel is astonishingly well paced, which comes as a
surprise to wary readers; and it concludes happily, which is no
surprise to readers accustomed to living vicariously the agony and the
ecstasy of the heroines' dilemmas. Since music is important in one
heroine's life, as it was in Mrs. Child's, she has consciously drawn
parallels with Bellini's opera *Norma*; she even anticipates a ploy
Mark Twain will use with far greater satiric effect in *Pudd'nhead
Wilson.* However, the framework of the romance is found in two
stories she wrote some years before: "The Young West-Indian" in *The
Coronal* and "The Quadroons" published in another anthology, *Fact
and Fiction* (1846).

The cast of characters is not really a large one, yet their lives for
various reasons are touched by incidents of slavery: the fair-skinned
heroines Rosa and Flora, octoroon daughters of a West Indian
woman of mixed blood and a New England entrepreneur whose
business dealings confine him to New Orleans; the heroes Alfred
Royal King, who lives up to his noble name and always does the right
thing even though it may cause some pain to his Brahmin conscience,
and Franz Blumenthal, an industrious and compassionate immigrant
to New Orleans who has none of the acquired prejudice of race
native-born Americans are heir to; Mrs. Lila Delano, the recently
widowed Boston benefactress who befriends Flora, and later Franz;
Gerald Fitzgerald, the dissolute Southerner addicted to wine and
women who keeps Rosa as his mistress until he can find a suitably
well-off heiress to marry. In the lives of these principal characters, the
lives of the minor characters are interwoven: a French teacher and an
Italian music master, a greedy merchant and his society-minded
daughter; slave traders and abolitionists; and cameo appearances by
William Lloyd Garrison, Wendell Phillips, and John Brown. The
story these characters play out in New Orleans, in the sea islands off
the coast of Georgia, in Boston and Rome, and on Cape Cod defies
ready summary. Highlights no doubt satisfy the mildly curious reader
today.

When the heroines' father suffers financial reverses and dies
penniless, his property is sold to satisfy his creditors. Up for sale on
the auction block are his well-educated daughters, Rosa a singer and
Flora an artist, who have never been told the circumstances of their
birth. Since their mother was never manumitted, by Louisiana law
"the child follows the condition of the mother." As property they will

command several thousand dollars apiece. To forestall the sale the children's teachers commit them to the protection of Fitzgerald, who promises marriage to Rosa and safety to Flora on his remote island plantation. Once established on the island hideaway, the three live for a time an idyllic existence, until Fitzgerald's money is gone and before he makes passes at Flora. The precariousness of Rosa's situation—as mistress and not as wife, since Fitzgerald postpones the marriage—comes to her when he makes longer and longer trips from the island in search of a proper wife.

When Flora is threatened by Fitzgerald, "who says he will carry [her] off to Savannah to sell [her]" unless she accedes to his wishes, she seeks the help of Mrs. Delano, who is by chance visiting at another plantation on the island. Mrs. Delano, the reader discovers, is the former sweetheart of the girls' father; the two young people had never married since he had been found unsatisfactory as a suitor by her parents because he had no money. Subsequently he had gone to New Orleans, made a fortune, had a liaison with the quadroon woman, and fathered the girls; Mrs. Delano had married a man of her parents' choosing. The woman befriends Flora, adopts her as her own daughter since she can apparently pass as white, and spirits her away. Henceforth begins what Flora refers to as "always running away"; and Mrs. Delano, a good woman, practices one deception or concealment after another to protect her "blameless and accomplished young [daughter]." Ultimately they arrive in Rome where Flora continues her art lessons.

Meanwhile, it is assumed by Rosa and Gerald that Flora has been killed by alligators which infest the island's ponds. Fitzgerald returns from one of his trips with a wife—an heiress—to occupy the "great house." As he confronts Rosa, her scorn equals that of Norma when Bellini's heroine discovers the perfidy of Pollione.

Alarmed by the strength of character which he had never dreamed she possessed, he said: "In your present state of mind, there is no telling what you may dare to do. It becomes necessary for you to understand your true position. You are not my wife. The man who married us had no legal authority to perform the ceremony."

"O steeped in falsehood to the lips!" exclaimed she. "And *you* are the idol I have worshipped!"

He looked at her with astonishment not unmingled with admiration. "Rosa, I could not have believed you had such a temper," rejoined he. "But why will you persist in making yourself and me unhappy? . . .

"And I give you undivided affection," he [added]. "By all the stars of heaven, I swear that you are now, as you always have been, my Rosa Regina, my Rosa*munda*."

"Do not exhaust your oaths," rejoined she, with a contemptuous curl of the lip. "Keep some of them for your Lily Bell, your precious pearl, 'your moonlight sylph.'"

". . . But Rosa, dearest, you cannot, with all your efforts, drive from you the pleasant memories of our love. You surely do not hate me?"

"No, Mr. Fitzgerald: you have fallen below hatred. I despise you."

Rosa bears Fitzgerald's son, and Mrs. Fitzgerald also bears a son a few months later. The remorseful husband promises to manumit Rosa so that the boy will be free, but he delays, as he had with their sham marriage. In a climactic scene, similar to one already played out before in *The Rebels*, Rosa takes matters into her own hands; when the Fitzgeralds's nurse comes to visit Rosa's housekeeper, bringing the baby with her, Rosa seizes an opportunity. ". . . Turn[ing] toward the babes, she gazed upon them for a long time. There they lay side by side, like twin kittens. But ah! thought she, how different is their destiny! One is born to be cherished and waited upon all his days, the other is an outcast and a slave. My poor fatherless babe! He wouldn't manumit us. It was not thoughtlessness. He *meant* to sell us. 'He *meant* to sell us,' she repeated aloud; and again the wild, hard look came into her eyes." In a deranged, apparently trancelike state, she switches the babies, although this fact is not openly declared until much later in the novel.

Soon after, Rosa, too, is spirited away by her former teachers in New Orleans, who after great difficulty get her safely aboard a vessel bound for Europe; in Italy they give her an assumed name and groom her as an opera star. She makes her debut in Rome in *Norma*, where the audience is clearly charmed not only by her bel canto voice but by her sensitive interpretation of Bellini's tragic heroine. She is aided in her success ironically by her lover. As she begins the aria "Ah! bello a me ritorna del fido amor primiero," she sees him in the audience; and the anguish of her former life is relived as she sings with great intensity the next aria, "Oh non tremare, oh non tremare, o perfido." After the bravas die away, she becomes the prima diva in European opera houses and concert halls. At this point in the story Alfred Royal King enters the narrative again.

Although King had met Rosa and Flora in their home many years before and had promised them, "in memory of our fathers' friend- ship . . . [any] command of [his] services, as if I were a brother," he has lost contact with them during the intervening years. In Rome he renews the friendship with Rosa and becomes her manager. Although both sisters are often in sight and sound of each other in the city, they never get together as Part I of Mrs. Child's romance of the republic concludes.

Nineteen years lapse. Rosa has married King, without his completely overcoming certain Brahmin scruples. "'What would my dear prudential mother say, to see me leaving my business to agents and clerks, while I devote my life to the service of an opera-singer?—an opera-singer, too, who has twice been on the verge of being sold as a slave, and who has been the victim of a sham marriage!' But though such queries jostled against conventional ideas received from education, they were always followed by the thought: 'My dear mother has gone to a sphere of wider vision, whence she can look down upon the merely external distinctions of this deceptive world. Rosabella must be seen as a pure, good soul, in eyes that see as angels do; and as the defenceless daughter of my father's friend, it is my duty to protect her.'" And Flora has married Blumenthal, whom Mrs. Delano has set up in business. Since the women have always passed as white, their backgrounds are carefully guarded; yet select friends of the family know the circumstances. The Kings and the Blumenthals with Mrs. Delano return to America, residing in Boston; Rosa and Flora do not fear for the safety of their children since the laws of Massachusetts protect fugitive slaves who seek their freedom. Rosa's "son" has apparently died; but young Fitzgerald—a comely young man, somewhat dissolute like his father, who is living for a time with his wealthy grandfather in Boston—has a strangely maternal feeling for Rosa, whom he meets in Boston society, and a more than sisterly feeling for the Kings' daughter Eulalia. She returns his affection. To keep the young people apart, King takes his wife and daughter to Cape Cod for a summer holiday where the Blumenthals and Mrs. Delano are also summering. And here the two sisters are reunited. Yet Rosa's happiness is agonized as she thinks of Eulalia and Fitzgerald. For a time she accepts the possibility of an incestuous marriage between the children, but at last she confesses her duplicity first to her husband and then to Fitzgerald.

When the young man discovers who he really is, he is angry: "I am not so much of a philosopher . . . [as to] find it easy to endure the double stain of illegitimacy and alliance with the colored race." Then, "this has come upon me so suddenly that I feel stunned." Then, in character appropriate to a novel of domestic sentiment, he is magnanimous:

[Rosa] raised her expressive eyes to his with such a look of love, that he could not refrain from giving her a filial kiss and pressing her warmly to his heart. . . .

[But his] countenance changed as he [remembered]: "My only unhappiness is the loss of Eulalia. That disappointment I must bear as I can."

"You are both very young," rejoined she; "and perhaps you may see another—"

"I don't want to hear about that now," he exclaimed impetuously, moving hastily toward the window, against which he leaned for a moment. When he turned, he saw that his mother was weeping; and he stopped to kiss her forehead, with tender apologies for his abruptness.

"Thank God," she said, "for these brief moments of happiness with my son."

"Yes, they must be brief," he replied. "I must go away and stay away. But I shall always think of you with affection, and cherish the deepest sympathy for your wrongs and sufferings."

King informs Mrs. Fitzgerald (her husband is now dead), who refuses to accept the turn of events; but her father threatens to disinherit "the nigger." King promises young Fitzgerald his assistance but admonishes him "to devote yourself assiduously to some business, profession, or art. Never be a gentleman of leisure. It is the worst possible calling a man can have. Nothing but stagnation of faculties and weariness of soul comes of it."

Now it is discovered that Rosa's "son" is not dead, and King sets out to find him, aided in his effort by Fitzgerald, who accidentally comes upon him in the course of war duty—since the Civil War has now broken out. "George Falkner" has married a mulatto girl and has made his home with a Quaker farmer in upstate New York. King goes to the Friend's home and brings back the wife, whom Rosa now educates. By this time King has done so many kindnesses for so many people that his brother-in-law is prompted to say: "You are rightly named Royal King. . . . [You] do things in such princely style." "In a style better than that of most royal kings," replied [King], "for it is simply that of an honest man." During the course of the war, Fitzgerald is killed, dying a hero's death and nursed in his final agonies by his long lost brother. He is given a hero's burial,[1] and his sacrifice calls for other sacrifices: Blumenthal and his son and King all join the Union army.

The novel, now over 400 pages, is hastily concluded. The war over, the Blumenthals and King return safely, except that King has lost a leg in battle. King befriends Rosa's "son," sending him and his wife off to Europe. When the young man asks him if he knows "anything about my parents," King informs him that he is the son of a slaveholder, that his mother's identity he cannot reveal because of "a pledge of secrecy which it would be dishonorable for me to break," and that he is "unmixed white." The novel ends with a patriotic program planned by the sisters in honor of their returning heroes.

II   *". . . Estimate People . . . according to*
Their Real Value . . ."

Aside from the patriotic pyrotechnics at the novel's end, which may amuse the reader today, *Romance* is written with a rather steady hand—the characters themselves supplying the dramatic focus for the story. And for the first time Mrs. Child creates truly believable characters, and the reader becomes attached to them. Rosa and Flora are far more real than Mary Conant, Lucretia Fitzherbert, and the lovely but idealized Philothea. The girls because of the "false position in which they were placed by the unreasoning prejudice of society" immediately engage the reader's sympathy; unlike their quadroon mother who "quietly accepted the fact [of slavery], as human beings do accept what they are powerless to overcome," they rebel against a chattel existence and resent a status other than free. Rosa's pride is deeply wounded when Fitzgerald refers to her as his "property," and Flora threatened with the prospect of being sold quickly seeks the help of Mrs. Delano. She has become the more wary of the two because she must resort to her own stratagems and fall back on native ingenuity to protect herself. Rosa has a sense of security her sister is not to feel for some time: first her love for Fitzgerald, later the protection of her teachers in Europe, finally her marriage to King. Flora, under the watchful care of Mrs. Delano, is always apprehensive as is Mrs. Delano herself who often seeks advice from friends as how best to secure the safety of her "adopted" daughter. The time is the late 1830s, when fugitive slaves were returned to their masters and Europe was a far better haven for slaves than Canada. Even in Europe, however, secrecy and appearance are maintained by the girls' guardians: Rosa has been transformed into a Spanish woman in dress and looks because of her darker skin; and Flora, heavily veiled in public, is confined to her room when guests become too interested in her. Only with the increased activity of the abolitionists and the disinclination, particularly by the citizens of Massachusetts, to return runaway slaves to the South, as well as the protection and the influence of rich benefactors, is it considered expedient by the guardians to risk a return to America; still, there are those men like young Fitzgerald's grandfather who "stand by the Constitution" and do not "pretend to be wiser than Daniel Webster . . . who said in Congress that 'he would support, to the fullest extent, any law Southern gentlemen chose to frame for the recovery of fugitive slaves.'" Until emancipation Mrs. Delano and to a lesser extent King do not breathe easily, when their families are wholly safe in their native land. That society classifies Rosa and Flora as Negroes seems altogether arbitrary and meaningless—an ironic commentary on the wrongheadedness of men's conventions.

Mrs. Delano is believable to the reader as well, a woman caught in "a strange combination of circumstances," where regard for Flora's freedom takes precedence over "the conventional rules of society" and her "aversion to all sorts of intrigues and mysteries." Her love of Flora's father and the realization that Flora may well have been her own daughter provides still another incentive for her conduct. She does, however, feel a sense of obligation to those self-same "conventional rules of society"; and when a well-intentioned young man wishes to keep company with Flora, Mrs. Delano must in honesty acquaint him with the facts. When he accuses her of "pass[ing] such a counterfeit on society," she counters with a human assessment of the situation: "[Flora's] beauty and vivacity captivated me before I knew anything of her origin. . . . She was alone in the world, and I was alone; and we adopted each other. I have never sought to introduce her into society." The suitor recognizes the poor choice of words he used to characterize Mrs. Delano's love for her adopted daughter and apologizes, yet still wonders how a woman of "her education and refined views of life" can overcome "*such* obstacles." "It requires no apology," she replies. "I am aware that society would take the same view of my proceeding [as] you do. As for my education, I have learned to consider it as, in many respects, false. As for my views, they have been greatly modified by this experience. I have learned to estimate people and things according to their real value, not according to any merely external incidents." And when Flora with her blessing marries Blumenthal, she sets him up in business—not to secure his favor or Flora's love but to provide the husband with material advantage. Money talks. Along with Hobomok, the Boston rebels, Anaxagoras, and Philaemon, she is one of Mrs. Child's characters of conscience who decries the conventions of society or defies the laws of the land to maintain the human family. She is Mrs. Child and the other women of her age who stoutly defended the Negro during the dark years of slavery.

Equally credible is Gerald Fitzgerald, who, unlike Mrs. Delano, is a victim of the system, "the conventional rules of society." Although he is typed as the profligate young Southerner, he is given greater individuality than Somerville; Fitzgerald's touchstone, like Somerville's, is pride: pride in himself and pride in conforming to the expected mores of his culture. Pride demands that he must have a slave mistress, yet pride also demands that the relationship must be discreet. Even though he is "madly in love" with Rosa, he "dreads the scorn of proud relatives" should he consider marriage to one of an inferior race. Thus Rosa's misfortune is his triumph; he has the best solution for his world: "he had satisfied her scruples by [a sham] marriage, [and] he could hide her away and keep his own secret; while she, in the fulness [sic] of grateful love, would doubtless be satisfied with any arrangement he chose to make." And for a time he is convinced that he and Rosa are happy on the island hideaway, which he has transformed into a replica of Rosa's New Orleans home. But when his small inheritance is squandered, pride demands that he must find a marriageable wife; the daughter of a wealthy Boston merchant is his choice, a haughty woman whose idea of rising in society includes being mistress of a plantation. Fitzgerald succeeds in concealing from his wife any knowledge of his mistress; and pride leads him to believe that Rosa aware of her station will accept the role she has been playing all along. He is annoyed when she remonstrates and cannot understand her sudden anger. Pride urges his appeasing her, promising to visit her often. "You will find me as affectionate as ever; and . . . I will provide amply for you," he tells Rosa with confidence. But Rosa is obstinate; when she denounces him, pride answers her anger: "You are my slave. I bought you of your father's creditors. . . . I can sell you any day I choose. . . ." The threat delivered in pride's anger is immediately repented, yet it is pride once again in maintaining esteem in his wife's eyes, later in the eyes of his creditors, that motivates him to further deceits. His remorse over Rosa is deep, but pride is deeper. When love for his wife wavers, when her father holds back money, when Rosa is the toast of Europe, pride goads him to offer his love again, still on his terms. The Southern ghosts, which Walter Hines Page will later write about,[2] torment him. He does indeed suffer the "tortures of the damned"—victim of pride, inherited and acquired, he cannot control. He is not unlike Faulkner's anguished young men of Yoknapatawpha County.

The hero of the story, Alfred Royal King, is typed as well, but he never achieves individuality. Introduced to the reader on the first page of the novel, he does not reappear until the story is well under way, when he becomes an ancillary to the plot. He comes "from the land of Puritans"; his manner is "grave." He has wisdom and intelligence beyond his years, and formality and caution govern his relationship with people. When he discovers the circumstances of the girls' birth, he is not so much "disenchanted" as he is embarrassed, since he is placed in the position of having to introduce them to society. Later on, he congratulates himself that he had not joined the girls' father in a business partnership, because "bad customs often lead well-meaning men into wrong paths." He remembers clearly his father's advice: how fortunate he is to be "brought up amid the free churches and free schools of New England." He shares his father's, and region's, abhorrence of slavery—"a cumulative poison in the veins of this Republic . . . [which] would some day act all at once with deadly power." This man of sterling principle, who delivers his settled convictions in settled conversations, is another paragon of virtue, like young Osborne in *The Rebels*. He is a moral prude, whom Mrs. Child asks the reader to admire. That the reader admires him for his stand is without question; that the reader accepts him as a real-life character is another question.

A comment made about Mrs. Delano is far more appropriate when transferred to King: "A perfect specimen of Boston ice." One can hardly imagine a more unlikely marriage than that of King and Rosa—the smug patrician and the olive-skinned octoroon. It could only happen in the pages of a sentimental fiction (and once again, Mrs. Child seems to endorse miscegenation, a "catastrophe" no more acceptable in America in the 1860s than it was in the 1820s). When Rosa tells him that "[her] mother was a slave, and that her daughters inherited her misfortune," King responds with magnanimity although to the modern reader the avowal smacks of sanctimoniousness.

"I am aware of it," he replied. "But that only makes me ashamed of my country. . . . Fortunately, my good father taught me, both by precept and example, to look through the surface of things to the reality. I have seen and heard enough to be convinced that your own heart is noble and pure. Such natures cannot be sullied by the unworthiness of others; they may even be improved by it."

Confidence is the basis of their marriage, yet one perceives a certain irritating vanity in his plan to make Rosa the darling of Boston society. He is noble, he is predictable, he is inestimable as a hero in a romance, but he is an insufferable boor—stiff, cold, arrogant.

Runner-up candidate for insufferable boor is young Fitzgerald, whose transformation from profligate to paragon is no less than remarkable. "Dark-complexioned," he like his mother can pass as white; and he does not consider very long the awful consequences of confessing his race. Such an act is indeed a dilemma, but he really can't lose. If his grandfather disinherits his "nigger" grandson, King stands ready to support him; if his foster mother rejects him, Rosa is filled with a mother's love. Society is no doubt the decisive factor, because society demands respectability. Although his leave-taking of Rosa suggests deceit and relief, his decision is not solely his to make. Of course, he is removed from the scene, to cause no embarrassment to anyone, by a hero's death in the war.

Mrs. Fitzgerald's decision is certainly society's. When she is informed of Rosa's changing the babies, she announces to King that it would be "very disagreeable . . . to have a son who had been brought up among slaves. If I wished to make his acquaintance, I could not do it without exciting a great deal of remark. . . . I have no wish to see him. I have educated a son to my own liking. . . . If you would cease from telling me that there is a stain in his blood, I should never be reminded of it." She does not care what the circumstances of her real son's situation are and reminds King "to keep him at a distance from me . . . for if he resembles Gerald so strongly, it would of course give rise to unpleasant inquiries and remarks." Mrs. Fitzgerald's reaction may have caused some distress to Mrs. Child's readers, nursed as they were on the concept of mother love; but Mrs. Fitzgerald perseveres in her determination, even relieved when her foster son is killed in the war because the knowledge of his birth dies with him. When George Falkner is found, she informs King: "I have but one request to make. It is that this young man may never know he is my son." She contrasts sharply with Mrs. Delano: Mrs. Fitzgerald who sees money and social position as a way to insure respectability in society and Mrs. Delano who regards money and social position as a means to discharge one's responsibility to the human family.

Such coldness of heart strikes deeply at an ugly aspect of human nature, but even more deeply at the credibility of Mrs. Fitzgerald. Presented as a social climber, a society matron, daughter of the nouveau riche to whom appearance is everything, she is precisely the kind of woman Mrs. Child herself could not—indeed, would not—tolerate. The author's peculiar contempt for such butterflies controls the one-dimensional nature of her character, a caricature who has only a role to play.

III *". . . [It] Cost Me Many a Headache . . ."*

Such characters are often the stock-in-trade for the vendor of domestic romances, and the trials and tribulations of the characters

make for moments of triumph and despair for the teary-eyed readers.
Mrs. Child was adept at handling pathos in her shorter fiction, as
"The Kansas Emigrants" dramatically suggests; yet pathos in a 400-
page novel palls the modern reader, probably the more sophisticated
reader in 1867 as well. *A Romance of the Republic* is a period piece,
out of fashion when she wrote it. Its relevance to her day, and to the
present day, is questionable. Given its limitations, what are its merits?

Read in its frame of reference, it is probably a "respectable"
novel—a word incidentally Mrs. Child's reviewers applied to *Hobomok*, *The Rebels*, and *A Romance of the Republic*. The obvious
theme of the story—the travails of slavery—is a continuing reminder
of a grim period in American life. And the specific theme of the
domestic romance—the sins of the fathers—is sounded early in the
story: "So one wrong produces another wrong; and thus frightfully
may we affect the destiny of others while blindly following the lead of
selfishness." The theme secured readers among the devotees of
domestic fiction. The distinguishing feature of Mrs. Child's story is
that she concocts a tale with relevance to a situation peculiar to nineteenth-century America. It is the tragedy of slavery that gives the
novel a stature *The Wide, Wide World* (1850), *The Lamplighter*
(1854), and *St. Elmo* (1866) do not achieve. Mrs. Child's experience
with fugitive slaves, at Isaac Hopper's way station in New York, her
dedication to antislavery, and her belief in equal rights for all classes
of Americans afford the incentive for writing the novel; and it is her
humanitarianism—her theory that "everybody ought to help in doing
the work of the world," as she has a character in the novel say—which
prompts the lesson the book contained, the lesson implanted in the
reader's mind through King's astute, if somewhat pedantic, review of
the facts in the case with young Fitzgerald:

With regard to an alliance with the colored race, I think it would be a more
legitimate source of pride to have descended from that truly great man,
Toussaint L'Overture, who was a full-blooded African, than from that
unprincipled filibuster called William the Conqueror, or from any of his
band of robbers, who transmitted titles of nobility to their posterity. That is
the way I have learned to read history, my young friend, in the plain sunlight
of truth, unchanged by looking at it through the deceptive colored glasses of
conventional prejudice. Only yesterday you would have felt honored to claim
my highly accomplished and noble-minded wife as a near relative. She is as
highly accomplished and noble-minded a lady to-day as she was yesterday.
The only difference is, that to-day you are aware her grandmother had a dark
complexion. No human being can be really stained by anything apart from
his own character.

It is a truth the reader can be reminded of. Perhaps Mrs. Child can be excused for the instrument she used, the domestic romance, to get her lesson across. Slavery was no longer an issue when she wrote the novel; the evil had been abolished; but its tragedy—the incidents in the novel, for example—continued to plague American society.

From one standpoint Mrs. Child's story raises an interesting question. Although one ought to judge a person's worth by his character, society often asks for deception. As Emily Dickinson puts it, tell the truth "but tell it slant." It seems on occasion that social expediency is not only the appropriate but the wise choice to make. As young Fitzgerald says in all frankness, it is not easy in society's eyes "to endure the double stain of illegitimacy and alliance with the colored race." So he keeps his secret. George Falkner marries a black woman; and as the story works itself out, he is truly the victim because he is never told who his parents are. It is social expediency. He is apparently happy in his marriage, yet will he continue to be knowing now that he is "unmixed white." The point is endlessly debatable, the issue remains an individual dilemma. Nevertheless, it is one of the more provocative questions Mrs. Child raises in the novel.

To return, the period piece had very modest sales; it was almost completely ignored by the reviewers. Although one reviewer, addressing his older readers, called it "a timely and interesting book,"[3] many reviewers who might have scanned it simply laid it aside or wrote a one-sentence summary like that in *Peterson's Magazine*: "A very good novel though inferior to 'Miss Ravenal's [*sic*] Conversion from Secession to Loyalty' . . . the best American fiction produced by the war."[4] The novel did not speak to readers in postwar America. Even Mrs. Child was disheartened by its reception, writing a friend: "When I had completed the book, I felt as if I could write another and better novel, and was full of earnestness to set about it, but the apathy of my friends took all the life out of me, and it has made me feel as if I never wanted to put pen to paper again."[5] She wrote out her disappointment to a close friend, Eliza Scudder, who had enjoyed it:

. . . I have been wanting to thank you for your letter about my book. It is by far the most appreciating and cheering letter I have had. Indeed it is the *only* one, that is both warmly sympathetic and discriminating. . . .

. . . [The story] was seething in my head [a year and a half] . . . though less than a year was spent in the actual writing, and copying. Laying the plot, so that it would come out right in all particulars, cost me many a headache, and many wakeful hours in the night. If I could have foreseen the apathy of my friends, I should probably have been too disheartened to have finished the labor.

Next to yours, the letter which has pleased me most was from Joseph Carpenter, the Quaker farmer in New York, in whose family I boarded a long time. He is the Joseph Houseman incidentally introduced in the book. I expected that Friend Joseph would consider so much fol de rol about music, and dancing, and love-affairs, as very unbecoming flightiness in a woman of my years, and that he would administer a gentle rebuke. But, to my surprise, the staid old Quaker wrote[:] "We are all deeply interested in thy *bewitchingly* interesting story. . . . Thee knows I was never very fond of romance or fictions; but thy story is so ingeniously put together, and it appeals so constantly to the best and holiest instincts of our nature, that it can not fail to penetrate the most obdurate heart."

On the whole I consider your letter and Joseph's as ample recompense for the toil of writing the book. Yours is, of course, far more discriminating, but both are *genuine* and *sympathetic*.[6]

Mrs. Child herself clearly offered the final estimate of the novel when she alluded to the letter of the Quaker friend who was the model for one of the characters. *A Romance of the Republic* was a "*bewitchingly* interesting story" and "so ingeniously put together" that it spoke "to the best and holiest instincts in our nature" and could not "fail to penetrate the most obdurate heart." It was an assessment appropriate for the domestic romance of the 1850s. Melodrama, high sentiment, heart appeal were the *modus operandi* of such fictions; such elements were always the fabric of Mrs. Child's imaginative tales. Here again, the real must be fanciful. The reviewers, and the readers, rejected the novel—as the reviewers at least had rejected *The Rebels* forty years before. She was once again embarrassed and "disheartened." Perhaps her chagrin over *The Rebels* was permissible; that novel was a jejune book. Yet *A Romance of the Republic* provided the amphitheater to comment frankly on the world around her, as she was so capable of doing in her nonfiction. Unfortunately, she chose to ignore the responsibility—disregarding the stern advice of the *Literary Gazette* reviewer "to discharge the universal debt . . . [of] making useful books."

CHAPTER 8

Philothea or Frugal Housewife: An Estimate

GRISWOLD in his literary anthologies did on occasion make insightful appraisals of his countrymen and countrywomen. Observing in Mrs. Child's work a "genial sympathy," he concluded that she had brought to it "something of her own spirit, which though meditative and somewhat mystical, [was] always cheerful and radiant."[1] These qualities which Griswold elaborated were the result of a set of fortunate circumstances which shaped her temperament and her personality. One that no doubt made the largest impression was a supreme confidence in the romantic idealism Emerson expressed so well: in particular, the importance of the individual. Another was a provincial pride, serene and conscious, of seeing things—to employ Emily Dickinson's phrase—"New Englandly." Life was measured by standards of conduct and conscience appropriate to her native soil. Another was the heritage of the Puritan forefathers: the adjuration in the writing of such men as Cotton Mather and Jonathan Edwards, and Benjamin Franklin, too, to do good. This concept was her religion, her practicing faith; and she did not need the stimulus of an established church to channel her service to others.[2] Another associated with the same heritage was the Yankee virtue of hard work, the strict necessity of doing "the deadening drudgery of the world."[3] Among these drudgeries was antislavery, which fired a zeal that spilled over into other reforms as well.[4] It was for Mrs. Child a happy blend of the ideal and the real.

Added to these circumstances were a good mind, a fiercely protected independence, a firm determination, a feisty aggressiveness, and a large heart. She was an impassioned spokeswoman; and if, as her friend Lowell said, "her heart at high floods swamps her brain now and then," she saw no other way than to go at a cause with

159

all her energy and intellect. Lowell thoughtfully added: "[the world] is richer for that when the tide ebbs agen."[5]

Such circumstances, formed during her most impressionable years, shaped Mrs. Child's rich intellectual life and her moral awareness. They never altered, they rarely modified. Her life was one piece, and evidence of that life was in all she wrote. Hers was a fixed vision, as she said in one of her poems, to "kindly view/The world that I am passing through." It was a blend again of the ideal and the real.

This vision, of course, creates a real problem when one estimates her purely literary work because the blend becomes unmixed. She once told her friend Lucy Osgood that in her novel reading she preferred those books which gave pleasant and instructive "pictures of society."[6] Aside from Mrs. Stowe, she apparently read little in the fiction of her own American contemporaries. Cooper's novels she no doubt had read, remembering vivid descriptions of the *mise-en-scène* and thrilling adventure. That Cooper was saddened by the exploitation of Eden may have touched her indirectly, as some of the quieter descriptions of nature in her work, particularly in *Letters from New York*, suggests. Since she knew Poe during the New York years, even contributing to the *Broadway Journal*, she no doubt had read some of his "fictions," probably dismissing them, as did many in her generation, as mere fantasies or horror tales. Yet the work of her near neighbors in Concord, with the exception of Emerson, she seemingly ignored altogether: Hawthorne's tales of the inner life, Thoreau's systematic pursuit of the character of nature and the defiantly independent life,[7] and even Melville's stories of men pondering the values of society. Whitman's expansive love of man and woman may have embarrassed her, a reaction perhaps much like Whittier's to the poet's overt sexuality. Nevertheless, these writers were facing squarely in their narratives and verse the real-life issues to which she had devoted her life. They were, in fact, picturing society.

A few months before her death she read Albion W. Tourgee's *A Fool's Errand* and deeply resented the hero, who called himself a fool "for meddling with what did not concern him"; the novel—she wrote a friend—was "so calculated to undermine faith in right principles," because the author scoffed at justice and freedom, that she laid it aside, never "willing to lend it" to anyone.[8] Having worked in the real world, she realized what an oppressive burden it was to guarantee those principles, to root out bigotry and prejudice, to expose chicanery and corruption. Tourgee acknowledged the same fight and grimly despaired of winning. Yet he too was picturing society.

Mrs. Child did not want these candid pictures of society in the fiction she read. Mrs. Stowe's pictures in the regional sketches endorsed Mrs. Child's view of the fictive world—eccentrics or noble abstractions as characters, nostalgia or the backward glance as sentiment, life illuminated or heightened by the sympathetic artist. In the solitude of Wayland, with time she told Lucy Osgood she "willingly set aside [from] household chores" for novel reading,[9] she chose not to read the pictures of society many of her contemporaries were developing; their somber view of life, which she certainly admitted in the workaday world—in *The Frugal Housewife*, in *An Appeal in Favor of That Class of Americans Called Africans*, in *Letters from New York*—she preferred not to admit to fiction. Fiction was the ideal, not the real. Was not *Philothea*, she professed, "romance of the wildest kind"?

The preface to *Philothea* spelled out Mrs. Child's choice:

This volume is purely romance. . . .

The work has been four or five years in its progress; for the practical tendencies of the age, and particularly of the country in which I lived, have so continually forced me into the actual, that my mind has seldom obtained freedom to rise into the ideal.

The hope of extended usefulness has hitherto induced a strong effort to throw myself into the spirit of the times; which is prone to neglect beautiful and fragrant flowers, unless their roots answer for vegetables, and their leaves for herbs. But there have been seasons when my soul felt restless in this bondage . . . so I, for awhile, bid adieu to the substantial fields of utility, to float on the clouds of romance.

The state of mind produced by the alternation of thoughts, in their nature so opposite, was oddly pictured by the following dream, which came before me in my sleep, with all the distinctness of reality, soon after I began to write this work.

I dreamed that I arose early in the morning, and went into my garden, eager to see if the crocus had yet ventured to peep above the ground. To my astonishment, that little spot, which the day before had worn the dreary aspect of winter, was now filled with flowers of every form and hue! With enthusiastic joy I clapped my hands, and called aloud to my husband to come and view the wonders of the garden. He came; and we passed from flower to flower, admiring their marvellous beauty. Then, with a sudden bound, I said, "Now come and see the sunshine on the water!"

We passed to the side of the house, where the full sea presented itself, in all the radiance of morning. And as we looked, lo! there appeared a multitude of boats, with sails like the wings of butterflies—which now opened wide, and reposed on the surface of the water; and now closed, like the motions of weary insects in July;—and ever as they moved, the gorgeous colors glittered in the sunshine.

I exclaimed, "These must have come from fairy land!" As I spoke, suddenly we saw among the boats a multitude of statues, that seemed to be endowed with life; some large and majestic, some of beautiful feminine proportions, and an almost infinite variety of lovely little cherubs. Some were diving, some floating, and some undulating on the surface of the sea; and ever as they rose up, the water-drops glittered like gems on the pure white marble.

We could find no words to express our rapture, while gazing on a scene thus clothed with the beauty of other worlds. As we stood absorbed in the intensity of delight, I heard a noise behind me, and turning round, saw an old woman with a checked apron, who made an awkward courtesy, and said, "Ma'am, I can't afford to let you have that brisket for eight pence a pound."

When I related this dream to my husband, he smiled and said, "The first part of it was dreamed by Philothea; the last, by the Frugal Housewife."

There was never a serious question in Mrs. Child's mind: she was the Frugal Housewife who would gladly labor in the workaday world. But when the "practical tendencies" became more than she could bear for the moment, she escaped to her own fiction like the exquisite *Philothea* or read in her pictures of society. "[H]uman friends disappoint us. . . ," she once wrote her brother Convers, "but these quiet, reliable friends [i.e., books] always remain the same. . . ."[10]

As a realist grappling with the workaday world in her reform efforts, she accepted its contraries; yet the contraries were not subject matter for fiction. The soberer pictures of society her contemporaries were presenting—the sad realities—were subject matter for non-fiction. Fiction was to inspire, to elevate, to reassure: it was to confirm the ideal. The fictive world and the real world were to Mrs. Child two separate worlds with no bridge spanning between. Fiction was unreality. Nonfiction was reality, where with intelligence and moral suasion she argued, analyzed, cajoled, and humored her reader to convince. To the real world she made her commitment. She once told Convers that she would willingly "scour floors and feed pigs," and only on occasion would she "convers[e] with the angels," as much as she liked such an escape.[11]

Surely Mrs. Child was aware of the ambivalence in her view of writing, aware of the romantic vision which limited the development of her purely literary talent. She wrote Convers:

In a literary point of view, I know that I have only a local reputation, "done in water-colors." . . . I am not what I aspired to be in my days of young ambition; but I have become humble enough to be satisfied with the conviction that what I have written has always been written conscientiously; that I have always spoken with sincerity, if not with power. In every direction I see young giants rushing past me, at times pushing me somewhat rudely in their speed, but I am glad to see such strong laborers to plough the land and sow the seed for the coming years.[12]

Not that she could compete with the "young giants"; she probably could not. Her talent was largely undisciplined: her most effective writing was charged with an emotional fervor of the moment, like the *Appeal*; or was written under the pressure of deadlines, like the essays in the *Letters*; or was found in a novel like *Philothea*, some four or five years in progress. Like Cooper she wrote too much, and like Cooper she did not revise. Style in her nonfiction is homely and appropriate; style in her fiction is often tedious and effusive. *Philothea* seems the exception. When she had opportunity to compete with the "young giants," to write a realistic novel about postwar America, *A Romance of the Republic*, she refused it.

Thus for the modern reader Mrs. Child's strongest appeal may well rest with her nonfiction of the workaday world—the domestic manuals, the *Appeal*, and the *Letters*, where real problems are dealt with in clear, hard-hitting, energetic prose. As a journalist and a social critic, and as an humanitarian, Mrs. Child reaches the modern reader—"ready to die for a principle and starve for an idea," her friend Phillips said at her funeral.[13] This is not a bad legacy. Although one may question the nearsightedness of her viewing the world through New England eyes, that world was nevertheless in her impressionable years a land of prophets and doers who spoke of the ideal and also of the real life. Mrs. Child tried in her writing and in her service to others to extend her readers' "unboundable empire" and to make them aware of their capacity.

Appendix

Many of the letters in various collections relate to Mrs. Child's antislavery activities, her work for a variety of humanitarian causes, her opinion of politics and later of the war. Letters to Maria Chapman, editor of the antislavery magazine *Liberty Bell*, and Garrison record her association with the *National Anti-Slavery Standard*: her growing disaffection with her position as editor because of the politics of antislavery and her futile efforts to keep the *Standard* a nonfaction newspaper. The disagreements between Mrs. Child and Mrs. Chapman and Garrison led to a severing of their friendship, renewed apparently only once with Mrs. Chapman when the two women escorted Wendell Phillips, threatened by an angry mob, from an antislavery meeting in Boston. With Garrison correspondence was reestablished in the late 1850s. Mrs. Child had expressed some interest in "spiritual manifestations" and mediums, as had Garrison; and on one occasion she asked him to arrange a seance since the possibility of making contact with the spiritual world "excites a good deal of interest in my mind. I waver between belief and scepticism." She continued: "What I should like above all things would be to have a *mental* question, concerning a subject known only to myself and a departed friend answered. If *that* was answered, I could not resist the conviction that some agency beyond *this* world was engaged in it."[1] On another occasion, speaking of her most recent publication—a manual for the emancipated slaves, *The Freedmen's Book*, she said; "If I live to be ninety years old, and go on at this rate, I shall be the rabidest radical that ever fretted a throne or upset an image."[2] At the time of Child's death, Garrison wrote an encomium to his work in the abolitionist cause, acknowledging his "encouragement and counsel which enabled me to go forward in the work of emancipation." He concluded the letter with a generous compliment about her own work: "Few have written so well and so instructively as yourself."[3] Although the letters are interesting reading for the social historian, they are disappointing to the researcher looking for literary material.

However, there are other letters in which she speaks about herself and offers opinions of writers and writing. Sometimes insightful, the letters are often frank and mildly amusing. To Higginson, who had written asking her opinion of the biographical sketch he had prepared for *Eminent Women of the Age* (1868), she replied: "To tell you the plain truth, friend Higginson, I have never read a single word of it. I have never been able to get up the courage to do it. To read my own biography seems too much like being dissected before I am dead. I have always been talking, more or less, to the public; but I have never talked about *myself*. And I am strangely sensitive about any *personal* introduction to the public."[4] She did, however, offer him her correspondence "as a legacy" after her death, should he be interested in editing a selected volume.[5]

Some years before, she had steadfastly refused information to an editor of a biographical dictionary, insisting that no editor would take "any notice of me, or any other ultra reformer, if he can anyway avoid it."[6] Nor did she like to have her photograph taken, because she did not photograph well. A look of firmness in the face, a set expression in her features, was unflattering. In photographs, she complained to a friend, "my *mouth* does not show itself. The natural result of fighting thirty-five years for my brother Sambo is that my mouth easily assumes a stern, defiant expression; and as I have grown older, the lines have stiffened into that habitual look." All photographs, she added, show "a strong-minded, 'come-if-you-dare' expression."[7]

In fact, she resented intrusions upon her time and her privacy. She once told her brother: "If I were going to Europe, and letters of introduction to Wordsworth, Dickens, etc., were offered me, I would never present them, unless I happened by some accident to receive indications of a wish to be introduced, on the part of the men themselves. What right have I to intrude upon their time, and satisfy my impertinent curiosity by an inventory of their furniture and surroundings?"[8] She complained to friends about an "impudent reporter" who had interviewed her and then "informed the public of the figures in my carpet and the color of my gown, to which he appended some literary dates."[9] When Whittier complained of similar intrusions—the "numerous loafers who come . . . out of mere idle curiosity," he asked her, "How does thee manage to get time to do anything?" She advised him to get a bulldog and a pitchfork.[10]

To Wendell Phillips, she once wrote, perhaps echoing a personal sacrifice as well: "What a poet was lost to the world when you became a reformer! What volumes might have [been] concerning the regal beauty of the Rose and the vestal purity of the Lily of the Valley! But, jesting apart, reform *is* a heavy cart-load of stones for Pegasus to carry; and, do what we will, the world *will* not come right side up."[11]

In a lighter vein she provided a correspondent with a home remedy for dyspepsia: dried dandelion leaves to brew dandelion coffee or dandelion beer. "The mind influences the body, and the body the mind" peculiarly in a case of dyspepsia, she went on to say. "If I were you, I would *seek* whatsoever influences amused or cheered me; and, as far as possible, avoid depressing influences. It will do you good to laugh, or to hurra[h]. If you had the Fremont fever, it would doubtless prove medicinal. Whether shooting a Border Ruffian would help your *digestion* or not, I cannot affirm; but the bullet would doubtless lie heavy on your *mind*, and bring on *spiritual* dyspepsia, which cannot be cured with Dandelion Coffee, or Dandelion Beer."[12]

Humor was often directed against herself. She was relaying one time anecdotes about a local woman who sometimes worked for her. "Mrs. Moulton was here . . . when a package arrived on the 11th of February. 'I wonder,' said she, 'what makes folks send things to you on your birth-day.' . . . I replied, 'I suppose it is because I am a sort of public character.' She looked very much shocked, and said, 'What makes you say *that*?' . . . '[T]he public know me as a writer.' 'Oh, is *that* it?' she inquired. 'I thought a public character was a bad woman.'"[13] On another occasion she told her friend Lucy Osgood that her "right ear remains deaf, for which I am sorry; as I like to hear the right side of things."[14]

All the research that went into her books and articles, she told Parke Godwin, made her without doubt a woman of "vast and varied misinformation, and great moral requirements," adding that such investigations always gave "a terrible shaking to old customs and traditions."[15] After Lincoln's second election, she wrote Godwin that she was delighted in having a rail splitter as president and a tailor as vice-president. "I wish," she added, "a shoe-black could be found worthy to be appointed Secretary of State; and I should be all the more pleased if he were a *black* shoe-black."[16]

She read omnivorously, "galloping" from one book to another, even setting aside her own writing to finish "a *very* remarkable book."[17] One such book was *The History of England* by Macaulay, "surely . . . the prince of historians," who discovered "the true secret of making history interesting." Although she remembered Gibbon's history of Rome clearly from her reading in Norridgewock—his figures "march[ing] across the stage with stately tread, a theatrical procession in correct costumes," she felt as if she was "actually living in the midst of Macaulay's [historical personages]; as if he had met them in the street but yesterday, and should be sure to know them wheresoever they appeared."[18] To another friend she praised "Emerson's book on the English. It seemed . . . wise, discriminating, and eloquent."[19]

Mrs. Stowe's second novel *Dred* was "a great book, and a wise book, and a very *witty* book, and will exercise an immense power over the public mind for good." She was amused by the character Old Tiff, "the *real* hero of the book . . . [who] had a deal of '*human natur*' in him." She was also surprised that the book seemed "to hit *orthodoxy* almost as hard as it hit slavery. What sort of Calvinism is it that young Beecherdom swears by?" she wondered.[20] Confessing on another occasion that she was "blindly partial to Mrs. Stowe's writing," she "greatly like[d]" *The Pearl of Orr's Island*—not only the descriptions of childhood but the characters too, "all wonderfully true to human nature; especially in making the sinners so much more entertaining than the saints." Although the book was not as exciting as *Uncle Tom's Cabin* and *Dred*, "because the nature of the subject does not admit it," as a literary piece, it was superior—"a charming book; so fresh and natural." She observed too the difference between the characters she and her generation of writers had created and those in the fiction of younger writers—a difference between "prim old portraits" of the romancers and "life-like photographs" of the realists.[21] Although she noted the difference, Mrs. Child apparently preferred "portraits" in the stories she was still writing.

Among contemporary writers in Europe she had great respect for George Sand, referring to her as "my twin sister." Although Mrs. Child did not "presume to claim such close affinity with her remarkable genius," nevertheless "the grain of the wood is certainly the same in both of us." She added, however, a grateful aside: "She has lived in a very artificial and corrupt state of society; while I, thank God, was born in New England. . . ."[22] A similar respect she had for George Eliot, "no writer since Shakespeare [having] had such insight into human nature"; yet she used her insight, Mrs. Child believed, to far better purpose: "so thoroughly is her soul pervaded by loving sympathy for the *common* people." "Aristocracy is *always* my aversion," she wrote her friend Lucy Osgood, "whether in the form of English noble, Southern planter, or Boston respectable. . . . I say truly with Eppie, in *Silas Marner*, 'I like the working-people; I like their ways.'"[23]

She lamented that good novels, like those of Mrs. Stowe, George Sand, and George Eliot, were so scarce and often asked her friends to

send her "any *good* novel in paper covers, which you have done with
reading." Yet she warned them that the books must have merit; she
was not "entertained by fourth and fifth-rate company . . . prefer[ring] the solitude of my own thoughts to poor company."[24]

However, leisure-time reading was a precious commodity; the
Puritan ethic of up-and-doing hung heavily over her.[25] If it was not
writing for a particular cause, she confessed to a friend, it was "too
many puddings to make and garments to mend." One time she was
studying German with her husband—"a hard knot, which I have
made a vow to disentangle before I have done with it. It 'raises my
dander' to have anything defy me to master it. . . . If you ask me what
for, I can't tell you, except that I don't like to be beaten by anything,
and I do like to keep my mind in exercise."[26] Toil, whether mental or
physical, was a part of her life; and she managed whatever emergency
of the moment, even though it deprived her of dearer tasks. To her
niece Sarah Parson she was sympathetic when the young woman was
faced with moving once again. "It is a dreary business, and very
wearisome; as I know by experience; having moved twenty one times,
and with the burden of the work all on my own shoulders. How I *have*
papered and patched, and altered carpets, and cleaned off rust and
mould from things that had been packed! I feel like crying,
sometimes, when I think how much of life has been expended in that
way, while my mind was hungry for other pursuits."[27]

To the same niece she wrote some years later, when she was
confined to the house in Wayland, not to send her any more sermons
to read, because she was already "inundated," commenting that "in
one way or another, my soul is pretty well saturated with radical
ideas." One detects, however, a shadow of perplexity in the woman
who had all her life espoused liberality of belief, even concern for
those more conservative who died not share her views.

Well, the old *must* perish, in order that the new may grow. But it is rather sad
to see a time-honored faith, which men have spent ages in building up,
tottering to its fall, by reason of the earthquake cracking asunder its
foundation. The old Platonists, who saw a spiritual significance in their
ancient faith, must have felt this sadness, when they saw their magnificent
temples deserted, for the worship of an unknown foreigner, who had [been]
put to death in Judea. What is coming toward *us* to supplant St. Peters and
St. Pauls?[28]

The letters contain character sketches of friends and acquaintances, political figures and national leaders—amusing at times,
candid, sharp, and caustic, when she saw such people as agents of

tyranny or injustice or chicanery: proslavery advocates, militant abolitionists, Southern congressmen, Webster (after his defection). She was highly critical of Lincoln during the early years of the war, believing him to be the pawn of his Secretary of State, William H. Seward. Charles Sumner, a personal friend who had credited her with the facts and statistics he had used in his antislavery speeches in the Senate, was understandably praised. Again such portraits are more interesting to the social historian.

Of greater interest to the student of literature is her opinion of literary contemporaries. Many of the transcendentalists—themselves champions of antislavery—she greatly admired: Parker, the Channings, Ripley. She did not always agree with their methods and projects, telling her friend Loring at one time that he need not trouble himself about her joining "Ripley's Community" at Brook Farm. "I have had quite enough of hard work without any pay, in the course of my life."[29] She frequently attended her friend Emerson's lectures, but she told her husband after one such evening: "It had his usual characteristics, profound and striking sayings, mystical Pantheism, etc., very agreeable to listen to, but, as usual, unreportable."[30] On another occasion, when she was living in New York, Emerson and James Russell Lowell came to call, Emerson giving her tickets for the lecture series he was currently offering. The lectures, she told Loring, were as "refreshing as a glass of soda-water; but as usual, not satisfactory." She also resented Emerson's reluctance to enter the antislavery ranks; it was not "manly" of him.[31] She often felt exasperation with Emerson. His lectures and his essays were indeed inspiring; yet their message seemed not to take into account the problems and the pressures of the everyday world. In response to *Essays: Second Series*, which Emerson had sent her, she told a friend:

. . . As usual, it is full of deep and original sayings, and touches of exceeding beauty. But, as usual, it takes away my strength, and makes me uncertain whether to hang myself or my gown over a chair. What is the use of telling us that everything is "scene-painting and counterfeit," that nothing is real, that everything eludes us? That no single thing in life keeps the promise it makes? Or, if any keeps it, keeps it like the witches to Macbeth? Enough of this conviction is forced upon us by experience, without having it echoed in literature.[32]

Her annoyance with Emerson was the fact that slavery was a real issue—not "counterfeit"—and he stubbornly refused to enlist in the humanitarian cause. On another occasion, discussing his essays with her friend Loring, she confessed that she was often dissatisfied with

his views "so far as I understand them, but I am right well satisfied
that he should utter them." In reference to an idea in a specific essay,
perhaps "The American Scholar," she continued:

. . . Does it mean anything more or less than this: that when we seek to be led
by the experience and opinions of others, rather than by the dictates of our
own souls, we gain knowledge; but that virtue springs only from a reverent
listening to the voice within, and a resolute obedience to its counsels? I
generally receive *some* idea from what Emerson says; but . . . [he] reminds
me of what Lady Morgan said of Madame de Stael: "There is in her
composition something of the Delphic priestess. It has the energy and
inspiration, and the disorder. Sometimes mystic, not always intelligible, we
still blame the *God* rather than the Oracle; and wish that she were less
inspired, or we more intelligent."[33]

Bronson Alcott amused her. She related an anecdote to Lucy
Osgood, when she met him and Elizabeth Peabody "in the cars" to
Boston: "He spent most of the time in the cars, and in Boston streets,
defining for me what he conceived to be the distinction between
'personality' and 'individuality'; but when I parted from him I was not
very clear in my mind whether I was a person or an individual."[34] She
liked Mrs. Alcott, "a friend of my youth," and the daughters, particularly Louisa May and May Abba, her artist sister. Even though
"some people complain that they are brusque," she told a correspondent, "it is merely because they are very straightforward and
sincere. They have a Christian hatred of lionizing; and the Leo
Hunters are a very numerous and impertinent family." She admired
in them a quality she herself cherished: "They don't like conventional
fetters any better than I do."

There have been many attempts to saddle and bridle me, and teach me to
keep step in respectable processions; but they have never got the lasso over
my neck yet, and "old hoss" as I am now, if I see the lasso in the air, I snort
and gallop off, determined to be a free horse to the last, and put up with the
consequent lack of grooming and stabling.[35]

The most extensive correspondence with a literary contemporary
was with Whittier, whom she referred to as "one of the best
benefactors of my soul."[36] It was a friendship beginning in Boston, in
Convers's study, where Whittier and the young men from Harvard
had gathered. It was a friendship based on mutual respect and mutual
interests and mutual admiration.[37] They shared the abolitionist cause
together and what they believed to be Lincoln's myopic view of

the war. Early in the conflict she wrote him excitedly, prevailing upon him to write a song for the soldiers, much like "John Brown's Body," which had become a rallying song of the abolitionists. "Nothing on earth," she was convinced, "has such effect on the popular heart as Songs, which the soldiers would take up with enthusiasm. . . ." She then supplied him with an anecdote which an antislavery friend had passed on to her. A sentinel stopped "a lordly Virginian" in his carriage driven by his slave and demanded his passport. The Virginian directed his slave to give the pass to the "greasy mechanic," the sentinel from the North, who upon receiving it positioned the slave behind him. "Now *you* can turn back," said the sentinel. The Virginian protested, and the sentinel coolly asked, "Where *is* your order?" "My servant just gave it to you." "Oh," replied the sentinel, "that was an order to pass only *one*, and he has already gone with it." Thus, Mrs. Child delightedly informed the poet, the "haughty Southerner" lost not only his slave to freedom but his pass through enemy lines. "If the soldiers only *had* [some such] song, to some spirit-stirring tune," she went on to say, "proclaiming what they went to fight for. . . ."[38] Whittier apparently never incorporated the anecdote into a "song," yet particularly inspiring verse for the war he did write.

She often sent him copies of her verses, and he reciprocated by sending her copies of his poems, which she and her husband greatly enjoyed. "What a glorious, blessed gift is this gift of song, with which you are so lavishly endowed," she declared in one letter. "Who can calculate its influence, which you exert always for good!" Child, himself a versifier several ranks below his wife's rather feeble efforts, had written for the poet a couplet, which Mrs. Child enclosed in the letter.

> One bugle-note from Whittier's pen
> Is worth at least ten thousand men.[39]

The humanitarianism that motivated them both is eloquently expressed in a letter to Whittier a few years after the war. In reference to a naturalization bill before Congress, she applauded Sumner's efforts to have the word *white* stricken from it, so that Orientals could freely emigrate to the country. She went on to say: "I dislike and despise this petty 'Native American' feeling. God kept this continent hidden for centuries to make it a High School for all the nations. Let us fulfil [sic] the glorious mission, and be thankful. I welcome the Chinese. Their industry and patience will prove a blessing to this country. Let them build temples to Buddha, if they like. They would be scarcely more foreign to our thoughts and feelings than Altars to the Virgin Mary."[40]

Mrs. Child admired Whitter's talent, and he hers, apparently; nearly every letter between them carried some word of praise. "[I]t seems as if you were spiritually near me," she wrote, very late in life, "when I read what you write. I say to myself, That is just what *I* should write, if I had been born a poet. . . . It is my opinion that you, by some spiritual legerdemain, steal my thoughts and string them into verse."[41]

Notes and References

Preface

1. It is frequently suggested that James had Elizabeth Peabody in mind when he drew the portrait of Miss Birdseye. However, Mrs. Child is a more likely candidate.

2. Among unpublished works are these: Lloyd C. Taylor's dissertation, "To Make Men Free: An Interpretive Study of Lydia Maria Child" (Lehigh University, 1956); Berenice G. Lamberton's thesis, "A Biography of Lydia Maria Child" (University of Maryland, 1953); Geoffrey P. Roever's thesis, "One Woman's Quest for Freedom" (Harvard University, 1974).

3. George F. Whicher, *Literary History of the United States*, rev. ed., ed. Robert E. Spiller et al. (New York, 1953), p. 565.

4. Tremaine McDowell, ibid., p. 292.

Chapter One

1. She cites *Paradise Lost*, Book IV, 11. 635–38, where Eve says:

> My author and disposer, what thou bid'st
> Unargu'd I obey; so God ordains.
> God is thy law, thou mine; to know no more
> Is woman's happiest knowledge, and her praise.

2. *Letters of Lydia Maria Child* (Boston, 1882; rpt. New York, 1969), p. 1. Letter to Convers Francis dated Norridgewock, June 5, 1817. Hereafter, *Letters*, with page reference.

3. Helene G. Baer, *The Heart Is Like Heaven: The Life of Lydia Maria Child* (Philadelphia, 1964), p. 20. I am indebted to Mrs. Baer's work for some of the factual information in this chapter.

4. Thomas Wentworth Higginson, *Contemporaries* (Cambridge, Mass., 1900; rpt. Upper Saddle River, N.J., 1970), p. 112.

5. *The Juvenile Miscellany* Third Series, 6 (July-August 1834): 323.

6. *Letters*, p. 4. Letter to Convers Francis dated Norridgewock, November 21, 1819.

7. Ibid., p. 3. Letter to Convers Francis dated [Norridgewock], February 3, 1819.

8. Ibid., pp. 4-5. Letter to Convers Francis dated Norridgewock, December 26, 1819. Reference is to John Neal, probably his narrative poem "Battle of Niagara" (1818).

9. Ibid., p. 5. Letter to Convers Francis dated Winslow [Maine], March 12, 1820.

10. Ibid., pp. 7-8. Letter to Convers Francis dated Gardiner, May 31, 1820.

11. Cited in Baer, p. 39.

12. "The Rebels, or Boston before the Revolution," *United States Literary Gazette* 3 (January 15, 1826): 293.

13. *Letters*, pp. 9-10. Letter to a Rev. Allyn dated Watertown, September 28, 1826.

14. "Autobiography," p. 1, in Cornell University Library.

15. Ibid., p. 2.

16. Ibid., p. 3. A page from Child's journal has been clipped and pasted into the autobiographical fragment. Hence some words are not clearly decipherable.

17. Cited in Baer, p. 49.

18. "Autobiography," pp. 5-6. George T. Curtis, whose mother's home was opened to Maria and Child during their courtship, recalled another version of the proposal: ". . . About nine o'clock, he rode out of Boston on horseback, and instead of leaving his horse at a livery-stable, he tied him by his bridle rein to a post at my mother's front door, which opened directly on the street . . . and then he came into the parlor to see Miss Francis. My mother, she believed that the *Dénouement* had come, or was coming, retired to her chamber, and sent me to bed, Mr. Child pressed his suit most earnestly. The lady was a long time in making up her mind. Ten o'clock came, then eleven, then twelve. The horse, grown impatient and no doubt very cold and hungry, repeatedly put his forefoot upon the wooden steps and stamped away, as much as to say, 'Take me home, or let me go by myself.' Mr. Child went out once or twice to pacify him, then returned, and went on with the momentous conversation. At last, just as the clock was on the stroke of one, he went. Miss Francis, when the horse's foot-falls ceased to be heard, rushed to my mother's room, and told her that she was engaged to Mr. Child." "Reminiscences of N. P. Willis and Lydia Maria Child," *Harper's New Monthly Magazine* 81 (October 1890): 719-20.

19. "Autobiography," p. 6.

20. Ibid., p. 7.

21. The "Autobiography" describes one such dwelling on "a pier for boats, at Cottage Place, in Boston [now Roxbury], where we lived from 1832 to 1835, in a very small cottage, with a *very* small garden *filled* with flowers; the sea dashed under the windows, and was often sparkling with moon-beams when we went to bed. We used to call the humble little home Le Paradis des Pauvres." [n.p.].

22. Curtis, p. 720.

23. *Letters*, pp. 10-11. Letter to David L. Child dated Phillips Beach [Massachusetts], August 8, 1830.

24. *Biographies of Lady Russell and Madame Guion* (1832), *Biographies of Madame de Stael and Madame Roland* (1832), *Biographies of Good Wives* (1833).

25. Letter to Samuel J. May dated Wayland, September 29, 1867, in Cornell University Library. Hereafter, referred to as CU. Mrs. Child devoted an essay in *Letters from New York*, Second Series (1845) to Hannah Adams, author of several books on religious history, among them *The Truth and Excellence of the Christian Religion* (1804) and *The History of the Jews* (1812).

26. *Letters*, p. 17. Letter to Convers Francis dated New Rochelle, September 25, 1835.

27. Letter to Samuel J. May dated Wayland, September 29, 1867, in CU. Mrs. Child added: "I don't think I lost so much 'per annum' by espousing the anti-slavery cause. At all events, I think the indefinite statement that my literary prospects were much injured by it would have been better."

28. "Works of Mrs. Child," *North American Review* 37 (July 1833): 139.

29. Apparently the historian George Bancroft, or so Mrs. Child reported to Ellis G. Loring. Letter to Ellis G. Loring dated Northampton, December 5, 1838, in New York Public Library. Hereafter, referred to as NYP.

30. She wrote a correspondent who was enlisting her support in forming a women's emancipation society: "In this, and all other matters, each one must act in freedom, according to his own perceptions of right and wrong, advisable or unadvisable—being, first of all things, careful that he is not guided by selfishness." Letter to Elizabeth Phelps dated[?], January 1834, in Boston Public Library. Hereafter, referred to as BP.

31. *United States Literary Gazette*, p. 292.

32. *Letters*, pp. 21–22. Letter to Convers Francis dated Boston, October 25, 1836.

33. Letter to Ellis G. Loring dated Northampton, December 5, 1838, in NYP.

34. "Autobiography," p. 13.

35. Cited in Baer, p. 121.

36. *Letters*, pp. 29–30. Letter to Convers Francis dated Northampton, July 12, 1838.

37. Ibid., pp. 42–43. Letter to E[lizabeth] Pierce dated New York, May 27, 1841.

38. Letter to Ellis G. Loring dated New York, September 21, 1841, in NYP.

39. "I have not liked the term 'non-resistance,' for I have felt that the instinct for fighting was not wrong," she wrote Loring; "that it only needed to be *rightly directed*. Resist we ought, and that with all our might. The irrationality lies in stabbing and strangling *bodies* to win *souls*. We fight spiritual evils with material weapons." Letter to Ellis G. Loring dated New York, March 9, 1842, in NYP.

40. Letter to Ellis G. Loring dated New York, August 11, 1841, in NYP.

41. Letter to Ellis G. Loring dated New York, September 28 [1841], in NYP.

42. Letter to Maria Chapman dated New York, May 11 [1842], in BP.

43. Letter to Ellis G. Loring dated New York, March 6, 1843, in NYP.

44. Ibid.

45. "You have no idea what a 'd—iteration' is the life of an editor," she complained to Loring. Letter to Ellis G. Loring dated New York, August 11, 1841, in NYP.

46. Letter to Ellis G. Loring dated New York, July 27, 1841, in NYP.

47. Letter to Ellis G. Loring dated New York, August 11, 1841, in NYP.

48. "It was," she told Loring, "a beggarly business to work for benevolent societies." Letter to Ellis G. Loring dated New York, September 21, 1841, in NYP.

49. Letter to Ellis G. Loring dated [New York], October 1842, in NYP.

50. David L. Child to William Lloyd Garrison dated Northampton, May 18, 1843, in BP.

51. Letter to Ellis G. Loring dated New York, January 25, 1842, in NYP.

52. Cited in Baer, p. 160.

53. Letter to Ellis G. Loring dated New York, June 16, 1843, in NYP.

54. William Ellery Channing wrote: "I have been delighted to see in your 'Letters from New York' such sure marks of a fresh, living, hopeful spirit; to see that the flow of genial noble feeling has been in no degree checked by the outward discouragements of life." *Letters*, p. 45. William Ellery Channing to Lydia Maria Child dated [Boston], December 21, 1841.

55. Letter to Rufus W. Griswold dated New York, May 1, 1843, in BP.

56. The children's books and the contributions to periodicals, among them *The Columbian Lady's and Gentleman's Magazine* and *The Union Magazine of Literature and Art*, kept the readers satisfied. The pieces were similar to those by the editor of the *Union*, Mrs. Caroline M. Kirkland— moralistic, sentimental, tender: essays on temperance, nature, education, even domestic bliss.

57. *Woman in the Nineteenth Century* in *Margaret Fuller: Essays on American Life and Letters*, ed. Joel Myerson (New Haven, 1978), pp. 185–86.

58. Cited in Baer, p. 190.

59. Ibid., p. 203.

60. "Autobiography," p. 13.

61. Letter to Lucy Osgood dated Wayland, May 11, 1856, in CU. Lucy Osgood and her sister, the poet Frances Osgood, were daughters of an Unitarian minister.

62. Ibid.

63. Letter to Lucy Osgood dated New York, June 28, 1846, in CU.

64. Letter to Lucy Osgood dated Wayland, May 11, 1856, in CU.

65. Letter to Lucy Osgood dated Wayland, February 6, 1859, in CU.

66. Fragment to Lucy Osgood, n.d., in CU.

67. Cited in Baer, p. 249.

68. Letter to [Anne Weston?] dated Wayland, November 28, 1859, in BP. A number of letters of "abuse" were subsequently exchanged between Mrs. Child and Mrs. M. J. C. Mason, wife of the author of the Fugitive Slave

Law—a correspondence of vilification on both sides. Greeley also printed this correspondence in the *Tribune*. The Child-Wise correspondence and the Child-Mason correspondence are reprinted in *Letters*, pp. 103–37.

69. Letter to [Anne Weston?] dated [Wayland], December 22, 1859, in BP.

70. She wrote Lucy Osgood on another occasion: "I hope you will pardon me for being so ready to rear my 'porcupine quills.' You must remember what a deaf community we 'old abolitionists' have been preaching to, this quarter of a century. . . . I rear my quills, in the same way, for *any* class that I deem oppressed. I always rebuke those that sneer at the *Jews*, or call an Irishman *Paddy*." Letter to Lucy Osgood dated Wayland, January 16, 1859, in CU.

71. Letter to Samuel J. May dated [Wayland], February 26, 1860, in BP.

72. "Autobiography," p. 16.

73. For the first time in their twenty-eight years of married life, they were free of debt. Mrs. Child made modest improvements in the pre-Revolutionary structure with the cash settlement she received. Child did not question his wife's distribution of the money, although he had a legal right to do so. He did not question his wife's management of their yearly incomes, although he had a legal right to do so. The fact that women had so few rights under the law was a continual irritation to Mrs. Child. She wrote Loring the year of her father's death: "David has signed my will and I have sealed it up and put it away. It excited my towering indignation to think it was necessary for him to sign it. . . . I was indignant for womankind made chattels personal from the beginning of time, perpetually insulted by literature, law, and custom. The very phrases used with regard to us are abominable. 'Dead in the law,' 'Femme couverte.' How I detest such language! I must come out with a broadside on that subject before I die. If I don't, I shall walk and rap afterward." *Letters*, p. 74. Letter to Ellis G. Loring dated Wayland, February 24, 1856.

74. Cited in Baer, p. 263.

75. Letter to Lucy Searle dated Wayland, December 21, 1862, in CU.

76. Fragment to [Sarah Shaw] dated 1861, in CU.

77. Letter to Lucy Osgood dated Wayland, December 21, 1862, in CU.

78. Fragment to [Sarah Shaw] dated 1861, in CU.

79. Letter to [?] dated [Wayland], July 14, 1861, in CU.

80. Letter to Sarah Shaw dated Wayland, June 9, 1862, in NYP.

81. Letter to Lucy Searle dated Wayland, August 22, 1861, in CU.

82. Letter to Lucy Osgood dated Wayland, January 29, 1865, in CU.

83. Fragment to Sarah Shaw dated 1865, in CU.

84. She wrote Convers some years earlier: ". . . I know that I have only a local reputation, 'done in water-colors.'" *Letters*, p. 98. Letter to Convers Francis dated Wayland, August 8, 1858.

85. Cited in Baer, p. 303.

86. *Letters*, p. 261. Letter to Mrs. S.S. Russell dated Wayland, September 23, 1880.

87. "Autobiography," n.p.

88. *Letters*, p. 268. Reprinted as an Appendix is Phillips' funeral eulogy.

Chapter Two

1. [John G. Palfrey], "Yamoyden, a tale of the wars of king Philip, in six cantos," *North American Review* 12 (April 1821): 480, 484.

2. Higginson, p. 113.

3. Ibid., p. 115.

4. Rufus W. Griswold, *Prose Writers of America*, rev. ed. (Philadelphia, 1870), p. 426.

5. "Hobomok, A Tale of Early Times." *United States Literary Gazette* 1 (June 15, 1824): 71.

6. "Religion ought to be taught, not forced." "Heresy must be untaught, not permitted."

7. "Let the Jew believe, not I."

8. "I perceive that an immense good has been done to the human race by *religion*," Mrs. Child wrote a friend some years later, ". . . [but] what good has been done by *doctrines* concerning God and the soul, I am yet to learn." Letter to Lucy Osgood dated Wayland, May 11, 1856, in CU.

9. "Recent American Novels: Hobomok, A Tale of Early Times," *North American Review* 21 (July 1825): 95.

10. John Collier and James Hopkins live in Plymouth; hence, the Plymouth elders hear the case.

11. *North American*, p. 87.

12. Ibid., p. 94.

Chapter Three

1. "The Rebels, or Boston before the Revolution," *North American Review* 22 (April 1826): 402.

2. Ibid., pp. 401–402.

3. "The Rebels, or Boston before the Revolution," *United States Literary Gazette* 3 (June 15, 1826): 293.

4. *North American*, p. 401.

5. Higginson, p. 115.

6. *Literary Gazette*, p. 292.

7. Ibid.

8. Ibid.

9. *North American*, p. 402.

10. *Literary Gazette*, p. 292.

11. *North American*, p. 403.

12. Ibid., p. 401.

13. Ibid., p. 403.

14. *North American*, p. 403.

15. Higginson recalls that *The Rebels* "had in one respect a remarkable success. It contained an imaginary sermon by Whitefield and an imaginary

speech by James Otis. Both of these were soon transplanted into 'School Readers' and books on declamation, and the latter, at least, soon passed for a piece of genuine revolutionary eloquence." Higginson, p. 115.

16. *North American*, p. 401.

17. *Literary Gazette*, p. 293.

18. Alexander Cowie, *The Rise of the American Novel* (New York, 1948), p. 181.

Chapter Four

1. The second edition is entitled *Philothea: A Grecian Romance* (1845).

2. *"Philothea, a Romance," North American Review* 44 (January 1837): 85.

3. "Philothea; a Romance," *American Monthly Magazine* N.S. 2 (October 1836): 409.

4. Edgar Allan Poe, "Philothea: A Romance," *Southern Literary Messenger* 2 (September 1836): 259, 262. Poe reprinted the review in *Broadway Journal* 1 (May 31, 1845): 342–45, when the second edition was published.

5. Griswold, p. 427.

6. Evert A. and George L. Duyckinck, *The Cyclopaedia of American Literature* (Philadelphia, 1875), II, 211.

7. Baer, p. 84.

8. "Philothea. A Romance," *The Knickerbocker, or New-York Monthly Magazine* 8 (September 1836): 370.

9. Among others, Kenneth W. Cameron considers it a transcendental novel. His edition is entitled *Philothea, or Plato against Epicurus: A Novel of the Transcendental Movement in New England* (Hartford, Conn., 1975).

10. She also follows in broad outline Landor's history of Pericles, Aspasia, and their friends, with one exception: Alcibiades is more the pronounced hedonist in Mrs. Child's romance.

11. Frances Wright, *A Few Days in Athens* (New York, 1835), p. 152.

12. Mrs. Child wrote in an end-note to the novel: "If there are errors in the application of Greek names and phrases, my excuse must be an entire want of knowledge in the classical languages. But, like the ignoramus in the Old Drama, I can boast, 'Though I *speak* no Greek, I love the *sound* on't.'"

13. Mrs. Child's use of Landor's imaginary letters is particularly apparent in the trial scene of the novel, where Pericles pleads before the citizens' court that charges against Aspasia should be dropped. Cf. Walter Savage Landor, "Letters of Pericles and Aspasia" in Vol. 5 of *The Works and Life of Walter Savage Landor* (London, 1876).

14. Anaxagoras says in Landor's imaginary letters: ". . . [Pericles] thinks that power over others is better than power over himself." Landor, V, 375.

15. "Scholars will say this trial ought to have been before the Areopagus. But I was induced to choose popular assemblies, for the sake of more

freedom of description, and to avoid a repetition of what has been so often described. . . ." Mrs. Child's note.

16. "Anaxagoras is supposed to have been the first who taught the doctrine of one God, under the name of One Universal Mind." Mrs. Child's note.

17. As Cameron suggests, Aspasia may well be modeled after the free-love devotee, Frances Wright.

18. See Marquis James, *The Life of Andrew Jackson* (Indianapolis, 1938), pp. 508–19 passim.

19. Duyckinck, II, 211.

20. Anaxagoras says to Plato: "Ah, Plato! Plato! where will you find materials for your ideal republic?" The philosopher answers: "In an ideal Atlantis; or perchance in the fabled groves of Argive Hera, where the wild beasts are tamed—the deer and the wolf lie down together—and the weak animal finds refuge from his powerful pursuer. But the principle of a republic is none the less true, because mortals make themselves unworthy to receive it. The best doctrines become the worst, when they are used to evil purposes. Where a love of power is the ruling object, the tendency is corruption. . . ."

21. *American Monthly Magazine*, p. 409.

22. Griswold complained that "the author seems hardly to have caught the antique spirit: the philosophical tone of *Philothea* reminds us quite as much of Boston as of Athens." Griswold, p. 427.

23. *North American*, p. 83.

24. Anaxagoras (500?–429 B.C.) and Pericles (495?–429 B.C.) are contemporaries; Alcibiades (450?–404 B.C.) is a near contemporary; Plato (427–347 B.C.) plainly is not.

25. Carl Van Doren, *The Cambridge History of American Literature* (New York, 1943), I, 320.

26. Van Wyck Brooks, *The Flowering of New England* (New York, 1957), p. 196.

27. For the modern researcher interested in psychoanalysis, there are in the autobiographical fragment revealing passages about the sexual life, or apparent lack of it, between the Childs. "We always continued child-like in our love-making," Mrs. Child wrote. And in another passage in the autobiographical fragment, she added: "He was the most loving husband God ever bestowed upon woman. In his old age, he was as affectionate and devoted as he was when he was the lover of my youth; nay, he manifested even more tenderness. He was often singing: 'There's nothing half so sweet in life, / As Love's *old* dream.' Very often when he passed by me, he would lay his hand softly on my head, and murmur: 'Carum Caput!' . . . Once, when he said, 'I wish, for *your* sake, dear, that I were as rich as Croesus,' I answered, 'You *are* Croesus; for you are King of *Lydia*.' How often he used to quote that!" "Autobiography," pp. 8, 13–14.

28. Higginson, pp. 124–25.

29. The extracts are reproduced in Cameron, pp. 135–36.

30. Cited in Higginson, p. 125.

Chapter Five

1. Fragment to Lucy Osgood, n.d., in CU.

2. The first edition of 1,500 copies sold out in four months, and 300 copies were backordered. "I have had much better luck with it than I expected," Mrs. Child wrote a correspondent. Letter to Ellis G. Loring dated New York, October 25 [1843], in NYP.

3. Ralph Waldo Emerson, "Letters from New York," *Dial* 4 (January 1844): 407.

4. "Letters from New York," *United States Magazine and Democratic Review* 13 (October 1843): 443. A British reviewer was equally enthusiastic: "Over all Mrs. Child's writing is thrown the charm of a lively fancy and affectionate disposition. . . . Looking at the world . . . in a kindly and considerate spirit, she sees much to admire and commend, much to be thankful for . . . the whole [book] breathing a spirit of chivalric benevolence . . . outpourings of a heart which speak in sincerity, and with a love of human kind." "Mrs. Child's *Letters from New York*," *Chambers's Edinburgh Journal*, No. 617 (November 25, 1843): 358.

5. "Letters from New-York," *Knickerbocker* 22 (October 1843): 374.

6. "Mrs. Child's *Letters from New York*," *Athenaeum*, No. 798 (October 14, 1843): 977.

7. There is a fragment of a letter from Dickens to Mrs. Child on the subject of temperance, in which he staunchly defends his "cheerful glass of wine." Charles Dickens to Lydia Maria Child dated Regents Park, December 28, 1842, in BP.

8. On another occasion she visited an orphanage, "supported by the public. It gives [the children] wholesome food, comfortable clothing, and the common rudiments of education. For this it deserves praise. But the aliment which the spirit craves, the *public* has not to give. The young heart asks for *love*, yearns for love—but its own echo returns to it through empty halls, instead of answer."

9. Griswold, p. 427.

10. *Knickerbocker*, p. 374.

11. *Democratic Review*, p. 443.

12. "The holy teacher of Nazareth tells us to *attract* a man toward goodness by giving him a coat, if he needs it, instead of going to law to *punish* him for taking a cloak. This is what I mean by the Demon Penalty and the Angel Attraction. I believe whips and prisons are the discipline of the Devil, and make society worse, instead of better. You will ask the common question, How can we do without them? We cannot *now*; but we ought all to be working toward *producing* a state of things when it *can* be done. One thing is certain; whenever it is *practicable*, it will be *safe*." Fragment to Lucy Osgood, n.d., in CU.

13. John C. Colt—brother of the Hartford, Connecticut, firearms manufacturer Samuel Colt—was guilty of the crime. He had stabbed a printer, hacked up his body, salted the pieces, stuffed them in a trunk, and shipped the

trunk to himself under an assumed name to New Orleans. After Colt's suicide, Mrs. Child turned her attention to his common-law wife and infant son, writing John S. Dwight at Brook Farm in their behalf: ". . . She is almost heart-broken, and longs for seclusion, soothing influences, and instruction [in] how to do her duty. If you, with your large and liberal views, and your clear perception of human brotherhood, if *you*, at West Roxbury, reject her, where, in the name of our common Father, *can* I find a shelter for her poor storm-pelted heart?" Letter to John S. Dwight dated New York, December 1, 1842, in BP.

14. Slavery, the most abhorrent evil society condoned—and Mrs. Child's most urgent social reform—is not discussed in *Letters* at all, no doubt because her editorials in the *National Anti-Slavery Standard* were addressed to this oppressive wrong.

15. In a letter many years later she despaired for the plight of "our poor Indians." "How wickedly they have been treated and *are* treated. The agents and the soldiers of the U.S. cheat them in every way, abuse them in every way, violate their wives and daughters before their eyes, and if they become maddened to some act of retaliation, straightway an army is sent for to put down the Indians, on the charge that the savages are murdering white people. *We* have attended peculiarly to the wrongs of the negroes, and it seems to *us* as if they were *peculiarly* tormented; and indeed I think their condition *is* some degrees worse than any other victims of human despotism, but everywhere we look, the same problem presents itself—why *is* there so much suffering and so much wrong?" Letter to Sarah Shaw dated Wayland 1864, in CU.

16. *Letters and Journals of Thomas Wentworth Higginson*, ed. Mary Thacher Higginson (New York, 1969), p. 82.

17. "Letters from New-York, Second Series," *Knickerbocker* 25 (June 1845): 548. Excerpts from the essay on music appeared in *New York Mirror* 3 (October 11, 1845): 9.

18. Edgar Allan Poe, "Letters from New York, Second Series," *Broadway Journal* 1 (May 10, 1845): 296.

19. "The Great Idea, which Swedenborg revealed to my soul," she wrote her brother Convers about this time, "was the intimate and perpetual union between the spiritual and natural world. So deeply was that engraved on my mind, and written on my heart, that ever since I received it, the other world has seemed to me the reality, and this the shadow. If I can, in *quietude* and *cheerfulness*, forego my own pleasures, and relinquish my own *tastes* . . . [if] I can smother the rising anger, and melt wrath with love, I have written a glorious piece of music, to be sung in my Father's house of many mansions. Nay more, perhaps I am doing somewhat to make a holier music descend to *this* world, first in purified affections, and ultimately in written notes. In this view of the ever-active agency of spirit, how apalling [*sic*] is the responsibility of a human soul! how glorious its capabilities!" Letter to Convers Francis dated Northampton, January 8, 1841, in CU.

20. The anecdote has a basis in fact. Mrs. Child wrote a friend: "[Bronson]

Alcott and Charles Lane have . . . been here. Perhaps Lane is one of the best and greatest of men; but his countenance pleases me not. In the first place, it looks as if the washwomen had caught it and scrubbed it on a wash-board; and in the second place, there is an expression, which would make me slow to put myself in his power. The day after they called, W. H. Channing came to tell me that he and they would hold a sort of social 'palaver' together, that evening, at a room in Medical Hall. Not to slight the kind invitation, I went; but the air of the small room was so very stifling, that I turned and went off, knowing I should pay the penalty of a severe head-ache, if I remained half an hour. David and John [Hopper] tried it, for awhile, and then *they* left; David's patience giving way first. When he came home, I said, 'Well, how did the conversation impress your mind?' He replied, 'After I had been there a few minutes, I'll be cursed if I knew whether I *had* any mind at all.' 'What did they say?' 'I don't know.' 'What was it *about*?' 'I can't tell.' Being much urged to remember *something*, he at last said that 'Charles Lane divided man into three states: the disconscious, the conscious, and the unconscious. The *dis*conscious was the state of a pig; the conscious was the baptism by water; and the *un*conscious the baptism by fire.'

"In a few minutes, John came home, with a violent head-ache. 'Well, John,' said I, 'have they done you any good?' 'They've put my body and mind both in a devil of a muss,' [a N. York phrase for utter confusion], said he, 'and I wanted to kick 'em all.' 'What did they say?' 'They didn't know themselves— how should *I*?' 'What was it *about*?' 'Mind and body.' 'Well, what did they *say* of them?' said I, for I felt too mischievous to leave him in peace. For some time, I could learn nothing more, than that they said 'a snarl of things'; but being urged unmercifully, he at last stated that W. H. Channing held a discussion with C. Lane; that 'Channing seemed to think there *was* some connection between soul and body; but them Boston chaps, so far as he could understand 'em, seemed to consider the body all a damned sham.'

"So ended Lane and Alcott's visit to enlighten Babylon. . . ." [Hereon, portions of the letter are undecipherable, an editor (possibly, Whittier) boldly inking out passages; Hopper's comment—"and I wanted to kick 'em all"—is still distinguishable.] Letter to Augusta King dated New York, September 19, 1843, in CU.

Chapter Six

1. Cited in Baer, p. 45.
2. The poem later set to music still appears in children's songbooks.
3. Among others, there are rules for playing a game like "Blind Man's Buff" and those for playing "Bob Cherry": "One in the centre holds a cherry; while each one tries to catch it in her mouth. This simple game must be played with great good humour; if any crying or disputing begins, the play should stop at once."
4. "When roses are budding and blooming, is the time to lay by a treat for Christmas. Select from your rose trees such buds as are just ready to blow: tie

a piece of fine thread round the stalk of each; do not handle the bud, or the stalk; cut it from the tree with the stalk two or three inches in length; melt sealing-wax, and quickly apply it to the end of the stalk; the wax should only be just warm enough to be ductile; form a piece of paper into a cone-like shape, wherein place the rose; twist it at the ends to exclude the air; put it in a box, and put the box into a drawer: this is to be sure that air is excluded. In winter, take it out, cut off the end of the stalk, place it in lukewarm water, and in two or three hours it will have the freshness and fragrance of summer. If the room is very warm, it will answer to put it in cold water."

5. A reviewer in the *North American* commended Mrs. Child as a "faithful instructor and enlightener of the young." "To come down to the . . . demands of the youthful mind," he continued, "and to enter into its interests and feelings, especially when literary ambitions and success would seem to allure to higher walks . . . is an act, that reflects honor on the intellect of the person who performs it. We say nothing of the heart that prompts to this sacrifice,—for sacrifice it is." "Works of Mrs. Child," *North American* 37 (July 1833): 140–41.

6. Herbert Edwards, "Lydia M. Child's *The Frugal Housewife*," *New England Quarterly* 26 (June 1953): 249.

7. Sarah J. Hale, "The Frugal Housewife," *The Ladies' Magazine* 3 (April 1830): 189.

8. "Wash very often, and rub the skin thoroughly with a hard brush."

9. "During the next seven years, it went through twenty editions, or three editions a year; in 1855, it had reached its thirty-third edition, averaging a little short of one edition for thirty-six years." Seth Curtis Beach, "Lydia Maria Child" in *Daughters of the Puritans* (Boston, 1905), p. 94.

10. *North American*, p. 142.

11. Ibid.

12. Ibid., p. 163.

13. "The early writings of Thomas Moore ought to be avoided altogether," Mrs. Child warns. They are "like poison concealed in honey dew."

14. *North American*, p. 143.

15. The American women included in the volume are "Margaret Winthrop, wife of Gov. Winthrop of Mass., Mrs. Experience West, wife of Rev. Samuel West of Mass., [and] Mrs. Ann H. Judson, wife of Rev. Adoniram Judson of Mass., missionary to India."

16. "Biographies of Good Wives," *Southern Quarterly Review* 9 (April 1846): 539.

17. *North American*, p. 163.

18. Wendell Phillips recalled Boston's reaction to the *Appeal*: "Hardly ever was there costlier sacrifice. Narrow means just changing to ease; after a weary struggle, fame and social position in her grasp; every door opening before her. . . . No one had supposed that independence of opinion on a moral question would wreck all that." Cited in Milton Meltzer, *Tongue of Flame: The Life of Lydia Maria Child* (New York, 1965), pp. 42–43.

19. Sarah J. Hale, "An Appeal . . . ," *Ladies' Magazine* 6 (September 1833): 431.

20. "Mrs. Child's New Work," *The Liberator* 3 (September 7, 1833): 141. In the same issue appeared a letter to the editor, the correspondent praising "the disinterested benevolence, and the noble independence of a woman who could thus hazard her glorious reputation 'in an unpopular but most righteous cause.'" *The Liberator* the following week, Saturday, September 14, 1833, carried extracts from the *Appeal*.

21. "An Appeal in Favor of the Africans, by Mrs. Child," *Knickerbocker* 2 (October 1833): 320.

22. "New Publications," *North American* 37 (October 1833): 539.

23. "Slavery: An Appeal in Favor of That Class of Americans Called Africans," *North American* 41 (July 1835): 170–93 passim.

24. *Juvenile Miscellany*, p. 323.

25. Higginson writes: "As it was the first anti-slavery work ever printed in America in book form, I have always thought it the ablest. . . . I know that on reading it for the first time, nearly ten years after its first appearance, it had more formative influence on my mind . . . than any other." Higginson, p. 123.

26. Cited in Baer, p. 126.

27. Letter to Caroline Weston dated Northampton, March 7, 1839, in BP.

28. Letter to Maria Chapman dated [New York], Wednesday 11th, in BP.

29. Letter to Ellis G. Loring dated New York, March 6, 1843, in NYP.

30. Cited in Baer, p. 161.

31. *The Right Way, the Safe Way* (1860); other tracts are *An Anti-Slavery Catechism* (1836), *The Evils of Slavery and the Curse of Slavery* (1836), *The Anti-Slavery Almanac* (1843), and *The Patriarchal Institution* (1860).

32. After Whittier had written thanking her for sending a copy of the book, Mrs. Child in reply alluded to the young woman's story: "I am glad you liked 'Linda.' I have taken a good deal of pains to publish it, and circulate it, because it seemed to me well calculated to take hold of many minds, that will not attend to *arguments* against slavery. The author is a quick-witted, intelligent woman, with great refinement and propriety of manner. Her daughter, now a young woman, is a stylish-looking, attractive young person, white as an Italian lady, and very much *like* an Italian of refined education. If she were the daughter of any of the Beacon St. gentry, she would produce a sensation in the fashionable world. The Mrs. *Bruce*, with whom the mother is described as living in New York, is in fact Mrs. *Willis*; for my protegee has for many years been the factotum in the family of N[athaniel] P. Willis, the distinguished poet. He has mentioned her incidentally in 'Letters from Idlewild,' in the *Home Journal*, as 'our intelligent housekeeper,' our 'household oracle,' etc. He would not have *dared* to mention that she had ever been a fugitive slave." Letter to John Greenleaf Whittier dated Medford, April 4, 1861, in Library of Congress. Hereafter, referred to as LC. A recent edition of the narrative, with an introduction by Walter Teller, is available to the modern reader: [Linda Brent], *Incidents in the Life of a Slave Girl* (New York, 1973).

33. "The History of Religious Ideas," *Democratic Review* N.S. 6 (March 1856): 261–62.

34. "The Progress of Religious Ideas through Successive Ages," *The Christian Examiner* 25 (January 1856): 148–51 passim.

35. See Chapter 1.

36. "The Progress of Religious Ideas, through successive ages," *New England Magazine* 14 (May 1856), 319–21 passim.

37. "The Progress of Religious Ideas through Successive Ages," *Methodist Quarterly* 38 (January 1856): 155.

38. Letter to Lucy Osgood dated Wayland, May 11, 1856, in CU.

39. Ibid. She continued in the letter: "Perhaps I am too much prejudiced against theology. It seems to me to have done such an evil work in dividing nations, neighbors, and friends. I perceive that an immense good has been done to the human race by *religion*; by which I understand practical love and truth toward our fellow human-beings, and humble reverence with regard to the infinite and incomprehensible, which we call God. But what good has been done by *doctrines* concerning God and the soul, I am yet to learn. So it seems to me, but Brother Convers views it differently."

40. Letter to John Greenleaf Whittier dated Wayland, February 17, 1872, in LC.

41. *Christian Examiner*, p. 148.

42. Mrs. Child frequently quoted verbatim from John Winthrop's *History of New England from 1630 to 1649* (1825–1826); William Hubbard's *Narrative of Indian Wars in New England* (1775); Thomas Hutchinson's *History of Massachusetts-Bay* (1764–1828).

43. "Autumnal Leaves: Tales and Sketches in Prose and Rhyme," *Knickerbocker* 49 (February 1857): 199.

44. "I am glad of this, for two reasons," she wrote a friend; "glad to have the book going abroad to fulfil [*sic*] the kindly mission for which I intended it, and glad because the Freedmen will fare the better for it. I seldom have a passing wish for enlarged means except for the sake of doing more for others." Letter to Henrietta Sargent dated Wayland, January 8, 1865, in CU.

45. Ibid.

46. Ibid.

47. Cited in Baer, p. 279.

48. Cited in letter to Henrietta Sargent dated Wayland, January 8, 1865, in CU.

Chapter Seven

1. The novel is dedicated to Mr. and Mrs. Francis G. Shaw, parents of Colonel Robert G. Shaw who was killed leading his troop of black soldiers from Massachusetts in one of the engagements in the Civil War.

2. Walter Hines Page in *The Southerner* (1900) refers to the "Ghost of the Confederate Dead, the Ghost of religious orthodoxy, and the Ghost of Negro domination."

3. "A Romance of the Republic," *The Ladies' Repository* 27 (November 1867): 636.

4. *"A Romance of the Republic," Peterson's Ladies National Magazine* 52 (October 1867): 311.

5. Cited in Meltzer, p. 181.

6. Letter to Eliza Scudder dated Wayland, August 11, 1867, in CU.

Chapter Eight

1. Griswold, p. 427.

2. She once told Theodore Weld: ". . . That is the only true church organization, when heads and hearts unite in working for the welfare of the human race!" *Letters*, p. 258. Letter to Theodore Weld dated Wayland, July 10, 1880.

3. *Letters*, p. 40. Letter to Convers Francis dated Northampton, January 1841.

4. One reform, however, eluded her—the enfranchisement of women. On Election Day in 1864 she wrote Whittier: "To think that a drunken Irishman may decide the destiny of this great nation, while I, who have so long and carefully watched all the springs in the machinery of State, would be contemptuously thrust from the polls!" Letter to John Greenleaf Whittier dated Wayland, November 8, 1864, in LC.

A few years later she tried to enlist Charles Sumner's support for the vote for women: ". . . sooner or later, you will see clearly that our republican ideas cannot be consistently carried out while women are excluded from any share in the government. I reduce the argument to very simple elements. I pay taxes for property of my own earning and saving, and I do not believe in 'taxation without representation.' As for representation by proxy, that savors too much of the plantation-system, however kind the master may be. I am a human being; and every human being has a right to a voice in the laws which claim authority to tax him, to imprison him, or to hang him. The exercise of rights always has a more salutary effect on character than the enjoyment of privileges. Any class of human beings to whom a position of perpetual subordination is assigned, however much they may be petted and flattered, must inevitably be dwarfed, morally and intellectually.

"But I will not enlarge the theme. For forty years I have keenly felt my limitations as a woman, and have submitted to them under perpetual and indignant protest. It is too late for the subject to be of much interest to me personally. I have walked in fetters all my pilgrimage, and now I have but little farther to go. But I see so clearly that domestic and public life would be so much ennobled by the perfect equality and companionship of men and women in all the departments of life, that I long to see it accomplished, for the order and well-being of the world." *Letters*, pp. 208–209. Letter to Charles Sumner dated Wayland, [?] 1870.

5. "A Fable for Critics" in *The Complete Poetical Works of James Russell Lowell* (Boston, 1896), pp. 140–42 passim.

6. Letter to Lucy Osgood dated Wayland, May 14, 1866, in CU.

7. A review of *A Week on the Concord and Merrimack Rivers* and

Walden, appearing in the *National Anti-Slavery Standard*, may be Mrs. Child's. The reviewer commends Thoreau's individualism, his "aim manifestly . . . to *live*, and not waste . . . time upon the externals of living." In particular, it is the "more purely thoughtful passages"—the "noble" essay on friendship in *Week* and "What I Lived For" and "Higher Laws" in *Walden*—which impress the reviewer, who concludes: "The striking peculiarity of Mr. Thoreau's attitude is, that while he is no religionist, and while he is eminently practical in regard to the material economics of life, he yet manifestly feels, through and through, that the loftiest dreams of the imagination are the solidest realities, and so the only foundation for us to build upon, while the affairs in which men are everywhere busying themselves so intensely are comparatively the merest froth and foam." *National Anti-Slavery Standard*, December 16, 1854, p. 3. I am indebted for this information to one of my students, Robert W. Lamb.

8. Letter to Frank Shaw dated Wayland, [?] 1880, in CU.

9. Letter to Lucy Osgood dated Wayland, January 19, 1858, in CU.

10. Letter to Convers Francis dated Wayland, October 25, 1857, in NYP.

11. *Letters*, p. 40. Letter to Convers Francis dated Northampton, January 1841. On another occasion she wrote a friend: "I did not go to Mr. [John S.] Dwight's ordination, nor have I yet been to meeting. He has been to see me, however, and though I left my work in the midst, and sat down with a dirty gown and hands somewhat grimmed [*sic*], we were high up in the blue in fifteen minutes. I promised to take a flight with him from the wash-tub or dish-kettle any time when he would come along with his balloon. . . ." *Letters*, p. 29. Letter to Mrs. Ellis G. Loring dated Northampton, June 9, 1838.

12. *Letters*, p. 98. Letter to Convers Francis dated Wayland, August 8, 1858.

13. *Letters*, p. 268, Whittier in his tribute to Mrs. Child, "Within the Gate," says: "Yet, loving beauty, thou couldst pass it by,/ And for the poor deny/Thyself. . . ."

Appendix

1. Letter to William Lloyd Garrison dated Wayland, February 1, 1857, in BP. Although the reader today may discount the phenomenon of "spiritual manifestations" and regard Mrs. Child as somewhat credulous, it is perhaps well to bear in mind that she and her contemporaries experienced what for them seemed truly miraculous developments in communication: the telegraph, the transatlantic cable, the railroad. It seemed logical that some means of spiritual communication might be discovered as well. She speculates on such communication in *Philothea* and in several essays in *Letters from New York*: the relationship between minds and between mind and body.

2. Letter to William Lloyd Garrison dated Wayland, July 7, 1865, in BP.

3. Letter from William Lloyd Garrison to Lydia Maria Child dated Roxbury [Massachusetts], October 25, 1874, in BP. Mrs. Child wrote an

article on the abolitionist: "William Lloyd Garrison," *Atlantic Monthly* 44 (August 1879): 234–38.

4. Letter to Thomas Wentworth Higginson dated Wayland, February 21, 1871, in BP. Among other eminent women, there were sketches of Margaret Fuller, Florence Nightingale, Fanny Kemble, Elizabeth Barrett Browning, Jenny Lind, Empress Eugenie, and Queen Victoria.

5. Ibid. The correspondence was given instead to Wendell Phillips and eventually deposited in Cornell University Library.

6. Letter to Samuel May dated Wayland, January 26, 1857, in BP.

7. Letter to Sarah Shaw dated Wayland, April 8, 1866, in Bryant-Godwin Collection, NYP.

8. *Letters*, p. 63. Letter to Convers Francis dated New Rochelle, January 20, 1848.

9. *Letters*, p. 256. Letter to Henrietta Sewall dated Wayland, August 25, 1879.

10. *Letters*, p. 142. Letter to Sarah Shaw dated [Wayland?] 1860.

11. Letter to Wendell Phillips dated Wayland, June 4, 1876, in BP.

12. Letter to Francis Jackson dated Wayland, September 15, 1856, in BP. Reference is to the presidential campaign of 1856, in which John C. Fremont was the standard-bearer for the Republican Party, and to the disputes in the Kansas Territory, where proslavery "ruffians" successfully overcame "free-soilers."

13. Fragment, n.d., in CU.

14. Letter to Lucy Osgood dated [Wayland?] December 21, 1871, in CU.

15. Letter to Parke Godwin dated New Rochelle, August 22, 1848, in Bryant-Godwin Collection, NYP.

16. Letter to Parke Godwin dated Wayland, December 13, 1864, in Bryant-Godwin Collection, NYP.

17. Letter to Lucy Osgood dated Wayland, January 19, 1858, in CU.

18. Letter to Sarah Shaw dated Wayland, March 20, 1857, in CU.

19. Letter to Lucy Osgood dated Wayland, October 28, 1856, in CU.

20. Ibid.

21. Letters to Lucy Osgood dated Wayland, May 18, 1862; and Wayland, June 9, 1862, in CU.

22. Letter to Lucy Osgood dated Wayland, June 12, 1858, in CU.

23. Letter to Lucy Osgood dated Wayland, September 1, 1861, in CU.

24. Letter to Lucy Osgood dated [Wayland?] June 16, 1867, in CU.

25. She once described herself as "being rather a Puritanic person." Letter to Eliza Scudder dated Wayland, April 12, 1868, in CU. In the manuscript collection at Cornell University, there is an itemized list of Mrs. Child's activities for the year 1864: her correspondence; editing work; knitting/sewing for soldiers, for Child, for herself; cooking "360 dinners" and "362 breakfasts"; cleaning; preserving; visits to friends.

26. Letter to Eliza Scudder dated Wayland, November 29, 1867, in CU.

27. Letter to Sarah Parson dated Wayland, December 29, 1871, in CU.

28. Letter to Sarah Parson dated Boston, January 29, 1879, in CU.

29. Letter to Ellis G. Loring dated New York, March 22 [1842], in NYP.

30. Letter to David Lee Child dated [?] April 9, 1858, in CU.

31. Letter to Ellis G. Loring dated New York, February 21, 1843, in NYP.

32. Letter to Augusta King dated New York, October 30, 1844, in CU.

33. Letter to Ellis G. Loring dated Northampton, January 12, 1839, in CU.

34. Letter to Lucy Osgood dated [Wayland?], March 21, 1864, in CU.

35. *Letters*, p. 239. Letter to Sarah Shaw dated Wayland, [?] 1876.

36. Letter to Margery Curzon dated Wayland, May 24, 1860, in NYP.

37. She remembered their association in the antislavery movement: "Oh those were glorious times! working shoulder to shoulder, in such a glow of faith!—too eager working for humanity to care a fig whether our helpers were priests or infidels. That's the service that is pleasing in the sight of God." *Letters*, p. 142. Letter to Sarah Shaw dated [Wayland?] 1860.

To another correspondent she wrote: "The memory of the early antislavery days is very sacred to me. The Holy Spirit did actually descend upon men and women in tongues of flame. Political and theological prejudices and personal ambitions were forgotten in sympathy for the wrongs of the helpless, and in the enthusiasm to keep the fire of freedom from being extinguished on our national altar.

"All suppression of selfishness makes the moment great; and mortals were never more sublimely forgetful of self than were the abolitionists in those early days, before the moral force which emanated from them had become available as a political power." *Letters*, p. 258. Letter to Theodore Weld dated Wayland, July 10, 1880.

38. Letter to John Greenleaf Whittier dated Wayland, September 10, 1861, in LC.

39. Letter to John Greenleaf Whittier dated Wayland, January 21, 1862, in LC.

40. Letter to John Greenleaf Whittier dated Wayland, July 31, 1870, in LC.

41. Letter to John Greenleaf Whittier dated Wayland, January 20, 1876, in LC.

Selected Bibliography

PRIMARY SOURCES

1. Books

An Appeal in Favor of That Class of Americans Called Africans. Boston: Allen and Ticknor, 1833.
Autumnal Leaves. New York: C. S. Francis, 1856.
The Coronal. Boston: Carter and Hendee, 1832.
The First Settlers of New England. Boston: Munro and Francis, 1829.
The Freedmen's Book. Boston: Ticknor and Fields, 1865.
The Frugal Housewife. Boston: Carter and Hendee, 1830.
The Girl's Own Book. Boston: Russell [and] Shattuck, 1831.
The History of the Condition of Women in Various Ages and Nations. Boston: J. Allen and Company, 1835.
Hobomok, A Tale of the Times. Boston: Cummings and Hilliard, 1824.
Incidents in the Life of a Slave Girl. Boston: L. M. Child, 1861. Edited by Mrs. Child.
The Juvenile Miscellany. Boston: Allen and Ticknor, 1826–1834. Edited by Mrs. Child.
Letters from New York. New York: C. S. Francis, 1843.
Letters from New York. Second Series. New York: C. S. Francis, 1845.
Looking Toward Sunset. Boston: Ticknor and Fields, 1864.
The Mother's Book. Boston: Carter and Hendee, 1831.
Philothea, a Romance. Boston: Otis [and] Broaders, 1836.
The Progress of Religious Ideas through Successive Ages. New York: C. S. Francis, 1855.
The Rebels, or Boston before the Revolution. Boston: Cummings and Hilliard, 1825.
A Romance of the Republic. Boston: Ticknor and Fields, 1867.

2. Biography

BAER, HELENE G. *The Heart Is Like Heaven: The Life of Lydia Maria Child.* Philadelphia: University of Pennsylvania Press, 1964. Included in Mrs. Baer's bibliography is an extensive listing of Mrs. Child's contributions to magazines of the day, pp. 328–33.

3. Letters

Letters of Lydia Maria Child, ed. John Greenleaf Whittier. Boston: Houghton, Mifflin and Company, 1882; rpt. New York: Negro Universities Press, 1969.

SECONDARY SOURCES

[The bibliography of secondary sources is deliberately very selective. There are no full-length literary studies of Mrs. Child, except the present volume. Works concentrate rather on the public life and her interest in reform movements in mid-nineteenth-century America. What may be regarded as the most significant of these works is acknowledged below. Briefer notices and estimates of her life and interests are frequently referred to in the chapters of this study and are identified in the Notes and References. W.S.O.]

BAER, HELENE G. *The Heart Is Like Heaven: The Life of Lydia Maria Child.* Philadelphia: University of Pennsylvania Press, 1964. A biography emphasizing Mrs. Child's work in the antislavery movement and her strong commitment to reform—a valuable source for the student of American social history. Narrative method similar to that of Madeline Stern in her biography of Margaret Fuller, with incidents and events based on Mrs. Child's correspondence and essays and articles which appeared in the news media of the day. Liberal quotations from Mrs. Child's letters without specific acknowledgment of sources. Containing a selective bibliography of Mrs. Child's works as well as a list of histories, biographies, volumes of letters, and cultural studies drawn on in writing the book.

BEACH, SETH CURTIS. *Daughters of the Puritans.* Boston: American Unitarian Association, 1905. In addition to the essay on Mrs. Child, essays on Louisa May Alcott, Margaret Fuller, and Harriet Beecher Stowe, among others. Relying heavily on Whittier's biographical sketch to develop a merely factual account of Mrs. Child's life.

CONRAD, SUSAN PHINNEY. *Perish the Thought: Intellectual Women in Romantic America 1830–1860.* New York: Oxford University Press, 1976. A series of brilliant essays on a number of remarkable women, among them Margaret Fuller and Mrs. Child. Emphasizing the dilemma facing such women hindered by restrictions placed on them by a male-dominated society. Remarking particularly the dichotomy in Mrs. Child: the romantic in her view of life and the aggressive realist in her service to others.

HIGGINSON, THOMAS WENTWORTH. *Contemporaries.* Cambridge, Mass.: Riverside Press, 1900; rpt. Upper Saddle River, N.J.: Literature House/ Gregg Press, 1970. An expanded version of the sketch of Mrs. Child first published in *Eminent Women of the Age.* Chatty, informative, drawing in part on Whittier's biographical sketch, with a brief discussion of Mrs. Child's major work popular with her readers. Little critical comment; insightful only as to the character of the woman herself.

MELTZER, MILTON. *Tongue of Flame: The Life of Lydia Maria Child*. New York: Thomas Y. Crowell Company, 1965. Another biography concentrating on Mrs. Child's work in humanitarian causes. As in Mrs. Baer's biography, "All the quotations in this book are taken from authentic records. Thoughts put into Maria's head are never invented, but reconstructed from passages in her own letters or other writing."

TAYLOR, LLOYD C., JR. "To Make Men Free: An Interpretive Study of Lydia Maria Child." Unpublished dissertation submitted to History Department, Lehigh University, 1956. "Interpretive" is a key word in this two-volume biographical study, which manifestly extols Mrs. Child as writer, editor, reformer, abolitionist, champion of the underdog. A portrait of a woman without equal, larger than life, the result in part of the author's conjecturing.

THORP, MARGARET FARRAND. *Six Persuasive Women*. New Haven: Yale University Press, 1949; rpt. *Female Persuasion: Six Strong-Minded Women*. Hamden, Conn.: Archon Press, 1971. A series of essays on strong-willed women who spoke defiantly and clearly for women's participation in the affairs of the nation: Catherine E. Beecher (Harriet Beecher Stowe's older sister), "Grace Greenwood" (Sara J. C. Lippincott, poet and editor), and Mrs. Child among others. Abolitionists whose interest in antislavery led to their participation in other reforms. Essay on Mrs. Child suggesting her strengths as a writer—an ability particularly in the nonfiction to simplify ideas for popular consumption—and illustrating her great interest in people, which inspired the life of service to others.

WHITTIER, JOHN GREENLEAF. "A Biographical Introduction" in *Letters of Lydia Maria Child*, ed. John Greenleaf Whittier. Boston: Houghton, Mifflin and Company, 1882; rpt. New York: Negro Universities Press, 1969. A biographical sketch of Mrs. Child's life, emphasizing her antislavery work. "The letters in this collection constitute but a small part of her large correspondence." Also, Phillips's funeral oration, Whittier's poem commemorating Mrs. Child, a bibliography of Mrs. Child's writings.

Index

194